FARMERS' AND
FARM WORKERS' MOVEMENTS

Social Protest in American Agriculture

D1563647

Social Movements Past and Present

Irwin T. Sanders, Editor

Abolitionism: A Revolutionary Movement
by Herbert Aptheker

The American Communist Movement: Storming Heaven Itself
by Harvey Klehr and John Earl Haynes

The American Peace Movement: Ideals and Activism
by Charles Chatfield

American Temperance Movements: Cycles of Reform
by Jack S. Blocker Jr.

The Animal Rights Movement in America:
From Compassion to Respect
by Lawrence Finsen and Susan Finsen

The Anti-Abortion Movement and the Rise of the Religious Right:
From Polite to Fiery Protest
by Dallas A. Blanchard

The Antinuclear Movement, Updated Edition
by Jerome Price

The Charismatic Movement: Is There a New Pentecost?
by Margaret Poloma

The Children's Rights Movement: A History of Advocacy and Protection
by Joseph M. Hawes

Civil Rights: The 1960s Freedom Struggle
by Rhoda Lois Blumberg

The Conservative Movement, Revised Edition
by Paul Gottfried

The Consumer Movement: Guardians of the Marketplace
by Robert N. Mayer

Controversy and Coalition: The New Feminist Movement
by Myra Marx Ferree and Beth B. Hess

The Creationist Movement in Modern America
by Raymond A. Eve and Francis B. Harrold

FARMERS' AND FARM WORKERS' MOVEMENTS

Social Protest in American Agriculture

Patrick H. Mooney and Theo J. Majka

Twayne Publishers • New York
Maxwell Macmillan Canada • Toronto
Maxwell Macmillan International • New York Oxford Singapore Sydney

Farmers' and Farm Workers' Movements: Social Protest in American Agriculture
Patrick H. Mooney and Theo J. Majka

Twayne Publishers   Maxwell Macmillan Canada, Inc.
Macmillan Publishing Company   1200 Eglinton Avenue East
866 Third Avenue   Suite 200
New York, New York 10022   Don Mills, Ontario M3C 3N1

Library of Congress Cataloging-in-Publication Data

Mooney, Patrick H.
  Farmers' and farm workers' movements : social protest in American agriculture /
Patrick H. Mooney and Theo J. Majka
    p. cm. — (Social movements past and present)
  Includes bibliographical references and index.
  ISBN 0-8057-3869-X — ISBN 0-8057-3870-3 (pbk.)
  1. Trade unions—Agricultural laborers—United States—History. 2. Trade unions—
United States—Political activity—History. 3. Agricultural laborers—United States—
Political activity—History. 4. Farmers—United States—Political activity—History. 5.
National Farmers Organization (U.S.)—History. 6. United Farm Workers of America—
History. 7. Labor movement—United States—History. 8. Social Movements—United
States—History. I. Majka, Theo J. II. Series.
HD6515.A29M66 1994
331.88'13'0973—dc20   94-18178
                                                                      CIP

The paper used in this publication meets the minimum requirements of American
National Standard for Information Sciences—Permanence of Paper for Printed Library
Materials, ANSI Z39.48-1984. ∞™

10 9 8 7 6 5 4 3 2 1 (alk. paper)
10 9 8 7 6 5 4 3 2 1 (pbk.: alk. paper)

Printed and bound in the United States of America.

For our parents:
Thomas E. and Mary Susan Mooney
Joe W. and Jeanne E. Majka

Contents

Contents

Preface

Periodically Americans become conscious of the concerns of those involved in agricultural work. During the first half of the 1980s numerous foreclosures of smaller, independent farms captured the public's attention. Farm Aid concerts provided one means for those concerned to give some assistance to small farmers in need. During the 1960s and 1970s many Americans responded to the attempts of farm workers in California to unionize by boycotting table grapes, head lettuce, and several brand-name products in support of a successful strategy pursued by the United Farm Workers (UFW) union under the leadership of Cesar Chavez. Many Americans had earlier offered various forms of support for agrarian people and movements, such as during the Populist era of the 1880s and 1890s and the Dust Bowl migration to California during the 1930s.

Normally, however, the circumstances of smaller farmers and farm workers are absent from the consciousness of most Americans. Yet there is a rich tradition of efforts by both groups to act collectively to improve their common conditions. Social movements with predominantly urban constituencies have received the most attention by scholars as well as the general public. There is, however, a historical and intellectual need to study the legacy of agrarian movements if only because, as Wendell Berry (1994, 10) has recently claimed, "Eating is an agricultural act." Even though these issues and concerns have had little publicity in recent years, changes and events in contemporary life can be expected to set the context for the next cycle of agrarian protests. Agrarian social movements have primarily been responses to larger patterns in U.S. history. Both farmers and farm workers have been profoundly affected by changes in the organization of social life, the economy as a whole, and the cultural and technological state of society. Issues that have stimulated both farmer and farm labor movements have been tied to the impact of larger institutional forces, such as the increasing dominance of large-scale agriculture and changes in government policies. These movements also illustrate more general social patterns, such as immigration trends, political and ideological shifts in the larger society, and the continuing importance of ethnic relations.

We have treated farmer and farm labor movements as social movements and have not allowed their rural origins to obscure what they share in common with other groups and movements. While social scientists typically think of urban movements as the most likely to be at the forefront of social change, both farmer and farm labor movements have at times embodied the progressive ideals that are at the heart of the American identity. In their best moments, agrarian movements have sought to further the empowerment and self-determination of their constituencies, to transform social and institutional arrangements into more egalitarian ones, to challenge the dominance of powerful organizations that lack accountability to those whose lives they affect, and to create institutional avenues that facilitate greater participation by ordinary people.

Agrarian movements have generated alternative organizations, such as farm cooperatives and farm labor unions, whose purpose has been to give their constituencies more power and to better realize their ideals and goals in practice. At the same time these movements have also reflected the more limiting aspects of American culture and politics. Contradictions within individual movements have been symptomatic of the polarizing forces in the larger society. In a society divided along class, racial, and other lines, conflicting ideologies have given definition to competition over group interests. As a result, the history of farm movements also contains many examples of the disintegration of movements spurred in part by cultural and ideological differences as well as racial, ethnic, and geographical divisions. Nevertheless, rather than being marginal, rural movements have often been at the center of struggles for greater democratization in American society.

The Introduction gives an overview of the history of farmer and farm labor movements and describes our basic analytical approach derived from the general literature on social movements. The chapters that follow are devoted to the specifics of farmer and farm labor movements. Our coverage of each is chronological. In the Conclusion we turn our attention to threads of continuity in both movements. The four chapters on farmer movements were written by Patrick Mooney, and Theo Majka was responsible for the three chapters on farm labor movements. The Introduction and the Conclusion are joint collaborations. With respect to farmer movements, we consider the intriguing hypothesis of Carl C. Taylor that there is a unitary farmer movement with a coherent ideology acting as a basis of continuity for this movement from one era to another. For farm labor movements, we discuss a continuity provided by their emphasis on "control issues." In analyzing episodes of farmer and farm worker mobilization, we also focus on the ways in which similarities in social class and ideology provide historical continuity to these movements.

This book owes a great deal to Professor William B. Lacy of Cornell University, who originally conceived the project. Similarly, a debt of gratitude goes to Dr. Irwin T. Sanders, editor of Twayne's Social Movements Past and Present series, who has supported and encouraged the project wholeheartedly throughout its long development. Twayne editors Carol Chin and Barbara Sutton contributed their suggestions and their patience. Much of our description of specific movements and episodes of protest represents a review of historical literature, and we are indebted to the many excellent studies of specific movements and periods. Proofreading and indexing were done in an especially conscientious manner by Stevie Ann Hardyal.

Patrick H. Mooney would like to thank Professors Ron E. Roberts and Jerry Stockdale of the University of Northern Iowa for stimulating an early interest in the field of social movements and Professor Morton Rothstein, whose brilliant lectures on American agricultural history and farmers' movements in the University of Wisconsin's Department of History provided some of the most delightful seminars of my graduate education. Professor Donald Johnson and Lorna Miller of the University of Wisconsin's Department of Rural Sociology also provided a great deal of insight into many of the more contemporary movements. I also must express my appreciation to the Rural Sociological Society, whose Early Career Fellowship greatly facilitated my collection of farm movement literature and interviews with various farm movement leaders. Similarly, the University of Kentucky assisted my research by providing summer support. A number of colleagues have helped this project over the years by listening, reading, and criticizing my thoughts on these matters. David Hamilton read and commented on an entire first draft of the chapters on farmer movements. Louis Swanson provided opportunities for me to put some ideas to his graduate seminar in agricultural sociology. Constructive criticism has also come from many friends and associates: Ron Aminzade, John L. Campbell, Robert Jenkins, Jess Gilbert, Krzysztof Gorlach, A. Eugene Havens, Bertrand Hervieu, Scott A. Hunt, Matteo Marini, Maureen Mullinax, Ed Nelson, Andrzej Pilichowski, Curt Stofferahn, William Talbert, and Paul Weingartner. I would also like to thank the students in both my social movements and my sociology of agriculture courses for their reading and critique of early drafts of various chapters.

Finally, I would like to single out two particular sources of inspiration. First, Carl C. Taylor's provocative thesis of a unitary farmers' movement furnished an intriguing heuristic device for telling this story. Taylor had wanted to complete a second volume on the history of farmers' movements that would have taken us from 1920 to the late 1960s. Unfortunately, he never completed that manuscript, which would have provided great insight into these movements from a central figure in New Deal agricultural policy circles. I hope and believe that this manuscript is in the same spirit as Dr. Taylor would have written. Second, to all those activists who contributed their valuable time for interviews and to all the farm organizations who have indulged my presence at their meetings, I must extend both gratitude as well as an expression of appreciation for the hard work they have undertaken for goals in which they believe so strongly.

Theo J. Majka would like to thank Professors Richard Flacks and William J. Chambliss, both of whom stimulated my initial interest in the possibilities of connecting social problems and social movement issues with the farm labor movement. Both offered valuable advice and encouragement during various stages of this research. Of the many scholars and writers covering the history of California's agriculture, the works of Carey McWilliams and Clarke A. Chambers were major influences and sources of inspiration. William H. Friedland initially suggested the need to examine the internal factors behind the decline of the UFW during the past decade. John Leggett and Ken Barger have been part of a network of scholars with whom Linda Majka and I have exchanged papers and ideas on farm labor movements during the past several years. Linda's participation in the field interviews, documentary data collection, and analysis over many years has been central to the completion of this work.

Writers for the *Los Angeles Times,* the Riverside, California, *Press Enterprise,* and the *Sacramento Bee,* as well as Doug Foster, editor of *Mother Jones,* provided useful clues, analyses, and contacts during our field research. California state and federal labor board officials have generously shared their experiences and provided insights and information. Also, thanks are due to a number of former officials and staff members of the UFW and the Farm Labor Organizing Committee (FLOC), as well as farm labor lawyers and activists, for sharing their knowledge and observations. Steve Lopez's research on FLOC under my direction while a student at the University of Dayton was a catalyst for examining the different trajectories of FLOC and the UFW. The research and writing of my chapters were facilitated by a University of Dayton Summer Research Fellowship and a National Endowment for the Humanities Summer Stipend. Laura Hengehold of the Social Science Research Center at the University of Dayton contributed to the research on the UFW's decline. Tonya McKee helped with some last-minute research.

Chapter 5, on the depression-era protests, and Chapter 6, on the emergence and successes of the UFW, are largely based on research by Linda and Theo Majka during the 1970s. Chapter 7, on the decline of the farm labor movement in California and the successes of FLOC in Ohio and Michigan, is based on recent research by Linda and Theo Majka. This included a series of interviews over the past six years with many of the participants and knowledgeable observers of the UFW era. The research on which the farm labor chapters are based has been a collaborative project with Linda over the past 20 years.

Introduction

In our coverage of agrarian protests and social movements, we hope to accomplish several objectives. First, we seek to provide an overview of the fascinating history of the struggles of farmers and farm workers to attain their goals and effect changes. We try to analyze this history in an accessible and interesting manner. We also hope that our condensation of a rich history will not have lost the drama of certain events or the courage and charisma of the individuals who have participated in these movements. Second, we illustrate central concepts and issues in the social movement literature with examples from the history of agrarian struggles. Finally, we attempt a "critical" examination of this history. Similar to much of the literature on social movements, we have tried to understand these movements from the vantage point of the agricultural producers and the movement participants rather than from that of their economic and political antagonists. Attention is given to movement goals, qualities of leadership, mobilization strategies, and efforts to counter the opposition. While our sympathies are generally with small farmers and farm workers in their efforts to create better futures, we also record their shortcomings, misjudgments, and failures.

Farmers and Farm Workers

The social movements generated by the development of U.S. agriculture can first be distinguished as farmer movements and farm worker movements. While both types of social movements are grounded in agricultural production, divergent class bases separate these movements in terms of power, resources, organization, and

objectives. Generally speaking, farmer movements have been stimulated by changes in government policy or relations with large enterprises
such as banks and processors that have affected them adversely. As a
result, many farmer movements began by attempting to forestall or
reverse changes detrimental to the interests of small farmers. But
farmer movements also have extended their demands and goals
beyond existing social arrangements and have attempted to create
more democratic and egalitarian structures, as illustrated by the
Populist movement during the late nineteenth century.

By contrast, most farm worker movements have had as a primary
goal the restructuring of existing social arrangements to give farm
workers and their organizations leverage in negotiating more stable
and productive employment arrangements—an objective they share
with the labor movement. "Control issues" have been crucial among
farm worker demands. Farm workers have had a far more difficult
time, however, in translating their discontent and protests into anything more than temporary concessions. The poverty, migrant-work
patterns, and immigrant and minority status of many farm workers,
combined with the usual oversupply of labor in the farm labor market,
have made it difficult for farm workers to effect reforms. Also, employment of farm workers has been shown to vary by region (Pfeffer
1983).

Still, there are cases in which the distinction between these two
movements is ambiguous. For example, as a class form, sharecroppers in the post–Civil War South had characteristics of both farmer
and farm worker. We have chosen to treat social movements of sharecroppers as farmer movements primarily because the movements
reflect the sharecroppers' interest in moving toward independent
farmer status and have often allied with owners of small and medium-
sized farms. In some instances tenancy was seen as merely a stage of
the farm family's life cycle or as an uncertain "step" on the "agricultural ladder" leading toward ownership. That anticipation or objective has
not been the driving force of most farm worker movements. Instead,
farm worker protests have usually sought to improve conditions within the sphere of wage-labor relations. At least in this century, the most
significant farm labor movements have been concentrated in agricultural areas dominated by large agricultural enterprises. As a result,
establishing an independent farm has not been a realistic goal for
most farm workers; instead they have usually sought improved working conditions or mobility out of farm work. The farm worker move-

ments we examine are mostly those of agribusiness employees or those dependent on corporations. These movements display organizational characteristics similar to those of industrial workers and goals similar to those of the civil rights movement.

Farmer Movements

Agrarian social movements in the colonial and pre–Civil War period were dominated by violent protests over the distribution of rent, taxes, and interest. This conflict derived from the underdeveloped cash economy of the agricultural frontier and property restrictions on formal political participation. Often such violence was spontaneous; sometimes it was highly organized, drawing on military skills acquired, for instance, in the French and Indian War and the American Revolution.

Challenges to the appropriation of rent developed during the colonial period in regions where attempts were made to establish large estates. New York's Hudson River Valley tenant revolts, for example, began prior to the Revolution and continued sporadically until the mid-nineteenth century. The colonial Regulator's movement in the Carolinas was concerned with political control over taxes and fees. The Whiskey Rebellion in Pennsylvania was also a struggle over taxes. Shays' Rebellion in New England focused on the credit extended by local merchants as urban centers began to call in loans to these rural merchants. While these movements often began with lobbying and petitioning, violent conflict often resulted in the face of an intransigent opposition. Another strategy during this period was simply the tendency of individuals to flee the landlord, creditor, or tax collector and migrate toward the frontier.

The extension of suffrage and the closing of the frontier facilitated a shift from violent confrontation and individual flight toward increasing political action associated with voting. Depending on the regional competitiveness of parties, local mobilizations tended to focus either on third-party formation or independent-bloc voting to influence a dominant party. Such political pressure was tied to increased lobbying efforts.

Alliances with labor were common to many agrarian movements between the end of the Civil War and the farm depression of the 1920s. While farmer-labor alliances were unstable, they were also central to strong factions within certain movements. That tradition extended into the Farmers' Union, which has maintained a sympathy with organized labor to the present. The Nonpartisan League was initiated by Socialist party members who were unhappy with the party's assumption of a structural antagonism between agricultural and industrial producers that precluded the organization of farmers. The specific class opponents of these movements were the emergent forms of monopoly capital in both industry (farm inputs) and world markets (especially grains and cotton). This opposition led to sporadic efforts at boycotts and holding actions. These were subordinated to a more fundamental pursuit of cooperative development, however. The mobilizations in this period were engaged in the creation of purchasing or marketing cooperatives as a means of retaining greater portions of surplus.

In the early twentieth century the cooperative movement became firmly institutionalized. Veterans of the Granger movement and the Farmers' Alliance combined experience from the past with a new prosperity that provided the initial capital formation so lacking in late-nineteenth-century efforts at cooperation. Finally, the coupling of these opportunities with an increasingly powerful agrarian socialist influence in the Midwest and Great Plains pushed the state to facilitate formal cooperation as a means of co-opting this socialist strength. The creation of the Farm Bureau by agribusiness and the government represents the culmination of their attempts to manage grass-roots political action. In this case the selective economic incentives provided by a resource-rich cooperative organization permitted membership recruitment to a highly conservative politics and ideology, controlled from the higher levels of the organization. During the farm depression of the 1920s Republican administrations pushed cooperation as a means of preempting a return to the more radical demands of the past.

The institution of cooperation in the twentieth century led to further consolidation of lobbying as an effective political tactic. Cooperatives provided a financial and organizational resource base for such activities. Lobbying as a political tactic has been eroded by two factors, however: economic crisis and demographic decline. The farm depression prompted the less flexible dominant classes to push farmers' lobbying toward protest and to institute holding actions as a means of transforming market relations—as, for example, the Southern Tenant Farmers' Union and the Farmers' Holiday Association did to achieve collective bargaining. These movements reintroduced violent confrontation insofar as economic conditions forced elites to repress ten-

ant insurgency, and holding actions nearly always required the use of
force as an instrument of social control over the "free rider."

In the 1950s and 1960s a declining farm population began to recognize the demise of its voting power. The National Farmers'
Organization (NFO) emerged as a protest and collective bargaining
movement. In the late 1970s and the 1980s the American Agriculture
Movement (AAM) talked of a "farm strike" and then of production
control (Browne and Lundgren 1988). Eventually new organizations
like Prairiefire and member organizations of the National Save the
Family Farm Coalition and the North American Farm Alliance directed more attention to farmer relations with financial institutions as the
credit crisis demanded immediate grass-roots action to impede a dramatic wave of farm foreclosures and bankruptcies.

Cooperative class practices continued throughout the period.
Nevertheless, the NFO holding actions began to reveal the extent to
which cooperative enterprises had abandoned direct responsiveness
to their constituency (i.e., their owners) and adopted behavior almost
indistinguishable from private-sector agribusiness.

Since the 1970s there has been little or no tactical innovation in economic strategies, although some of the newer agrarian social movements have advocated the development of land trusts. The cooperative
movement has been marked by a continuing concentration that parallels agribusiness. The collective bargaining movement seems to have
reached a standstill, at least in the major commodities. The dearth of
innovative collective economic action is strikingly similar to the frontier period, with increasing off-farm employment replacing the escape
to the frontier as a means of struggle against monopoly capitalist domination of production and markets. The focus of the AAM, Prairiefire,
and the National Save the Family Farm Coalition has been political
and has sought to enhance agrarian political power by extending an
identification with broader "rural" interests. This strategy reflects a
rational adaptation to the demographic (and thus the political) decline
of full-time farmers and the growing significance of part-time farming
as well as the turnaround of population trends in some rural areas.

Farm Worker Movements

Compared with farmer movements, farm worker organizing has
been primarily a twentieth-century phenomenon. As agricultural capi-

tal has become increasingly concentrated and large agricultural enterprises have dominated certain agricultural regions, particularly California and other areas of the Southwest, the previous commonality of interests shared by farmers and hired farm employees became replaced by capital-labor relations resembling those in other productive industries. Driven by motives to increase profits, to maintain competitive positions in a national and now increasingly international agricultural marketplace, to rationalize production, and to increase labor productivity, large agribusiness enterprises have sought to maintain substantial control over conditions in the farm labor market. Generally, they have been beneficiaries of an abundant supply of labor that has exerted downward pressure on wages and inhibited worker protests and organization. To achieve this, agribusiness has used a variety of strategies. At different times agribusiness has attempted to influence immigration laws and their enforcement to preserve their access to low-wage labor; to replace a labor force that was increasingly organized with one that initially was more controllable; to hire undocumented workers in preference to domestics or new immigrants to replace those that were beginning to express discontent; to play one ethnic or immigrant group off against another; to introduce machine harvesters to preempt worker organizing efforts; to use political alliances to undercut farm labor laws; and, in general, to vehemently resist farm worker collective bargaining.

Farm worker responses have created a history rich in protests and organizing efforts undertaken by a variety of both radical and more moderate farm labor unions. Farm worker efforts to improve their positions have been particularly prominent in California. Agribusiness has been dominant in most of the state's agricultural areas for nearly a century, and California has been a major entry point for a variety of immigrant groups who worked in agriculture, including Chinese, Japanese, Asian Americans, Mexicans, and Filipinos. Most of the time, however, agribusiness has been successful in thwarting attempts at worker organizing and collective bargaining. Concessions, when granted, were usually temporary, many only for the duration of a particular harvest season. Also, governmental agencies and officials generally have assisted agribusiness in their struggle with farm labor organizations.

We have been selective in choosing which farm worker insurgencies to cover. While farm worker discontent and protests have occurred widely throughout the United States, most have been short and have not led to the kinds of prolonged efforts characteristic of social movements. One reason is that agricultural labor is in a structurally weak position. Farm workers do not possess the economic resources to endure long strikes. Many are particularly vulnerable to threats of discharge, and some fear deportation. The chronically over-supplied agricultural labor market has given agribusiness formidable leverage to exact compliance to prevailing wages and working conditions. Also, the migratory status of many farm workers reduces the incentive for achieving concessions from any individual employer and makes the migrants themselves harder for labor organizers to mobilize over time. Finally, agricultural labor is not covered by most federal labor legislation, such as the National Labor Relations Act, leaving farm workers vulnerable to actions by employers that would be illegal in other industries.

Necessary for the success of farm worker movements is the ability to build alliances with groups and organizations outside of agriculture. Such a situation is more likely during a liberal political climate when national concern with issues of social justice and support for social reforms becomes more prominent. External resources can then be freed up to assist in reforming the conditions of agricultural work. We will cover two such periods that have shown considerable potential for permanent reform, the depression era and the period of United Farm Workers (UFW) activism that began in 1965. Both of these efforts have been concentrated in California. In addition to their size and impact, the farm worker movements in California represent attempts to gain collective bargaining where large-scale agricultural enterprises are the dominant form of farming, far more so than in most other areas in the United States. We will also cover a spinoff of UFW efforts, the achievements by the Farm Labor Organizing Committee (FLOC) in Ohio and Michigan during the 1980s and early 1990s. FLOC's activities are significant because they involve a different kind of agricultural enterprise. Negotiations have involved bargaining among three parties: representatives of farm workers, individual farmers who are considerably smaller than their California counterparts, and large food corporations, such as Campbell Soup Co. and Heinz U.S.A., whose contracts with the smaller farmers give them considerable power over working conditions on large farms.

Agricultural labor protests were frequent during the Depression years in California and elsewhere. A number of farm labor unions flourished briefly in certain areas, and many had a specific ethnic iden-

tity, such as being a Mexican or Filipino union. The two most prominent unions in California were affiliated with national organizations:
the Cannery and Agricultural Workers Industrial Union (CAWIU)
with the Communist party and the United Cannery, Agricultural,
Packing, and Allied Workers of America (UCAPAWA) with the newly
formed Congress of Industrial Organizations (CIO). They were successful in part because they transcended ethnic loyalties and could
use resources of their affiliated organizations. Despite differences in
ideologies, both had similar goals: to negotiate contracts with agricultural employers that would increase wages, improve working conditions, and provide some guarantee of job security for regular workers.
Both, however, failed to translate temporary gains into long-term
reforms, which was in part due to repression by both local and state
authorities. The prominent anti-union activities by both powerful economic interests and government officials probably would have been
sufficient by themselves to prevent unionization. But weakness within
each organization also inhibited both unions from taking full advantages of opportunities for reform. Whereas urban industries began to
unionize during the 1930s and 1940s, the relationship between farm
workers and agribusiness failed to substantially change when the
depression era ended.

The current period has been dominated by the organizing efforts of
the UFW under the leadership of the late Cesar Chavez. This union's
campaigns began intensively in 1965, just after the expiration of a
series of bracero programs in which Mexican nationals were recruited
for harvest work throughout the Southwest. Drawing inspiration from
the civil rights movement, the UFW mounted a successful boycott of
table grapes resulting in 150 contracts in 1970 with growers producing
85 percent of California's table grapes and covering 20,000 jobs. The
contracts were notable in their emphasis on "control issues." These
included the institution of a union hiring hall intended to provide
worker seniority; strict enforcement of pesticide use, including the
banning of the still-legal and widely used DDT; institution of a formal
grievance procedure; formation of a health plan unprecedented for
most farm workers, including a fund to support elderly and disabled
farm workers; and changes in the working environment, such as providing for rest breaks, field toilets, and cool drinking water.

The UFW was immediately placed on the defensive, however, by
incursions by the Teamsters Union and proposals for restrictive legislation. When the table grape contracts expired in 1973, nearly all the

table grape growers signed contracts with the Teamsters without consulting employees. In response, the UFW developed a legislative strategy in which consumer support for a renewed table grape boycott and a boycott of head lettuce and Gallo brand wines was channeled into pressure for California legislation that would guarantee the rights of farm workers to organize and vote in unionization elections without undue threats or interference from any party.

The result was the 1975 California Agricultural Labor Relations Act (ALRA). Under its terms the UFW won the substantial majority of farm labor elections during the last half of the 1970s, and the Teamsters suspended their organizing efforts. The law faced considerable opposition, however. Funds to supervise the elections, certify the results, and investigate unfair labor practices were temporarily shut off. Also, many growers continued to resist serious negotiations. As a result, by January 1978 the UFW had won more than 250 elections, 180 of which were certified, but only had signed 80 contracts covering 25,000 workers.

Since 1980 the position of the UFW has been on a steady decline. Part of this erosion is due to a change in state administration in California and stiffened resistance by agribusiness to unionization. But also the UFW experienced considerable internal difficulties that resulted in the departure of much of the union's organizers and leadership. Instead of continuing its organizing campaigns, the union returned to a table grape boycott in the mid-1980s, but the boycott still has not reversed the UFW's decline. By the early 1990s the UFW had few contracts left and was simply struggling to stay alive as an organization. The death of Chavez in April 1993 left the union without a nationally recognized leader, but it also opens the possibility that a revitalized UFW or other unions can again take the initiative in organizing farm workers.

Somewhat different conditions and strategies have led to modest gains for FLOC in Ohio and Michigan. A boycott of Campbell-owned products combined with boycott endorsements from a number of influential religious organizations led Campbell to protect its public image and begin talks with FLOC. The results were three-party negotiations in which the tomato and cucumber farmers contracted to Campbell organized themselves into bargaining units to participate in talks with FLOC and Campbell representatives. A private, bipartisan organization, the Dunlop Commission, oversaw representative elections among farm workers. After the Campbell contracts were signed

Heinz, another major purchaser of tomatoes and cucumbers, began negotiations with FLOC and subsequently reached agreements similar to the ones with Campbell. By the early 1990s FLOC contracts covered more than 5,000 workers, modest by UFW achievements at the height of its influence but representing a substantial proportion of the tomato and cucumber harvest workers in Ohio and Michigan. While the UFW is struggling to survive, FLOC's ambitions are to end sharecropping arrangements in other states that put harvest workers at a disadvantage and organize migrant workers along the migratory routes originating in Florida and Texas and leading to the upper Midwest.

Analytical Approach

Our analysis of these two broad forms of agrarian movements has been especially influenced by two approaches to social movements: the resource mobilization and the political process models. These approaches contain a number of basic propositions about the nature of social movements (Jenkins 1983; McAdam 1982; Zald and McCarthy 1979). The resource mobilization approach focuses on how people can translate their discontent into forms of effective collective action. The relevant issues concern how people can organize, pool their resources, and create the pressure necessary for social change. Social movements need to mobilize a variety of resources to achieve success. A distinction is sometimes made between a social movement's internal resources and those resources that derive from sympathetic supporters or institutions external to the constituency.

Internal resource mobilization concerns include selecting issues and goals that fit best with the constituency, building solidarity among the constituency, developing effective leadership styles and organization, and utilizing whatever resources the constituency has to offer, such as time for protest activities and money for expenses. Questions concerning external resources include strategies for gaining publicity for the cause through media coverage, creating and sustaining a sympathetic public willing to offer various forms of assistance, promoting advantageous alliances with influential individuals and organizations, seeking political endorsements for movement goals, and soliciting donations for social movement organizations.

Our emphasis on strategic considerations assumes the rational character of most social movement actors. The contention that activists calculate the costs and benefits of various courses of action departs from common media portrayals and several theoretical approaches that view protest participants as irrational, emotionally or psychologically stressed, socially isolated, or deviant. Furthermore, movement activists are seen by both the resource mobilization and political process models as often drawing on indigenous organizational strengths and existing leadership and solidarity through established networks of interaction and communication. The key to setting these assets in motion and generating a social movement lies, in part, with changes in political opportunities provided by the larger socioeconomic environment.

The political process model analyzes social movements as adaptations to long-term structural transformations of the society, economy, or government. This focus is particularly useful in understanding the broad, historical patterns of farmer and farm worker movements. Striking changes in the larger political and economic environment have influenced the development of farmer and farm worker movements throughout U.S. history. These have included the introduction of new forms of production; changes in communication and transportation technologies; extension of suffrage to unpropertied males, women, and ethnic minorities; changes in immigration policy; migration patterns in settling the frontier; rural to urban migration; increasing concentration of capital; growing centralization of government; abolition of slavery; the impact of the depression; changes stimulated by the civil rights movement; and stages of the economic cycle. Structural changes have altered the balance of forces that open and close the windows of opportunity for agricultural producers to resolve their persistent grievances.

Both the resource mobilization and the political process models assume grievances to be longstanding rather than appearing suddenly. For example, the persistent character of farmers' grievances led Taylor (1953) to portray the various episodes of farmer movements as the unfolding of a single farmer movement, analogous to the labor movement. Also, Majka and Majka (1982), McWilliams (1939), and others have emphasized the continuity in farm labor demands over time, even though the ethnic character and immigration status of farm workers have tended to change periodically. The resource mobilization approach tends to regard the availability of new resources to the social movement as providing the means to pursue their interests—for example, the willingness of a substantial proportion of the population to support UFW boycotts from 1966 to 1975. In contrast, the political process model views new resources as only one form of changing political opportunities. This broader view includes two particularly significant variables in the larger political environment: changes in the ability of movement opponents to control the social movements and the emergence of "cognitive liberation."

The contention that grievances of social movements are ubiquitous is derived from the idea that the goals of social movements are shaped by institutionalized conflicts of interest with other actors (e.g., bankers, landlords, merchants, employers). The opponents of a movement are not always capable of a strong response. They may be temporarily weakened by economic conditions or political setbacks. More significantly, the elite may be divided among itself as to the relative threat posed by the social movements. Indeed, one faction of elite opponents may even benefit from losses inflicted on another elite faction. The cooperative movement, for instance, faced stronger opposition in the cotton South, where the landlord, merchant, and banker were often unified in a single person or family, than in the Midwest and Great Plains, where these roles were more often distinct and sometimes in conflict with one another over immediate interests. Also, the passage of California's ALRA in 1975 was made easier by a temporary split between the large agribusiness enterprises—most of whom wanted to continue resisting unionization—and major food corporations such as supermarket chains, many of whom wanted to end the instability that UFW strikes and boycotts had caused to the industry during the preceding decade.

McAdam's (1982) political process model reflects more recent tendencies in social movement theory to reconsider subjective as well as objective conditions. This is clear in his emphasis on the role of "cognitive liberation," a concept that refers to the emergence of new ideologies that alter the constituency's beliefs about the injustice or about the possibilities for successfully challenging existing conditions. Actual conditions may or may not change or may have changed long before or may be about to change. What is important is that potential activists develop an analysis of conditions that is more conducive to mobilization. While farmers themselves often "cannot see the forest for the trees," sometimes persons with marginal involvement in agriculture can transcend the routine, institutionalized way of thinking and present novel analyses of existing conditions that encourage a sense of injustice, or a translation of "personal problems" into "public issues," or create new hopes for success in solving old grievances.

In farmer movements a new understanding of problems and solutions can often be traced to a peripheral actor—a rural newspaper editor or minister, a seed salesman, a retired military official, an immigrant, a socialist, or a government bureaucrat. In farm worker movements a substantial proportion of the leadership has had experiences outside of agriculture, such as urban labor activism and the civil rights movement. For example, Cesar Chavez, the UFW head, previously was active in the Saul Alinsky–affiliated Community Service Organization, which was involved with grass-roots organizing in California's urban areas. We will consider both the role of ideology and fluctuations in political and economic conditions as significant components of the mobilization process. We will also point out when prevailing ideologies function to stifle mobilization.

While the chapters that follow do not often refer specifically to resource mobilization and political process, these two approaches have oriented our selection of critical aspects of each episode. For example, we will highlight the variety of ways in which both constituencies were mobilized for collective action and the alliances that were attempted to give movements more leverage. We will also focus on the relationships between individual movements and government and political leaders—specifically the possibility of translating discontent into political reforms and the not always beneficial impacts that these reforms have had on the movements themselves. Finally, we will describe structural changes in agricultural production that influenced the development of these movements and the possibilities for change.

The ubiquitous character of agrarian discontent lends itself to these approaches. Farm workers have never fared well economically and are not even protected by much of the legislation that covers wage workers in other economic sectors. Similarly, scarcely a generation of farmers can pass without experiencing some downturn of the farm economy. Thus, while certain problems may be continually in the consciousness of farmers and farm workers, the opportunity to act collectively toward resolution of those problems is contingent on the ability to mobilize political and economic resources as the means of asserting power against opposing interests. In a sense, ideology can also be considered a resource insofar as the analysis generated by the ideology triggers cognitive liberation and facilitates useful mobilization of political and economic resources. These ideologies—or what may be referred to as "master frames" (Snow and Benford 1988)—have been particularly important in shaping farmer movements. These ideologies have included "agrarian fundamentalism" (the belief that agriculture is more important to the economy than any other sector), "competitive capitalism" (the possibility of a market economy of private ownership without a few large-scale enterprises dominating any particular economic sector), and "producer ideology" (based on the primacy of human labor as the creator of all economic value) (Mitchell 1987, 201). (The role of ideology in farmer movements will be taken up in more detail in the Conclusion.)

Resources and Strategies

Economic resources, or the lack thereof, structure the available economic strategies of collective action. The repertoire of economic strategies in the history of U.S. farmer mobilizations include cooperative marketing, cooperative purchasing, cooperative production, boycotts, squatting, rent strikes, land trusts, holding actions, individualized participation in free-market transactions, and participation in state-directed production control and marketing. Economic strategies of the farm worker movements covered in this book are more limited. Generally, they have included labor strikes and other work-related tactics and consumer boycotts. The objectives have been improvements in wages, working and housing conditions, and job security, usually through collective bargaining and unionization.

Similarly, political resource bases shape collective political practices. Political strategies that have emerged among farmers include third-party formation, independent-bloc voting to influence a two-party system, protest, lobbying, collective bargaining, alliances with labor, regulation of monopoly, and squatters' associations. Farm worker political strategies have included building alliances with influential organizations and individuals outside of agriculture, such as labor unions, religious organizations, political leaders and city governments, civil rights groups, student organizations, and progressive community groups. The purpose of these alliances was to attempt to offset the ordinarily weak political influence of farm workers themselves.

The chapters that follow will describe more precisely events in each episode of agrarian mobilization and the nature of shifting strategic uses of variable resources. While each mobilization has its own specific character, we do not wish to view each episode as completely distinct from the next. Instead, we hope our discussion illustrates the historical flow of patterns of agrarian mobilization in the United States.

FARMER MOVEMENTS

Chapter 1

The Colonial Period to the Civil War

When North Americans consider the great farmer movements, it is usually the powerful Populist challenge of the late nineteenth century or the various regional mobilizations that took place in the Great Depression that come to mind. Since the founding of the republic, however, America's farmers have periodically engaged in collective actions designed to bring about desired changes. Indeed, the history of American farmer movements precedes the Revolutionary War and that revolution itself is difficult to understand without an awareness of the important role played by farmers. In observing the various social movements undertaken by farm people prior to the Civil War, we shall see that, from the very beginning, America's farmers were not always a unified group. Class divisions and social stratification fragmented the interests of that part of the population we generally refer to as farmers.

In colonial and Revolutionary America the farm population—the proportion of persons directly engaged in agricultural production—was very large. More than 80 percent of the residents of Revolutionary America were farm people. While the number of farmers continued to grow in absolute terms, as a percentage of the total population farmers declined to less than 60 percent of the population by the time of the Civil War (USDA 1940). Nevertheless, colonial and Revolutionary America was an agrarian society. The interests and actions of farmers, however divided, were essential to the American Revolution and to the subsequent construction of the new nation. We turn first to an examination of certain farmer movements that developed in colonial America.

Pre-Revolutionary Agrarian Movements

Sporadic revolt commonly precedes revolution. The instability of British America is reflected in the periodic upsurges of collective expressions of farmers' discontent. Historians' efforts to reconstruct the events of this period face many obstacles. Surely many revolts by these colonial farmers have gone unrecorded. Controversy also rages over interpretation of evidence that is often meager. Revolts and rebellions by tenant farmers in New York and by slaves in the South have provided the most evidence and thus have received the most attention. They are, by no means, to be understood as exhaustive of farmer movements in pre-Revolutionary America but only as representative of the types of movements generated by the respective class structures of the regions. To be sure, tenants also rebelled in southern colonies and slaves rebelled in northern colonies, while many independent farmers, landowners, and planters rebelled not against class domination, but against colonial political subordination and market restrictions. Furthermore, we can be sure that the subordinate classes of agricultural producers struggled in less spectacular, more hidden forms against local and regional elites. What James Scott (1990) has called "everyday forms of resistance" provided a cultural context from which more public expressions of protest and conflict emerged.

Taylor (1953) ties the first farmers' revolt in the colonies directly to conflict over the development of commercial (market-oriented) agriculture. The first uprisings involved tobacco, a significant export crop in colonial America. In 1621 British law granted its colonies a virtual monopoly on the sale of tobacco to England. This led to high prices for American tobacco which, in turn, encouraged farmers to increase their production. In a lesson American farmers were to "learn" again and again for the next 350 years, this increased production led to a rapid decline in tobacco prices. Holmes (1920) estimated this to be comparable to a decline from 55 cents a pound in 1618–20 to 6 cents a pound by 1639. Market barriers in this particular episode of overproduction resulted from the British demand that all colonial tobacco be shipped to England on irregularly available British boats, the lack of competition among British buyers (owing to a temporary chartered monopoly sold to one company by King James I), and the imposition of a tax on colonial tobacco.

Farmers collectively protested these restrictions on their markets. They also sought legislation that would stabilize prices and control production. They tried to organize collective-bargaining groups in which they would voluntarily commit themselves to restrict production and not sell their crop for less than an agreed on price. When these efforts failed, producers would sometimes engage in violence by destroying the tobacco of other farmers. These plant-cutting "riots" were directed primarily at those producers who failed to join the collective bargaining group. As Taylor (1953) notes, these events foretell much of the future of American agriculture and farmers' efforts at collective actions to resolve the problems created by their productivity.

This history will make clear that rational choices for an individual are not necessarily rational choices for the group of which that individual is a member. When tobacco prices were high, the logical response for an individual farmer was to produce as much as possible. That decision, however, repeated by all tobacco producers, results in overproduction and the high prices disappear. Such episodes have often led the group of producers to attempt to restrict their production to levels that the market can readily absorb. A particular dilemma faced by such collective action is that their very success at increasing prices for their goods increasingly gives rise to the *free rider*, which in this case is the producer who has not agreed to restrict production but who benefits from the increased prices created by other farmers' collective production control. This is an important concept for understanding farmer movements, as well as many other forms of collective action.

Taylor's association of farmer movements with the development of a commercial agriculture helps to make sense of American agricultural history, although commercial production should not be understood as a necessary condition of agrarian revolt in general. World history is full of peasant revolts against feudal lords in the absence of commercialized agricultural economies. Efforts to import or copy feudal forms of production in the United States also often resulted in uprisings of tenant farmers or sharecroppers against landlords. Unlike the colonial tobacco producers, these farmers do not appear to have been so immediately motivated by commercial interests as by the desire to own the land they worked on. Nonownership of the land they farmed may have posed a prior obstacle to these tenants' ability to participate in the market, since the bulk of any surplus they could produce was appropriated by the landlord.

The dominant settlement pattern in the agricultural regions of the northern colonies was what Main (1965) called subsistence farm communities. These communities of small-scale farming families did not produce any significant cash crop but merely exchanged goods and services within the simple division of labor of the local community. This type of settlement created a relatively egalitarian class structure in which the majority of these farmers owned the land they farmed and the simple tools they used. Main describes these communities as such: "Great wealth could not be or had not yet been accumulated; therefore no wealthy class was present. Neither did the landless laborers increase in numbers, for land was not very valuable and therefore could be easily obtained" (1965, 18).

There were also regions, however, usually of more commercialized agriculture, characterized by much more inequality in the class structure. These are areas where uprisings of colonial farmers were much more common. The Hudson River Valley of what is now New York State was one such region. The inegalitarian character of this region can be traced to its origins as a Dutch settlement, although the British continued the policy of providing huge grants of land to wealthy and influential families. These families then acquired landless European immigrants to labor as tenants on the manors. Since this was very much like the European feudal system from which most of these peasants were escaping, the instability of such settlement should not be surprising. While most northern colonial farmers possessed farms of less than 100 acres, the manors of the Hudson River Valley consisted of thousands, sometimes hundreds of thousands, of acres. Kim (1978) has documented many of these manors. The largest, Rensselaerwyck Manor, belonged to the Van Rensselaer family, contained 850,000 acres and was supplemented by another smaller manor, Claverack, of 250,000 acres. The Livingston family acquired about 160,000 acres in one Livingston Manor. Cortlandt Manor consisted of about 86,000 acres, while Philipsburgh Manor held 92,000 acres. There were many more such grants—some smaller ones to other individual families, some of equivalent size to groups of families who held them in partnerships.

Mark's (1940) history of these manors indicates that the development of these large manors was intended to reproduce the European landed aristocracy and feudal relations in America. Similarly, it was a means by which colonial governors enriched themselves. The legal and illegal means by which these large holdings were consolidated provided the governor all sorts of opportunities to pocket fees and bribes and to grant himself (under the names of paid collaborators) large acreages.

The Revolt of the Palatines

One of the first agrarian uprisings precipitated by these conditions involved the Palatines, a German immigrant group who had fled to England in 1708, then relocated to New York in 1710, where they were bound to the production of wood products. This servitude was in exchange for passage to the colonies and was to be further rewarded, when resettlement costs were reimbursed, with 40 acres of land and seven years of freedom from taxes. This arrangement with Governor Robert Hunter was troubled from the start. Nearly one-sixth of the Palatines died en route. The survivors found themselves located next to Livingston Manor, instead of other land near Schoharie, to which they believed they were entitled through their agreement with Hunter.

According to Mark, they were forced to work "in gangs under military supervision" (1940, 111). In protest, the Palatines collectively refused to continue working. An armed contingent of Palatines threatened to leave the region for Schoharie. Hunter's troops successfully disarmed the Palatines but could not, in the long run, end the work stoppage nor contain the Palatines' emigration from the settlements. Over the next decade most of the Palatines dispersed to frontier regions. Some of them began to work on Livingston Manor under conditions of credit-dependency or debt-peonage. Some Palatine families remained on the original settlement and actually received land of their own in 1724. Many of them went to Schoharie, where they came in conflict with rival claimants to the land that had since been given or sold by Hunter to wealthy land speculators. When these speculators demanded that the Palatines either "purchase, lease or vacate the land," the Palatines destroyed the home of one of the speculators, beat up the speculator's son, broke the sheriff's ribs, and dragged him through two pig sties (Mark 1940, 114). Hunter's successor eventually removed most of the remaining Palatines, and the rest of the Schoharie land was distributed to several of the most prominent land speculators of the era.

The revolt of the Palatines is somewhat atypical of the agrarian movements that arose from the inequalities of colonial New York. This is due, in part, to the lack of clarity with respect to their class position. It might be argued that the Palatines are better classified as indentured laborers than as farmers, although farming as independent owners seems to have been their primary aspiration. Regardless, their actions exemplify the significance and power of civil disobedience as a form of protest. Their capacity to collectively refuse to work as well to sow their crops in direct violation of executive orders was probably strengthened by their status as a minority ethnic group. This exemplifies the way in which subcultural characteristics can sometimes be translated into a resource base for solidarity. In this sense the cohesiveness of a distinct minority community can function to reduce the free rider problem. This is perhaps especially the case when the number of persons in the subordinate group is relatively small and live in close physical proximity to one another.

Tenant Revolts

Tenant farmer revolts occurred in other regions of colonial America where single families held titles to large tracts of land, such as in eastern New Jersey in the mid-1700s and earlier in Maryland, Virginia, and the Carolinas (Taylor 1953). The manors of New York, however, seemed to be particularly prone to uprisings by this subordinate class. Mark (1940) claimed that the large size of the landholdings and the often illicit means of their consolidation contributed to tenant resentment. Sometimes these uprisings were merely intended to obtain the security of a long-term lease rather than renting from year to year at the whim of the landlord. The objective was sometimes the termination of the tenants' feudal obligations of providing service or labor on the personal estate of the landlord. At other times, however, these uprisings aimed at the elimination of the landlord-tenant relationship altogether. In these movements tenants sought to dispossess the landlords and to acquire ownership themselves.

The legitimacy of these large landholdings was undermined not only by the unscrupulous manner of their acquisition and by the inequality itself, but also by legal disputes between colonies over jurisdiction of land. The manors of colonial New York were subject to such a controversy. Colonial Massachusetts also claimed much of the land just east of the Hudson River. The speculators and ambitious politicians of Massachusetts were more than willing to use the New York tenantry to further that colony's expansionary interests. Massachusetts had a more egalitarian agrarian landholding pattern than New York (Main 1965) and according to Kim, the relative deprivation of the New York tenants encouraged these anti-landlord movements: "Living right next to colonies in which a freehold land system prevailed undoubtedly sharpened their perception of the contrast between the two systems and made their status look worse than it actually was. Moreover, their frequent intercourse with New Englanders exposed them directly to the highly contagious culture of that region" (1978, 293).

Indeed, the landlords and conservative propagandists of the era often labeled the rebellious tenants "levelers" (Mark 1940), a derogatory term referring to their interest in eliminating the status and class inequalities based on the privileges of property. To be sure, not all of the Massachusetts supporters of the New York tenant revolts were motivated solely by an interest in social equality. Many were wealthy speculators in their own right, who saw an opportunity to acquire vast undeveloped areas in New York. The granting of freehold privilege to the relatively few tenants of these manors was well worth the price of overturning the legal claims of the New York landlords to these manors. Complicating the jurisdictional disputes were the claims of Native American groups that they had not been reimbursed adequately, if at all, by the manorial lords. The Massachusetts speculators were also quite ready to use these people as pawns in their expansionary politics. One such speculator, David Ingersoll, found that much of Livingston Manor had never legally been acquired from the Mohicans. The tenants also supported the Mohican claims since the tribe was willing to lease the land for periods of 999 years, as opposed to the one-year lease common on the manors (Mark 1940).

The form that these tenant revolts took is exemplified by what we might today call a rent strike. In 1751 the tenants of Livingston Manor collectively refused to pay their rent. Furthermore, they contended that the parcels they had been farming as tenants now belonged to them as owners and that the titles to such land had been granted by the government of Massachusetts. Livingston's response, typical of landlord reaction, was to request the New York colonial government officials to evict the tenants as trespassers on property recognized by

New York law. In retaliation, the Massachusetts government began to arrest loyal Livingston tenants and to give those tenants' land to farmers willing to take a Massachusetts title.

These events demonstrate how the state or government provides a resource that can be mobilized by specific classes. The government of New York provided the landlords' legal claims to the land as well as armed forces to arrest those who violated those claims. The government of Massachusetts provided similar resources to the tenants. The situation is unique insofar as specific land areas usually fall under the jurisdiction of a single government. Thus whatever class dominates that government controls that land area. Observers often fail to see the state as the resource of a class because, in the more common case, only one government is recognized, and class domination is obscured by presenting itself as the state. This character of government is made clear in border disputes and in revolutionary movements that establish parallel governments. Indeed, the American Revolution and the Civil War are examples. In the Revolution the rule of an alliance of English nobility and merchants in the form of the British government was challenged with the Declaration of Independence and armed resistance by an alliance of an aspiring new class of urban and agrarian entrepreneurs as well as a class of small independent farmers and artisans. In the Civil War the South seceded and established a parallel government that ultimately could not defend itself militarily against the Union forces. That such events also usually generate violence in the resolution also reveals the character of government or the "state," as Weber defined it: "a human community that (successfully) claims the monopoly of the legitimate use of physical force within a given territory" (1946, 78). Thus the coercive nature of class domination—a quality also commonly obscured in everyday life—is also made apparent in disputes over territorial jurisdiction.

A series of arrests and counter-arrests by New York and Massachusetts authorities continued for several years, escalating at times into violence with armed resistance to arrest, armed efforts to free the imprisoned from the jails, and the burning and destruction of tenants' crops by small private armies employed by the landlords. Mark (1940) claims that by 1755 the tenant revolt had become a "miniature border war" with the destruction of tenant homes and the killing of a rebellious Livingston Manor tenant by a New York sheriff's deputy. The Massachusetts government claimed jurisdiction over the matter, charged the deputy with murder, offered a reward for his capture, and unsuccessfully demanded that the New York government turn the deputy over to Massachusetts for trial. At a seeming impasse, the conflict gradually began to decline with the escalation of the French and Indian War (1754–63) and the diversion of both colonial governments' attention and resources to that common battle. Tensions remained high, however, and the class conflict between tenants and landlords did not simply disappear.

During the French and Indian War the Stockbridge Indians played a more significant role. A Native American by the name of Van Gelder, who had been a key leader in the tenant revolt, led an armed group that kidnapped manor workers and killed two men. Livingston Manor's iron foundry was making weapons for the British in the war. Whether Van Gelder's interests were still simply to oppose the manor lords or to assist the French and Indians is not certain. The Stockbridge Indians continued to sell manor land to Massachusetts settlers during the war. This helped lay the basis for a renewal of the conflict after the war in the "Great Rebellion of 1766" (Mark 1940), which in turn made for some very interesting class politics in the American Revolution.

The tenants' desires to become owners of their land led to a resurgence of rebellion following the French and Indian War. While many of these farmers probably believed they had legally purchased these lands, others were likely to have simply been interested in seizing the opportunity to become landowners. Regardless, civil disobedience and violence were almost inevitable since the tenants had little in the way of legal and political resources to pursue justice in the courts or legislature. The judges were almost entirely drawn from the landlord class, and property ownership was a requirement for both jury membership and for voting. Thus, the rent strike and the subsequent armed defense of the land they occupied once again became the mode of revolt.

Another potential resource for the tenant farmers was to form an alliance with the growing movement for independence that was developing in cities like New York and Boston. Mark (1940) contends, however, that the tenants must have been very disappointed with the failure of an alliance with the Sons of Liberty, an organization composed primarily of merchants, artisans, and mechanics seeking to end the market restrictions of a colonial economy. While the tenants "liked to think of themselves as rural Sons of Liberty" (Mark 1940, 138), some leaders of the Sons of Liberty actually sat on courts that con-

demned the tenant rebellion. The failure of this alliance, foreshadow-
ing the character of the emerging society, suggests the significance of
divergent fundamental class interests (Wright 1978). The history of
farmer movements is filled with attempts, mostly unsuccessful, at
alliance between urban, industrial workers and farmers. That two
groups are in simultaneous rebellion against a common enemy does
not necessarily make them allies. The tenants were challenging basic
economic principles of the developing capitalist economy: the ownership of another person's means of production (i.e., the land) and the
entitlement of property owners to a share (in this case, in the form of
rent) of the surplus production. Rebels, such as the Sons of Liberty,
did not commonly seek such a radical egalitarianism. They primarily
fought the political entitlement to surplus in the form of colonial
exploitation. This did not directly challenge class exploitation or the
economic entitlement to surplus.

The ideology that informed this revolt is revealed in literature that
Mark (1940, 140) discovered in similar anti-rent strikes in New Jersey.
This ideology contends that "no man is naturally entitled to a greater
Proportion of the Earth, than another" and that once land is improved
by labor it is "made the Property of that Man who bestowed his labor
on it, from whom it cannot afterwards be taken, without breaking thro'
the Rule of Natural justice; for thereby he would actually be deprived
of the Fruits of his Industry" (quoted in Mark 1940, 140). This ideological appeal to natural rights found its way into the writings of Thomas
Jefferson and was retained as a fundamental premise of American
agrarian ideology, or what is sometimes called Jeffersonian or agrarian democracy. The radical egalitarianism of the doctrine, however,
and the notion that the entire value of one's production should be
retained by the laborer who produced it are in basic contradiction to
the principles of capitalist economy.

In a capitalist economy a share of the value of the product is guaranteed to the propertied even though they themselves have not
labored to produce anything of value. In agrarianism a "producer ideology" (Mitchell 1987) remains a potent element in the history of
American farmer movements. U.S. agriculture has always been an
object of attempted capitalist domination, but many American farmers
have also stubbornly, though not always successfully, resisted efforts
by nonproducers (landlords, bankers, employers) to intrude on their
independence and to acquire a share of the surplus produced by the
farmers themselves. In turn, the dominant class has actively opposed

the producer ideology since colonial times. The landlord Livingston, recognizing the fundamental threat to the propertied elite presented by such ideas, wrote in 1766, "If you give anything by compulsions of this sort, you must give up everything" (quoted in Mark 1940, 40).

The wealthy played a dominant role in the early formulation of the American government. Consequently, the state has proven to be a very unreliable ally or resource for American farmer movements. As we have noted, behind the authority of the state is the power of a monopoly on the use of violence. In the New York tenant rebellion of 1766 the authority of government and thus the power of landlords to maintain their rule was undermined by the unreliability of local militias, composed mostly of small farmers. The widespread character of the rebellion (Connecticut farmers were also refusing to repay creditors and petitioning for an equal division of property among citizens) required outside forces to quell the revolt by apparently well-armed farmers who now also had more military experience from the French and Indian War. The result was considerably more bloodshed than in previous rebellions. The tenants, however, did not find as ready a resource in Massachusetts this time as the ruling elites of both colonies seemed to temporarily unite in the face of the tenants' radical threat to their property ownership. Eventually, most of the leaders of the rebellious farmers were arrested and imprisoned.

The trial of one leader in particular, William Prendergast, seemed to have captured the essence of the rebellion. The colony's supreme court was composed of men, all of who "were amongst the greatest landlords and land speculators of the colony" (Mark 1940, 145). Prendergast was tried on charges of high treason and was not, surprisingly, found guilty. In his defense, Prendergast claimed that if opposition to government was treason, then none of the members of the court were innocent, as they were all rebels against England. His sentence was to be hung, cut down while still alive, have his internal organs and genitals cut from his body, and then his body was to be cut into four sections (quartered). This sentence was unable to be executed since the sheriff could find no one to do the job, and was later commuted by the king, perhaps as part of a strategy to seek the sympathy of tenants for the British in the rapidly developing confrontation between Whig forces and the king.

The conflict continued off and on throughout the year, forcing the military to place troops in rural households. These troops, however, were increasingly in demand to put down the growing urban rebellion.

The force exerted by the landlords and the government in dealing with the rebellion led many of the tenants to simply leave New York for more western frontiers or to the unsettled region of what is now Vermont. This migration from New York no doubt exacerbated already existing concerns of New York's government and commercial classes for the relative underpopulation of the colony. The harsh tenancy of the manors was not attractive to small farmers when the frontier of an entire continent lay before them. Following the French and Indian War this frontier became a more effective resource for small farmers since it functioned as an outlet from such conditions. The struggle to make this land available for family-sized farming was, however, one that would span the next century.

The hostility bred by conditions of the manor system and the class struggles between landlord and tenant in colonial New York created a curious twist in the politics of collective class action in the American Revolution. Lynd's (1967) study of New York farmers' role in the Revolution discovered that the decision of tenants to side with the British or with the Revolutionaries was not based on Whig or Tory political ideology. Rather, tenants simply allied with the enemies of their landlords. The Livingstons of Livingston Manor, for instance, were leaders in the struggle for independence from Britain. Their tenants sided with the British. In neighboring Dutchess County, however, where the landlords were Loyalists, the tenants joined in the rebellion.

Thus the tenants of New York can be said to have acted as a class but were divided among themselves. How was this possible? Both sides in the Revolution held forth the promise of confiscation of their opponents' lands and redistribution to the tenants. This basic economic interest pushed aside political ideology in determining military alliance. At the economic level the tenants acted—or perhaps we should say reacted—in a unified manner against their landlords. The landlords, on the other hand, had more autonomy to choose their cause on the basis of their political ideology. Thus at the political and military level, tenants found themselves in opposition to one another. Lynd contends correctly that it was "precisely because they were so radical economically, the tenants at Livingston Manor opposed their Whig landlords politically" (1967, 77). This division of the tenants, however, helped to ensure continuation of landlord-tenant relations of production in the aftermath of the Revolution. A tenant alliance at the political and military level in this critical conjuncture might have permitted a strong challenge to the very existence of tenancy in the new nation. In this sense their radicalism was diminished. They were no longer demanding an absolute termination of this form of exploitation, only an end to their own individual tenancies.

Slave Revolts

The nature of slavery suggests that any time a single slave sought to escape bondage, we might speak of revolt. Since our interest here is in social movements, we would focus only on collective actions on the part of slaves to change the conditions of their slavery. In some cases this meant escape to nonslave regions; in other cases this meant a rather shortsighted armed (usually only swords and clubs) insurrection against their owners. The latter rebellions were rather quickly put down by the superior weapons and resources of the larger slave society, which provided assistance to the particular plantation facing revolt. Aptheker (1969) documents at least 250 reported slave revolts and contends that slave rebellion increased whenever the agricultural economy was in recession. This was because agricultural slave owners' response to depressed markets was to increase production (thus increasing the slaves' workload) and to restrict even further already stringent living conditions. Aptheker argues that "exciting or unusual events" (1969, 11) often encouraged slave revolt. Certainly the American Revolution was one such event. The spread of Revolutionary politics and the talk of freedom, equality, natural rights, and entitlement to the fruits of one's labor enhanced the hopes and aspirations of colonial slaves for their freedom.

Rebellion against slavery predates the Revolutionary period, however. Aptheker (1969) claims that the first community in the American South to have slaves was also the first to experience revolt. This occurred in a Spanish settlement in South Carolina in 1526, when slaves rose up and killed some of their owners in escaping to freedom with the region's Native American population. In British colonial America slave revolts did not become particularly important until the early 1700s with the development of large-scale rice and indigo production. Before this, tobacco was the main agricultural export crop and was more commonly produced by whites under conditions of debt peonage, indentured servitude, or tenancy.

In the eighteenth century, as slavery expanded, so did the collective struggles of blacks for freedom. While some individuals and groups did escape—and these rebellions may have helped outlaw slavery in some states (e.g., Pennsylvania and Massachusetts)—these movements were not, of course, directly successful in eliminating slavery as an institution. Slave society dealt harshly with slaves in revolt. The treatment of New York's rebellious tenants must be considered mild in comparison with the summary executions of slaves who challenged the class relations of slavery. Just as most of the slave revolts had a leader, most also seem to have had a traitor. Slave owners shrewdly offered freedom to slaves who betrayed their fellows in revolt. Slaves who were willing to reveal secret plans could themselves acquire freedom, but only at the expense of their fellow slaves. South Carolina, an important colonial agricultural producer, experienced a number of slave revolts around 1740. Aptheker (1969) notes that this led the colonial government to tax slave importations and to use the funds to obtain white Protestant settlers to farm the land.

Unfortunately, a full treatment of slave revolt is beyond the bounds of this book on farmer movements. Although most slaves farmed and much of southern agriculture depended on slave labor, the breadth, complexity, and peculiarity of this oppressive institution gave rise to unique movements (e.g., abolition, the underground railroad, and movements to return to Africa); this struggle against slavery has been treated in a separate volume.[1]

The Regulators

Inequalities in southern agriculture also existed between the eastern, commercialized, slave-based plantation economy and the western subsistence farm communities on the frontier. In North Carolina the economic, political, and social inequality between these agrarian structures culminated in a rebellion of small farmers who were known as "the Regulators." Their objectives were not specifically related to agriculture but rather at the elimination of political injustices derived from the eastern planters' domination of the legislative, judicial, and executive branches of the colonial government. The eastern counties, for instance, had one representative for every 1,700 persons, while the growing western counties had one representative for every 7,000 persons (Lefler and Powell 1973).

The hostilities came to a head over the refusal of the Regulators to pay taxes and fees. Fees were a primary source of income for government officials. Few of these officials were elected by the citizenry.

Most had either purchased their office or had received it as a gift from the king or the governor. The small farmers of the western frontier communities resented what they saw as arbitrary and excessive collection fees. These farmers also resented the passage of tax legislation in which they felt their interests were underrepresented, owing to the disproportionate representation in the legislature. In fact, taxes and fees worked a particular hardship on these back-country farmers, not simply because they were poor but because their communities were based largely on a noncash, subsistence and barter economy.

As often happens in social movements, the first victims of collective actions were not the real enemies of the participants but merely persons who represented or symbolized the dominant class or the undesired trends. In 1765 about 100 angry farmers attacked and beat a group of surveyors near Sugar Creek, North Carolina. The next year the farmers began to circulate a paper calling for collective refusal to pay fees and taxes. This prompted legislation to regulate the fees of some lower-level public officials. By 1768 the movement had acquired the name "Regulators" and became more formally organized around the goal of gaining control over their local government. Their primary resource in this endeavor was still simply civil disobedience, a collective refusal to pay taxes until this objective was achieved. When a Regulator's horse was confiscated for nonpayment of taxes, however, about 70 Regulators went to Hillsborough and fired their guns into the roof of Colonel Fanning's house. Shortly after this the Regulators published an apology, signed by 500 citizens, that still sought democratization but through peaceful means. One leader of the Regulators was a Quaker by the name of Herman Husband, whom Powell (1949) compares with India's more recent anti-colonial leader, Mahatma Gandhi, in his belief that nonviolent civil disobedience is the most powerful weapon of otherwise powerless subordinate classes.

In 1769 the frontier farmers elected Regulator leaders to the legislature. Their underrepresentation continued, however, as did the scattered disorders and resistance along the frontier. In Hillsborough the court docket was full of Regulator cases and the Regulators came together to occupy the court. At first peaceful, the situation soon became a riot. The judge fled, and other court officials were whipped and dragged through the streets. Colonel Fanning, identified by the movement as their principal opponent, was whipped in the streets before the Regulators destroyed his house and burned his papers (Lefler and Powell 1973). The next day the Regulators kept their promise to obtain justice on their own, since they could not get it in the courts. They held mock trials in the courthouse, dispensing justice as they saw it.

When the legislature passed stronger laws for dealing with the resistance and expelled Husband from his elected seat, the Regulators simply attracted more members. All of this culminated in a battle between some 1,400 militia men and 2,000 Regulators at Great Alamance Creek in 1771. Though both sides suffered nine dead, the better equipped and organized militia dispersed the Regulators. The arrest and execution of a number of Regulators' leaders led to the demise of the organization. Many of these farmers fled further into the frontier hills of what is now Kentucky and Tennessee, seeking to escape the domination of nondemocratic government, the tax collector, and the developing commercial agriculture. Lefler and Powell (1973) contend that most of the Regulators went on to fight against the British in the Revolution. While the Regulators surely hoped that the Revolution would bring the democracy they had been fighting for, historians debate whether Alamance was the first battle of the Revolution. At one level it was a struggle against "taxation without representation," and, as Powell (1949) argues, it gave an inspirational example of courageous resistance against the British colonial government. The Regulator movement does not, however, seem to have had any explicit aspiration for independence from Britain. This is not to say that the latter was a grander goal than the objectives of the Regulators. The Revolution did not eliminate the inequalities between the eastern commercial agriculture and the western frontier subsistence farmers. Struggles between these factions would continue for years to come.

Shays' Rebellion

The achievement of political independence from Great Britain did not necessarily entail the achievement of economic independence. The American economy had developed as a British colony and continued to depend heavily on trade with England. After the Revolution, however, Britain terminated many of the advantages of colonial status, such as trade with the British West Indies. At the same time New England merchants imported, on credit, huge quantities of English goods that overloaded the still underdeveloped American market. When British wholesalers began to demand payment on the goods extended to the New England merchants, the New England merchants turned to the retailers to whom they had extended goods on credit. The retailers then sought to collect on the thousands of small credit extensions they had made to individual customers. Although these retailers and their customers were located in both urban and rural areas, problems arose especially in the rural areas, where a full-fledged money economy had not yet developed.

In the frontier subsistence communities the economy was often still primarily based on barter. Farmers would exchange their crops for goods from local retailers. To the extent that any surplus could be transformed into cash, that money was often necessary to pay the taxes imposed by the states, which were still suffering the expenses of the War of Independence. Thus local retailers' sudden demands for payment in hard currency worked a particular hardship in the New England back country. In this credit crisis, the conflictual nature of the relationship between creditor and debtor was made clear. The powerful opposition of these two forces has encouraged some historians to refer to the farmers' rebellion against creditors and the state governments that functioned at the behest of the creditors and merchants as a "class war" (Starkey 1955, 5) in which both debtors and creditors were "class-conscious" (Kaplan 1952, 48; Taylor 1953, 167)—that is, aware of themselves as two groups with fundamentally opposed political and economic interests.

Szatmary (1980) divides Shays' Rebellion[2] into four phases: (1) political protest, (2) armed assaults on debtor courts, (3) radicalization of reformist goals toward revolutionary objectives, and (4) a form of what Hobsbawm (1981) has called "social banditry" against the economic and political elite. The chain of debt that began with British wholesalers' demands on American merchants often ended in the debt courts of the frontier. Szatmary (1980) found that one out of three adult males in many western Massachusetts counties were taken to court by local merchants in efforts to obtain hard cash with which to repay the British. The inability of these subsistence farmers to provide such payment is reflected in Szatmary's finding that 72 percent of customers of one rural community's store paid their bills in goods and labor, without any exchange of money. Szatmary also contends that the increasing tax burden legislated by a government that overrepresented the wealthy, urban merchant class was disproportionately carried by small farmers, laborers, and artisans.

Without money to pay even small debts and the refusal of merchants to accept payment-in-kind (cows, crops, etc.), many small farmers faced the loss of their land. This was, for them, intolerable. Many of these farmers had recently fought for independence and had no intention of returning to tenant status or allowing America to slip back into a quasi-feudal agrarian class structure like the "old country." A petition of the farmers of Conway, Massachusetts, expressed this fear: "To be tenants to landlords, we know not who, and pay rents for lands, purchased with our money, and converted from howling wilderness, into fruitful fields, by the sweat of our brow, seems to carry with it in its nature truly shocking consequences" (quoted in Szatmary 1980, 33–34). When farmers did not face foreclosure on their property, they often faced the jail cell. The death of indebted Massachusetts farmer and Revolutionary War veteran, Timothy Bigelow, in a Worcester County jail served to heighten tensions and further encourage political mobilization for reform measures to relieve the burdens of the credit crisis.

In this first phase farmers attempted to work through legal political channels. The most commonly advocated reform was for the states to produce paper money that would be the equivalent of gold and silver. This would increase the money in circulation, inducing an inflationary effect and ease the payment of farmers' debts. Another reform advocated by New England farmers was the passage of tender laws, which would allow the payment of debts with goods rather than money. The debtor courts were also an object of demands for reform. While these courts were later to become primary targets of the rebellion, in the early stages farmers were usually simply requesting that the debtor courts (Courts of Common Pleas) be staffed with elected committees instead of appointed justices of the peace (Szatmary 1980).

These reforms were advocated against a background of hostility toward what seemed an unfair system of taxation. This anti-tax sentiment coincided with anti-lawyer attitudes. At one level this disdain for the legal profession reflected the economic conflict and the farmers' encounters with lawyers as they were prosecuted in the courts. At another level, however, this sentiment may reflect the deeper cultural clash that Szatmary (1980) contends lay behind this rebellion. Szatmary argues that Shays' Rebellion represented not only a class conflict but a battle of two cultures, or ways of life. The hostility toward lawyers, then, indicates a critical sensitivity to and awareness of the process by which commercial society sought to subjugate the society of the frontier subsistence community. As Weber has pointed out, the development of a rational legal system is necessary to the development of a commercialized capitalist economy (Weber 1978; Collins 1986). Szatmary writes,

Merchants and professionals looked with horror upon the disruption of the legal process. In their eyes, the forced closings of the courts undermined the contractual basis of law, thus making property insecure and eventually leading to a general economic leveling. The blurring of socioeconomic divisions would in turn signal the complete destruction of a commercial society, ushering in anarchy and finally a tyrannical despotism by the lower classes. (1980, 70)

Thus lawyers not only represented this cultural penetration but were clearly implicated in the struggles against creditors and tax collectors. To the extent that these communities were underrepresented in legislatures and courts dominated by the wealthy, lawyers were also seen as the executors of unjustly developed laws.

In general, the first phase of the rebellion was peaceful, although there were sporadic attacks on tax collectors and attempts to free indebted farmers from prison. The refusal of the elite to permit reform, however, pushed the farmers to violence. The issue of paper money or passage of tender laws were as much against the interests of the merchant class as they were in the interests of the farmers. The advocacy of paper money was criticized by the commercial interests as immoral. The tender laws were opposed, since they would institutionalize barter at a time when merchants could not dispose of the farmers' goods due to the restriction imposed on trade by the British. Particularly interesting is the reversal of the commercial class's advocacy of institutions of local democracy. County-level conventions had been an important mechanism of mobilization in the Revolution and were enthusiastically endorsed by the Whig leadership. As these conventions became the source of discussion and advocacy of monetary, legal, and tax reform, however, the elite began to oppose them. Szatmary notes the irony of a "Freeman" writing in a 1786 Massachusetts publication: "When we had other rulers, committees and conventions of the people were lawful—they were then necessary; but since I myself became a ruler, they cease to be lawful—the people have no right to examine my conduct" (1980, 47).

Since eligibility to hold political office required the possession of a certain amount of property, the Massachusetts state government was dominated by men of wealth. These legislators not only refused reform but also increased their opposition to local democracy. Farmers were told by leaders such as Noah Webster that they should live more frugally, work harder, drink less, and save their money for the tax collector and creditor. Only in Rhode Island did the legislature pass tender laws and issue paper money. In that state the merchants themselves sometimes engaged in a civil disobedience campaign by refusing to accept the paper money. The rural interest that had gained power in the Rhode Island legislature passed laws banning merchants who refused paper money from holding political office and threatened state ownership of commercial enterprises. As a result Rhode Island was relatively free of the disturbances that plagued Massachusetts in the mid-1780s. Smaller reforms were achieved in Vermont with the 1785 passage of a tender law and in New Hampshire with the issue of paper money to be used only for tax payments. Massachusetts, however, firmly resisted reform and soon became the center of an armed rebellion.

When the farmers of Massachusetts finally took up arms, their primary objectives were the closures of the courts that handled debt suits. Their awareness of the pre-Revolutionary farmer movement in the Carolinas is reflected in their adoption of the name "Regulators" for themselves. While the fear of property loss or incarceration for nonpayment of debt were immediate causes for mobilization, the rhetoric of speeches and writings often focused on the loss of autonomy and freedom. In the minds of these farmers, the virtues of independence were only possible with individual ownership of property in the means of production—a fundamental tenet of agrarian democratic philosophy. While this notion has continued even to the present generation of American farmers, these farmers in early America had much fresher memories of feudal dependence and peonage.

In August and September of 1786, just prior to the harvest, thousands of New England farmers engaged in armed disruption of court proceedings. Since the rural courts did not meet in October anyway, the protest subsided until November, when the harvest work was finished. As these attacks were scattered throughout the countryside, there was usually little opposition offered and thus little bloodshed. The farmers often realized their short-term objective of closing the debtor courts and stopping the processing of debt suits.

The networks of organization included neighborhood friendships, kinship, and print media. In these subsistence communities, neighbors commonly exchanged and cooperated in production activities.

They also usually shared a common church, school, and social life. Under such conditions the refusal to participate in collective action (against courts whose judges were usually outsiders) would more likely be seen as deviant than the participation in such action, even though illegal. Then, too, kinship networks extended across and between the New England states. These, as well as newspapers and pamphlets, were a source of information about actions in other states. This information facilitated the spread of collective actions as successful and unsuccessful tactics were learned by a large audience. These actions provided demonstration effects, constituting not only a learning mechanism but a source of inspiration for new actions in other communities.

Taverns and inns also served as a communication resource facilitating network development. Taverns had served a similar function in the Revolution and again they provided a gathering place for travelers to informally exchange news from other regions. In general, tavern owners and innkeepers were more likely to identify with the community than with the outside. Thus taverns often provided a place for organized meetings of rebels. Such an arrangement no doubt made for better business as well as better speeches.

Another resource of the farmers was their military experience. Many of these people had just fought in some capacity in the Revolution. Tactics and strategies were often clearly planned, and actions were usually organized in a disciplined military manner. The rebels simply marched on the court, dismissed the proceedings, and occupied the premises. There was rarely extraneous activity. This discipline was important in nullifying the opposition's propaganda that the farmers were rioters. A symbolic resource assumed by the rebels was a sprig of evergreen. To Massachusetts citizens, the pine tree had long symbolized independence and liberty. The appropriation of this symbol from the Revolution sought to legitimize the rebels by casting their actions as a continuation of the pursuit of the goals of the Revolution.

The dominant class, however, had resources of their own. Not only did they have access to print media, but they controlled the legislature and, to some extent, the military as well. Szatmary found the propaganda campaign waged by the creditors, merchants, and state government to contain three basic themes. The first accused the rebels of wanting to end the right to private property in the pursuit of a redistribution of wealth, or a "leveling revolution." This position seems highly untenable, even in the most radical phases of the rebellion. The rebels' ultimate goal was, in fact, defense of their private property against creditors. To the extent that they sought greater equality, it was an equality based on private property, in which all citizens, not just the few, held property. Rather than seeking a redistribution of the elite's wealth to the commoner, they are perhaps better characterized as seeking to prevent a redistribution of the commoners' wealth to the elite.

The second theme was that rebellion against the state would lead to anarchy and then to tyranny. This was the same argument advanced by the British and Tories during the Revolution. At that time the elite had rejected such logic. From the rebels' point of view, they were seeking to further democracy and fight tyranny. The loss of property to the creditors would not only threaten their economic independence but also terminate forms of access to political power, such as eligibility to hold political office. Indeed, the Massachusetts legislature had recently increased the property (wealth) qualifications by 50 percent. Small farmers' loss of property would allow even greater consolidation of economic and political power by the wealthy.

Finally, the dominant class also accused the rebels of conspiring with Great Britain to undermine the Revolution in order to set up a monarchy in America. Apparently, some rebels did agree with British officials in Canada to acquire weapons, although the deal was never completed. The suggestion that the rebels sought to reinstitute a British monarchy runs against the very logic of the rebellion. The idea that people who so recently fought to eliminate British rule would now seek to reestablish that rule is difficult to imagine.

The domination of most state legislatures by merchants and creditors not only prevented the reforms advocated by the farmers but resulted in strong repressive measures against the farmers once they took up arms. Massachusetts and Vermont passed Riot Acts that outlawed the assembly of more than 12 armed persons. Vermont's Treason Act provided the death penalty for participation in insurrection. New Hampshire also restricted freedom of assembly. While in other states the law-enforcement officials and militias were fairly reliable in arresting and dispersing crowds of rebellious farmers, the Massachusetts militia (composed mostly of small farmers) refused to respond to the governor's command to repress the assaults on the courts. Thus Massachusetts made a plea to the Confederation

Congress for outside military assistance. Under the Articles of Confederation there was no national standing army. Certain persons, later to be leaders of the federalists, sought to use the situation in Massachusetts as a means of advocating a stronger central government, backed by a single military command. These forces were still too weak, however, and when only Virginia appropriated assistance to Massachusetts the plan collapsed. Thus the merchants and creditors began to organize a privately financed army to quell the increasing disturbances. Some of the elite themselves joined in this army, while others committed their sons or even their servants.

The legislature's harsh response to the insurrection in the form of increasingly repressive acts—such as suspension of the writ of habeus corpus, riot and treason acts, and the assignment of captured rebels to the personal service of more loyal citizens—had, meanwhile, radicalized the farmers. They were now discussing revolution when they had once limited their talk to reform. In 1787 the farmers began to organize an assault on the federal arsenal in Springfield, Massachusetts, as a first step in overthrowing the state government. This became the point of a major confrontation between a well-organized rebel force of over 2,000 men and an army of 4,400 organized by the mercantile elite. The latter were joined by another 1,000 loyal militia men. Although the rebel forces were skillfully organized, a messenger was intercepted by opposition troops and the planned simultaneous three-pronged assault on the arsenal failed when one regiment did not get the message to delay the attack by one day. For the next week the privately financed government troops pursued the rebels, who, while trying to regroup, resorted to the looting of selected rural merchants' stores for supplies. A number of minor skirmishes occurred before 3,000 government troops surprised a contingent of 2,000 rebels in a snowstorm. Consistently outgunned and generally taking the worst in each skirmish, the rebels abandoned plans to overthrow the government. The state responded with a new wave of repressive legislation. Shays' followers were banned for three years from public office and from employment as school teachers or innkeepers; they could not vote or serve on juries.

Thus the rebellion entered a fourth stage of "social banditry." Assaults were launched against the property and persons of a selected commercial elite. This mostly consisted of looting and burning homes and stores, kidnapping merchants and lawyers, and freeing debtors from jail cells. This form of conflict led to many smaller skirmishes, although one incident in which government troops sought to free 19 kidnapped retailers and professionals from Stockbridge ended up in the bloodiest battle of the rebellion, with 30 farmers and three government soldiers killed.

This final phase of the rebellion gradually faded with the rebellion as a whole. Aside from simple military defeat, Szatmary gives several reasons for its demise. The next election ousted half of the incumbents in the legislature, including the governor, and despite the legal disqualification of Shays' followers, many of them were in fact elected to local office. Although this eliminated much of the hostility toward individual politicians such as the hated governor, James Bowdoin, the legislature did not relent in its oppression of the rebels. Neighboring states that had once provided refuge for Shays' rebels began to restrict such shelter. Clearly outgunned by government troops, a critical blow was dealt with the final British refusal to supply arms to the rebels. As with other rebellions in early America, many of the farmers simply moved farther into the frontier to establish new subsistence communities. Finally, in 1788, Massachusetts experienced an economic upturn with exports exceeding imports. This relieved a great deal of the pressure on the credit market, reduced foreclosure proceedings, and thus removed one of the major causes of the rebellion.

Shays' Rebellion displays some of the problems of governance under the Articles of Confederation. These events were certainly on the minds of many leaders as the forces gathered to centralize government under the Constitution. A particular concern was the unreliability of state militias in putting down local rebellions and the inability to obtain outside forces to suppress the insurrection. A stronger federal government with a national army was seen by many of the elite as a means of circumventing such dilemmas. The ratification of the Constitution changed the nature of the American government so that farmers' protests would thereafter be mostly directed at the federal government rather than state governments. The issues and concerns, however, remained remarkably consistent with the pre-Constitution past. Farmers' movements continued to primarily center on control and distribution of their surplus production, on their relations with creditors, and on defenses against threats to their sense of independence—an independence that hinged on the ownership of the land they farmed.

The Whiskey Rebellion

Not long after the adoption of the Constitution, federalist dominance was challenged by revolt against certain forms of taxation. The Whiskey Rebellion was centered in but not restricted to western Pennsylvania. This agrarian mobilization focused on opposition to a tax that was imposed on the production and sale of liquor. As was the case in Massachusetts with Shays' Rebellion, western Pennsylvania was a cash-poor economy. The grains that grew well there were not easily transported as grain to the eastern seaboard markets. Thus farmers distilled the grains into alcohol for a more cost-effective product that could provide the cash needed to make certain purchases as well as pay other taxes. Similar efforts at taxing liquor before the Revolution (i.e., 1684, 1738, 1744, and 1772 [Taylor 1953]) had been repealed owing to widespread protest. This law was drafted by Treasury Secretary Alexander Hamilton, who was eager for more revenue for the U.S. Treasury. Hamilton was already seen negatively by many small frontier farmers owing to his advocacy of dispersing public lands in large parcels to the nation's wealthy rather than adhering to the Jeffersonian strategy of disposal to large numbers of small farmers (Cochrane 1979). This tax was seen as discriminating against the small, independent frontier farmer and as a renewed threat of "another central government gone awry" (Slaughter 1986, 227).

The rebellion began in the early 1790s when citizens initiated such abuses as tying tax collectors to trees, tarring and feathering them, taking their money and horses, cutting their hair, and whipping them. One county even passed resolutions demanding that its citizens simply treat these tax collectors with contempt and not speak to them. The conflict escalated to acts of arson against the barns and homes of tax collectors and then to armed conflict between farmers and government revenue agents. As in Massachusetts, these conflicts resembled organized guerrilla warfare as leaders on both sides shared Revolutionary War experience. The killing of rebel leader Major McFarlane by government troops under the direction of Major Kirkpatrick further escalated the conflict by evoking sympathy for the rebellion on the part of larger numbers of prominent citizens in the region.

The conflict moved toward the possibility of a large-scale battle as between 5,000 and 7,000 rebels amassed and President Washington ordered nearly 13,000 federal troops to prepare to march on western Pennsylvania. Last-minute assurances by local leaders that order could be restored without military force were dismissed as being too late, and Washington himself went with the troops to discipline the rebellious farmers. Washington left some troops in the region to carry out the work of documenting stills used for liquor production (Taylor 1953). Some leaders of the rebellion were tried, convicted, and eventually pardoned. Many other farmers in the region, however, simply fled into the wilderness, pushing the frontier westward. Ironically, government expenditures to maintain troops in western Pennsylvania provided the largest infusion of cash the region had ever seen. This alleviated some of the pressures of the tax and provided capital with which cash-poor farmers, and in fact many of the soldiers, could buy land. This proved highly lucrative not only for Hamilton's Treasury but also for the eastern speculators, in whose interest his land policy worked. Among those who benefited from this development was Washington himself, who had only one month before the rebellion renewed his efforts to sell his frontier property. Slaughter concludes that the suppression of the Whiskey Rebellion not only increased the value of Washington's landholdings by 50 percent but that a resurvey revealed that these holdings included "hundreds of acres more than he had previously declared or paid taxes on" (1986, 224).

This rebellion did not end farmers' resistance to taxation or to centralized government. Only a few years later farmers in eastern Pennsylvania rose up under the leadership of auctioneer John Fries against property taxes. These taxes were believed to be designated for preparation for war against France, a nation toward which both farmers and Jefferson tended to feel rather friendly. Furthermore, the taxes were negatively perceived, as they were designed around an old English custom of counting the number of windows in a dwelling as a means of assessment. Again, the result of Fries's Rebellion was federal military intervention in which the worst abuses were perhaps the beatings of newspaper editors who supported the rebellion.

Jefferson's election as president partially redirected these tendencies. Jefferson appointed a Whiskey Rebellion sympathizer as his treasury secretary, and one of the editors who had been flogged by troops in Fries's Rebellion became an advisor in his administration. More importantly, land policy moved in the direction of disposal in ever smaller parcels that were more accessible to less wealthy farmers, rather than just eastern speculators. Nevertheless, as with tax policy and the issue of government centralization, this tension between settler and absentee speculator continued to shape the structure of agrarian movements. As we shall see throughout this book, such strains have persisted as important issues in agrarian politics to the present day.

Until the closing of the frontier to settlement, however, there existed an escape for embattled farmers and their children to hopes of a new life of independence and prosperity. Perhaps this explains, in part, the relative absence of major episodes of agrarian mobilization (aside from some squatter's associations and the migration itself) during the first half of the nineteenth century.

Chapter 2

Response to Monopoly Capitalism, 1860–1900

The victory of Union forces over the Confederacy in the Civil War secured a major transformation in the social relations of agricultural production: the abolition of formal slavery in the American South. The dynamics of capitalist economies require continued territorial expansion (Harvey 1982), and slavery posed an obstacle to continued capitalist development in the United States. Thus slavery had to be eliminated if there was to be a coherent governmental role in facilitating capitalist penetration of the South. The abolition of slavery alone was not, of course, a sufficient condition for assuring a free, competitive market in human labor. Deeply embedded racism and continued economic inequality created the exploitative system of sharecropping that posed a new and different obstacle to capitalist development in the southern United States—an obstacle that persists today. Race plays an important role in the development, and lack of development, of agrarian social movements in the South. Race was a means by which the dominant classes could divide the producing classes, and when black and white sharecroppers showed signs of unity, the landlords and merchants were sure to take notice.

Another clearly significant development in the post–Civil War period was the beginning of the end of the frontier. In the first half of the nineteenth century there was relatively little collective social action on the part of farmers, although the act of settlement of the midwestern and south-central states could be classed as a social movement of sorts and did entail some political agitation for government land disposal policies that made possession of land by farming families easier (Cochrane 1979). Between the end of the Civil War and the turn of the century, however, the frontier closed. Farmers increasingly turned to one another in collective action to remedy their social, economic, and political problems. One of the first of the post–Civil War agrarian social movements was the Grange, an organization that has survived to the present.

The Grange (Patrons of Husbandry)

Aside from the problems of racial inequality, farmers in the South faced several serious problems that restricted their ability to prosper immediately after the war. The first of these was the crop lien system that was the basic source of credit in a region whose limited capital reserves had been seriously drained by the war. Local merchants, who were also very often large landholders, provided production supplies (and often basic consumption goods as well) to farmers on credit in exchange for assurance that the crop would be sold to that merchant. This tended to eliminate competition for production, and because crops rarely sold for more than the cost of needed supplies, a dependency developed that approached peonage. This state of affairs was exacerbated by the dependence on a single crop, cotton, which not only exhausted the soil but impeded the growth of basic foodstuffs, in turn increasing dependence on the merchant. Monoculture also led to overproduction and then to declining prices. Southern agriculture was also relatively disadvantaged by the slower development of railroads than was the case in the North.

As in the South, midwestern farmers often saw merchants and buyers as their enemies in the marketplace. In many areas there was only one retail dealer and one outlet through which to sell their production. Thus opposition to "monopoly" and "middlemen" also became a rallying point for organization. The comparatively more capital-intensive character of midwestern grain production also generated hostilities toward the manufacturers of farm implements and to a resentment of the patent system itself, which precluded competitive production of rather simple machinery. This same demand for machinery led farmers to resent the protective tariffs that existed for manufactured goods but not for agricultural produce. Thus these tariffs increased the cost of production for farmers, while their grain and cotton sold at unprotected world market prices. The differing impact of tariffs sometimes impeded alliances between farmer and laborer.

While the crop lien system was not as common in the North, many farmers were still in debt and often surrendered large portions of their earnings to agents of eastern capital, who added their own commissions to the interest charged the farmer (Buck 1913). The instability of the currency also lent to the problems of the farmer. Buck contends that farmers had to pay debts "with money worth from 15 to 20 percent more than the actual value of that which had been borrowed" (1913, 20–21). The Panic of 1873 made money even more scarce and depressed prices further. Another source of resentment among the farm population was taxation. While the financing of the war effort had increased taxes, much of this antagonism seemed directed at the use of tax dollars to subsidize the private railroads over which the taxpayers had no control. Disagreement with the way in which tax dollars were spent also led, of course, to complaints about the representation of farmers' interests in Washington, D.C., and in state capitols. Buck (1913) points out that while 47 percent of the population were farmers in 1873, only 7 percent of Congress were farmers. That this was a time of considerable corruption and scandal in the federal government only added fuel to the fires of disgust with existing political powers.

Into these conditions stepped a relative outsider, Oliver Hudson Kelley, a clerk in the U.S. Department of Agriculture. Kelley, a Yankee, had been sent on a three-month fact-finding trip to the southern states. This trip apparently confirmed his belief in the need for a national association of farmers. Kelley's model for this association was derived from his own experience as a member of the Masonic Order. He, along with several other clerks in Washington, believed that the rituals and fraternal qualities would bind farmers to one another in their political and economic struggles. Gardner (1949) contends that Kelley's Masonic connections did indeed assist this Yankee's research in the hostile post–Civil War South.

Kelley's hard work and perseverance laid an organizational basis, first in the upper Midwest, that soon swept the original idea of a fraternal and educational society away in a far larger social movement. This organizational foundation provided a means by which local leaders could mobilize their fellow farmers toward economic and political objectives that do not appear to have been conceived by Kelley but rather rose from the economic and political conditions we described.

Among the most important of these were the development of cooperative purchasing and marketing services and political action in the
interests of the farm population, especially with respect to regulation
of the railroads.

Ironically, while southern farmers hoped for increased railroad
transportation, northern farmers were mobilized to collective action in
attempts to regulate the railroads that they felt had unfair advantages
over them in both market transactions and political clout. Indeed, railroad regulation legislation became one of the Grange's primary objectives.

By 1870–71 the Grange, or the Patrons of Husbandry, had begun to
develop in the eastern and southern states, although its strength was
still in Minnesota, Iowa, Wisconsin, and Illinois. Soon thereafter the
Grange began to gain strength on the West Coast, a development
owing primarily to its facilitation of cooperative services. Although the
Grange seems to take great pride in its open admission of women to
membership and office, it did not overcome the barrier of race in the
South, where black farmers were not permitted to join. While such discrimination is regrettable for a social or fraternal organization (the
Grange's originally intended form), it can be disastrous for an organization that aspires to cooperative economic or political power. This
division within the producing classes and the greater ability of local
creditors/merchants to foreclose on farmers as a penalty for joining
the organization served as impediments to the Grange in the South
that were not encountered in the North and East.

By 1873, within five years of Kelley's initial organizing, control of
the Grange and its leadership had passed from the "little band of government clerks" into "the hands of farmers themselves" (Buck 1913,
57). Two aspects of the initial idea of a social and fraternal order carried over to the transformed Grange, however, and presented structural obstacles to the new political and economic agenda of the
"movement." On one hand, the Grange's constitution permitted the
admission of "any [white] person interested in agricultural pursuits,"
which led to the formation of some Granges by grain dealers and middlemen in New York City and Boston, for example. Another obstacle
was posed by the prohibition of the "discussion of political or religious
questions in the work of the order" (Buck 1913, 58). While this rule
seems to have been in the spirit of preventing political divisiveness or
religious discrimination, it also was a formal hindrance to the pursuit
of political activity. To the extent that the Grange was successful in

politics, it was most certainly due to a highly selective enforcement of this bylaw, (e.g., it was used to revoke the charters of the Boston and New York City Granges). One of the more interesting positive functions of the Masonic-like organization of the Grange was in its emphasis on the importance of secrecy with respect to the rituals and passwords of the order. This practice seems to have facilitated the functional need for secrecy in negotiation and acquiring input goods through cooperative purchasing at wholesale prices, not available to nonmembers.

As we have noted, the individualized character of most agricultural production lends to the development of strong individualism in agrarian ideology. This individualism tends to increase the free rider problems encountered by organizations that need solidarity in order to be effective in political and economic action. The Grange adopted a motto that reflected this tension: "In essentials, unity; in non-essentials, liberty; in all things, charity" (Buck 1913, 64). This recognized the need for the submission of the individual to the group's collective interest if farmers were to develop political and economic power, while also allowing for individualism in other areas of life and culture.

In 1874 the Grange adopted a Declaration of Purposes that claimed only monopoly forms of capitalism to be their opponent. Along these lines the Grange movement overlapped with the development of Independent, Farmers, and Anti-Monopoly parties—political organizations that are sometimes collectively referred to as the "Granger Movement." The railroads were a primary target of this general anti-monopoly fervor. One of the more successful cases of Grange political activity was in Illinois, where local granges merged with other local organizations to found a coalition known as the Illinois State Farmers' Association, which in turn was part of an Anti-Monopoly party. The success of this political action was impeded by the refusal of the Grange to officially involve itself in political action, thus splitting both the Illinois State Farmers' Association as well as the Grange itself as members left to join the more avowedly political organization. Candidates running on the Illinois Anti-Monopoly party ticket in the 1873 elections won in 53 of the 66 counties in which they ran, disrupting the traditional two-party system. Similarly, in Iowa, Minnesota, and Wisconsin these farmers' or anti-monopoly reform parties attracted large numbers of members of the other parties. The Republican party especially suffered abandonment of farmer members for the third party's anti-monopoly platform. Continued success in state elections in

1874 provided enough influence to pass legislation that curbed some of the power of the railroads in several midwestern states.

Most of these legislative reforms were lost by 1876—overturned either by the state judiciary or through the recapture of state houses by Republicans in the national elections of 1876. The power of these parties was primarily at the local and sometimes the state level. There was no effective national-level organization that could unite various regional or commodity interests. Farmers in the West and the South, for instance, were still in need of increased rail transportation and were far less enthusiastic about restricting the railroads at this time (McNall 1988). According to Buck (1913), the most damaging factor to the continued success of the movement was that the anti-railroad and other reform legislation did not work well in the depression of the mid-1870s, thus dampening enthusiasm for further reforms guided by such ideology. In the Midwest other new, more explicitly political organizations were developing.

Perhaps the Grange's most lasting contribution lay in the field of developing economic cooperatives. In the early days of the organization many of these efforts at cooperation collapsed. Sometimes this was simply because cooperative action forced local merchants to become competitive with the cooperative, and a deal was struck between local farmers and the merchants. In other cases the cooperatives expanded too quickly, and market fluctuations caught them overextended. Some local granges were simply exploited by unscrupulous merchants in far-away cities. Once the Rochdale Plan of Cooperation was adopted as the model for Grange cooperatives, however, success was more common (though surely not certain). The Rochdale Plan was developed in England and involved the creation of a stock company with shares sold only to members in limited amounts with each member having only one vote in management regardless of volume of shares or business transacted. Sales were made at competitive retail prices, with profits first distributed as a limited payment of interest on stock then divided among purchasers in proportion to the amount of business transacted, with the exception that nonmembers received only one-half of such refunds. Abrahamson contends that these basic principles of cooperation have "stood the test of time" and provide the "basic principles of cooperation" even today (1976, 50).

Efforts by granges to develop cooperative manufacturing, on the other hand, led to consistent failure and even to the ruin of many local granges, contributing to the Grange's usurpation by other organizations arising from the increasingly radical political climate. Nevertheless, many of those subsequent organizations learned a great deal from the organizational successes and failures of the Grange.

The Peak of Agrarian Populism

The last two decades of the nineteenth century is the most heavily researched and debated area in the history of U.S. farmer movements. Such movements spawned hundreds of newspapers; their participants were photographed, and the movements varied, with the class structure, a great deal from state to state. While all this has permitted historians more access to these movements than to those we have heretofore considered, interpretations have varied, thus giving rise to even more literature. Causes are attributed to economics, to politics, to ideology, and even to psychology. The nature of the movements is seen by some as conservative, even fascist; by others as progressive, even socialist. Several works have informed our view of this time, particularly Schwartz (1976), McNall (1988), Goodwyn (1978), and Taylor (1953).

In the latter 1800s agrarian politics took a strong turn toward third-party tactics. In part this reflected the increasingly peripheral class position of farmers in an economy marked by rapidly developing industrialization and a tendency toward monopoly capitalism. Both major parties served to create a post–Civil War government that focused more on the facilitation of capital accumulation than on advancing the democratic practice of politics and economics. The farmer movements of this period represented a fundamental challenge and alternative to the status quo. As McNall has written, this was a struggle "over the very meaning of America" (1988, xii). Although these movements as such failed to achieve the broader objective of reconstructing a democratic society, many of their demands were legislated in the progressive reforms of later decades (e.g., graduated income tax, women's suffrage, equal access to credit, civil service reform, regulation of monopoly).

A brief period of prosperity ended with the Panic of 1873. Many farmers had benefited little from this prosperity and believed that the financial crisis was due to a shortage of circulating currency. These farmers joined a third-party movement known as the Greenback party, which stood for an increase in the money supply. In both the North and South many farmers were deeply in debt. Inflation would benefit them by reducing the ratio of their debts over their assets. In 1873 farmers failed to obtain a congressional appropriation of increased money supply. For the rest of the century farmer movements would remember this failure as the "Crime of '73." The Greenbackers' electoral politics anticipated the third-party efforts of the various farmer movements that arose in the 1880s.

Third parties have always been at a severe disadvantage in the United States. The winner-take-all structure of the electoral process means that the most a peripheral group can usually hope for is to push one of the two dominant parties closer to its own position. The relative success of "third parties" in state and local elections is, in fact, usually a matter of influencing a second party to challenge a local one-party system. Thus in Republican-dominated Kansas we might find Populists merging with Democrats, while in Democrat-dominated southern states Populists might ally with Republicans. At the national level, however, this sectional split created an impasse, for a true third party would be pushed out of the electoral process unless it was able to form an alliance with one of the two dominant parties.

The Farmers' Alliance

The Farmers' Alliance originated in several places. Distinct organizations arose at about the same time in response to increasingly concentrated market conditions. These organizations soon found themselves with some common interests and thus sought to join together as a united front. At the state level, each alliance tended to reflect the class and structure specific to the region. Such structures, in turn, reflected the social organization of production around that region's primary agricultural commodities. While this permitted considerable unity among southern alliances and among their northern counterparts, the differences between the agrarian structures of North and South ultimately impeded unity between these two regional factions. The following discussion parallels the literature, which tends to focus heavily on three states where the Alliance was especially strong: Texas, North Carolina, and Kansas.

The origin of the Alliance is often traced to Lampasas County, Texas, in 1877, where farmers organized an association, first called the Knights of Reliance, that was patterned very much after the Grange. This group, which soon changed its name to the Farmers' Alliance, sought to recover strayed and stolen cattle and to reconcile differences between farmers and ranchers. According to Taylor (1953), many of the larger landholders were attempting to enclose lands with fences—a process that would restrict the traditional open range or communal grazing rights that benefited smallholders. This organization coincided with the rise of a Greenback movement, and immediately the organization confronted the issue of partisan politics. A failed attempt at political action led to the demise of the Lampasas Alliance in 1880, as Democratic party loyalty triumphed over the insurgent group. But by then the idea had spread to more frontierlike regions north of Lampasas.

The movement began to engage in cooperative purchasing and marketing as a means of combatting the crop lien system. In 1883 S. O. Daws was hired as an organizer and "traveling lecturer." By 1884 the Alliance had been reborn, primarily around the "trade store" where all Alliance members would agree to trade with only one merchant in exchange for reasonable prices (Goodwyn 1978). This was a means of instituting some measure of competition among the merchants. Daws, in turn, recruited William Lamb as a "state lecturer." In addition to advocating cooperative enterprises, Lamb pushed for coalition between the Alliance and the Knights of Labor, who were organizing railroad workers. Taylor (1953) claims that the number of suballiances grew from 50 in 1884 to 2,700 in 1886.

The Alliance also began "bulking" the sale of their cotton. This involved pooling their production and forcing cotton buyers to compete amongst themselves for Alliance cotton. Clearly many Alliance members were familiar with and had learned from the failure of the Grange's cash-only form of cooperation. The Alliance sought to more directly confront the exploitative crop lien system—that is, to alter the basic social relations around which production was organized. As it was, cooperative purchasing and marketing could only benefit those unencumbered by the lien system (Schwartz 1976) since the law forbade tenants and debtors to seek access to land from anyone other than the landowner to whom they were indebted. Thus many believed that a political solution was needed to coincide with the economic solution of cooperation. Lamb's pursuit of a coalition with railroad workers was part of this desire for a broader political movement.

By 1886, however, part of the Alliance leadership was losing touch with the rank-and-file. As lecturer, Lamb was in touch with the membership. He undercut these leaders by advocating a boycott of the railroad in support of a railroad workers' strike. Goodwyn claims that a letter written by Lamb in rebuttal to the conservative Alliance leadership's criticism of this action served as the beginning of "Alliance radicalism-Populism" (1978, 39). For Goodwyn, this meant that the conception of the farmer as small capitalist had given way to an image of farmer as worker—that is, that farmers, as producers, had more in common with the emerging propertyless working class or proletariat than with the propertied, nonproducing capitalist class. Farmers as a group can be seen to have one foot in each class or to exist as a distinct class (Mooney 1983). This ambiguous identity of interests with respect to the larger society's class structure explains, in part, what otherwise seems to be the contradictory ideology of agrarianism. Indeed, not only the ideology but also the politics and the economics of agrarianism are rife with the apparently contradictory tensions of a group that, by belonging to both classes, belongs to neither (Mooney 1988).

Eventually, despite assistance from the Alliance in the form of money and food, the strike was broken by the replacement of workers under armed guard. The Knights of Labor never regained the strength they had before this strike. This unstable coalition of farmers and workers was typical of many future alliances. The more radical Populist wing of the Texas Alliance pushed a split within the organization by succeeding in passing the "Cleburne Demands" in 1886. According to Goodwyn (1978), five of the demands dealt with labor issues, all of which were sympathetic to the working class; three of the demands were attacks on the interests of the railroads; two of the planks addressed financial issues and were essentially the Greenback party program; and five demands dealt with land policy, advocating return of forfeited railroad lands to the public domain for sale to settlers and urging the prohibition of land ownership by foreign capital. There was also an attack on dealings in agricultural commodity futures and a resolution encouraging lobbying activity in the farmers' interests. The conservatives, opposing the radical substance of the demands and their potential threat to the Democratic party, formed a splinter organization, the Grand State Farmers Alliance.

Dr. Charles W. Macune, whom Goodwyn calls "the boldest single theorist of the agrarian revolt" (1978, 332), ascended to a position of diplomatic leadership that at least temporarily healed the division. Macune was a strong advocate of cooperative economic enterprise and believed cooperation could counter the monopoly power of "organized capital." Macune's presidential address in 1887 captured the hopes of the Alliance:

I hold that cooperation, properly understood and properly applied, will place
a limit to the encroachments of organized monopoly, and will be the means
by which the mortgage-burdened farmers can assert their freedom from the
tyranny of organized capital, and obtain the reward for honesty, industry and
frugality, which they so richly deserve, and which they are now so unjustly
denied. (quoted in Taylor 1953, 198)

In early 1887 Macune succeeded in passing a bold program for
expansion of the Alliance that captured the imaginations and put aside
the differences of Alliance members assembled in Waco, Texas.
Macune proposed an ambitious plan for a single statewide Alliance
Exchange that could function as both a centralized purchasing mechanism as well as a single marketing outlet for all the state's suballiances. Where suballiances were unable to force competition among
local merchants and cotton buyers, the Exchange would provide a
resource that members could fall back on. Macune bolstered this plan
with proposals to hire representatives to go beyond Texas to organize
all cotton-producing regions and to merge with an existing organization known as the Louisiana Farmers' Union (Schwartz 1976). These
paid organizers are early examples of what McCarthy and Zald (1987)
have called "social movement entrepreneurs." Many of them quite
simply became professional organizers, and their income was directly
dependent on the number of suballiances they organized.

The Louisiana Farmers' Union arose in 1880 from the initiative of
about a dozen farmers who took care of their parish cemetery and
decided to form a farmers' club open to all denominations. Their
agenda appears to have been political as well as economic from the
start. The declared objectives of the Louisiana Farmers' Union were
to better educate themselves with respect to the technical skill of
farming, to oppose "class legislation" and corruption in government,
and to get rid of "professional politicians" (Taylor 1953, 200). The
organization declined temporarily but was resurrected in 1884. In
1887 the union, with a membership of somewhere between 4,000 and
10,000, merged with the Texas Alliance. This "merger"—which
"amounted to an absorption" of the Louisiana Farmers' Union by the
much larger Texas Alliance—became known as the National
Farmers' Alliance and Co-operative Union. Macune was elected its
president (McMath 1975, 34).

When Alliance organizers reached North Carolina in 1887 they
found the North Carolina Farmers' Association rapidly developing in

the vacuum created by the successful Democratic party assault on the Knights of Labor's interracial recruitment of farmers. The leader of this North Carolina Farmers' Association, L. L. Polk, a former state commissioner of agriculture and editor of the *Progressive Farmer*, joined the North Carolina Farmers' Alliance, which in 1888 absorbed the North Carolina Farmers' Association. The success of the Alliance organizers in North Carolina and across the South probably owed a great deal to the wisdom of sending transplanted Texans back to their native states, usually beginning in their native county. By 1887 there were Alliances in Texas, Louisiana, Missouri, Mississippi, Alabama, and North Carolina (McMath 1975).

By 1889 the expansion of the Farmers' Alliance had proceeded to include merger with the second largest farm organization in the nation, the Agricultural Wheel. The Wheel was centered in Arkansas but had strength in Tennessee, Missouri, Kentucky, and Alabama. The merger of the Wheel and Alliance was somewhat more complex than the merger with the Louisiana Farmers' Union. This was due not only to the independent strength of the Wheel but also to the fact that the Wheel was a more radical populist organization than the Alliance, with stronger ties to organized labor. The militant politics and high level of class consciousness of the Wheel is readily apparent in the declaration of principles of the Brothers of Freedom, a farmer and laborer organization absorbed by the Wheel in 1885: "The laboring class of mankind are the real producers of wealth . . . oppressed by combinations of capital and the fruits of their toil absorbed by a class who propose not only to live on the labors of others, but to speedily amass fortunes at their expense" (quoted in Taylor 1953, 206). This merger created a larger organization that was known temporarily as the Farmers' and Laborers' Union of America.

The strength of the class-consciousness of the Wheel is evidenced by its admission of blacks. This openness, however, was surrendered by the Wheel as part of the merger with the Alliance. As McMath has noted, the Alliance "systematically ignored" almost half of all southern farm people by excluding blacks (1975, 44). Black farmers did organize parallel Alliance groups in many parts of the South, but always within the constraints imposed by white supremacy. Several black organizations emerged, apparently independently, in the latter 1880s. The best known of these was the Colored Farmers' National Alliance. Radicals in the white Alliances, many of whom envisioned an interracial organization, often lent their experience in helping black

Alliances get started and often persuaded state Alliances to permit blacks the use of their cooperative exchanges. Goodwyn contends that the fact that the Colored Farmers' Alliance could reach as many black people as it did "was a remarkable political and cultural achievement" (1978, 123). Not only did these black farmers confront formal exclusion from membership in the Alliances, but their informal affiliation threatened the only semblance of a power base they did have— their position in the Republican party. The necessarily covert nature of their organization impeded the development of the broader movement culture, with its public protests, picnics, speeches, summer camps, and cooperative stores. Furthermore, nearly two-thirds of the black farm population was denied access to education and was thus illiterate (Mitchell 1987). Consequently, along with the secrecy imposed by white supremacy, the black movement lacked the widespread development of an alternative press that was so vital to the white Alliance movement. These facts also mean, of course, that the development of the Colored Farmers' Alliance remains "shrouded in mystery" (Goodwyn 1978, 122).

In the 1880s another organization that used the name "Alliance" developed in the northern part of the nation—the National Farmers' Alliance. Often referred to as the Northern Alliance or Northwestern Alliance, this organization was begun in 1880, independently of the southern Alliances, by Milton George, an agricultural journalist in Chicago who published the farm journal *Western Rural and American Stockman*. George financed the National Farmers' Alliance out of his own pocket and simply sent charters, free of charge, to local clubs who requested membership. The organization was from the beginning openly political, oriented toward lobbying for railroad and anti-monopoly legislation (McMath 1975).

After a brief initial success—particularly in Nebraska, Kansas, and the Dakota Territory—the National Farmers' Alliance nearly collapsed as wheat prices rose in the early 1880s. In the mid-1880s, however, as grain prices declined, this loosely structured organization became the vehicle for mobilization against monopoly. McMath (1975) and Goodwyn (1978) both claim that cooperative enterprises developed by local National Farmers' Alliance chapters were important in creating the economic incentives and organizational networks that led to this political mobilization. McNall (1988) has more recently challenged this contention, claiming that, in Kansas at least, cooperatives were of little significance in providing a basis of mobilization. Indeed, the organization was quite different from the southern Alliance. Coincident with its top-down origins, members did not have to be active farmers, and there was little of the ritual and secrecy associated with the southern Alliance. The class structure of the upper Midwest and frontier northern plains, too, was quite different. Though farmers were in debt, they were not generally subject to the crop lien system—that is, their creditors were not local merchants/landlords who dominated their day-to-day existence. Their communities were characterized by far more equality and, as McNall (1988) shows for Kansas, higher levels of social mobility than was the case in the cotton South. Furthermore, the absence of a large black farm population simplified the social structure of these northern regions.

As the Texas Alliance spread to the Southeast, some of its leaders also sought northern expansion and by 1887 were seeking mergers with existing Northern Alliance organizations and organizing southern Alliances in the Wheat Belt, especially Kansas, where land prices collapsed in 1887–88. By 1889 the Kansas chapter of the Northern Alliance was "absorbed" by a small southern Alliance (McMath 1975). In the Dakotas a particularly strong cooperative network was developed that included credit and hail insurance as well as purchasing and marketing services. Farmers' efforts at developing their own elevators and warehouses were defeated by strong opposition from the railroads and elevator companies. By 1890 the Dakota Alliance had also switched allegiance to the southern Alliance network, leaving the North's National Farmers' Alliance much the smaller organization as the two groups attempted to come together to formulate a national political agenda. We turn now to a brief description of some tactics employed by the Farmers' Alliance movement.

The Exchange. Schwartz has called the Farmers Alliance exchanges "the most ambitious counter-institutions ever undertaken by an American protest movement" (1976, 219). The exchanges had the potential to replace the cotton monoculture and to transform the class structure of the South by eliminating middlemen and developing countervailing power against creditors and the railroads. Schwartz describes the Exchange as "massively simpleminded, but subtly ingenious" (1975, 219). Before the growing season, local suballiances drew up lists of their supply needs and provided these orders, "along with crop liens, mortgages, and cash, to the state business agent. The accumulated securities offered by the entire statewide membership provided collateral for yearlong credit from banks and manufacturers" (1975, 219). The state Exchange then bought supplies directly from the manufacturers. At harvest, cotton was bulked and sold collectively and directly to exporters or manufacturers.

The plan worked so well at first that it threatened the merchant class of Texas, who, in turn, mobilized a counterattack. Most merchants were also heavy users of credit from urban banks. These merchants made it clear at a joint meeting with bankers in April 1988 that their downfall would endanger the banks' investments in their businesses. Shortly thereafter the Exchange was declared ineligible for credit, and no bank would lend it money. This coalition of merchant and finance capital helped to defeat the Exchange. Short of building an entire independent economy with their own factories and credit, the Alliance Exchange was doomed. While some dreamed of such an expansion, the hard reality of a shortage of initial capital pushed more and more Alliance members to consider a political solution to their conflict with the dominant class.

Jute Boycott. Among the farmers' costs of marketing cotton was the jute "bagging" in which the cotton was wrapped for shipping and storage. In August 1888 the few companies that controlled jute bagging production colluded to raise the price from 7 cents to 11.75 cents per yard. At this time the Alliance happened to be strong enough at state levels to organize a boycott of the "jute trust." Outside the jurisdiction of an increasingly detached national leadership, the leaders of 11 state Alliances met and agreed to use only cotton bagging. The boycott spread rapidly; in some cases state Alliances invested in the production of cotton bagging. The boycott was effective in the first year, forcing jute prices down below 7 cents per yard (Schwartz 1976). The next year, however, the jute interests countered by getting local merchants to refuse to accept cotton in any wrapping except jute. Again, solidarity on the part of the dominant class defeated the Alliance. Success in combatting one opponent only revealed another, more powerful opponent at a higher level. In this case it was the Liverpool, England, market, through which the "largest part" of U.S. cotton passed. Liverpool accepted only jute bagging, as much of the jute was grown in India, a British colony, and shipped in British vessels and manufactured and sold by British industry. Thus U.S. ports could only accept jute bagging. Still, the pressure from the state and local Alliances kept the price of jute at around 7 cents per yard through 1890. In Schwartz's analysis, longer-term success in this project was possible but was impeded by the Alliance leaders' increasing interest in political, rather than economic, solutions. This group of national leaders, Schwartz contends, feared alienating the newspapers, which could in turn damage their personal political ambitions

The Subtreasury Plan. The lack of capital and the turn to political solutions led Macune to develop what Goodwyn has described as a "breathtakingly radical" (1978, 301) proposal: the subtreasury plan. In 1889 Macune proposed this "system of currency designed to benefit everyone in the 'producing classes,' including urban workers" (1978, 91). The subtreasury plan advocated the establishment of "warehouses and elevators in which farmers could store certain non-perishable commodities. Upon depositing his crop, a farmer would receive negotiable treasury notes equal to 80% of the crop's value. He would pay 1% interest per month on the notes, plus minimal storage fees, but could withdraw his crop for sale at any time" (McMath 1975, 90). The subtreasury plan would not only have the effect of creating the inflation sought since the Greenback movement but would free farmers from merchants-creditors-landlords and give them greater control over the sale of their product. In justifying this provision of capital, advocates of the subtreasury plan often called on an agrarian fundamentalism, arguing that the nation's agricultural production should be as worthy a means of backing up the dollar as gold (Taylor 1953). Equalizing access to credit in this way would indeed have been, as Goodwyn has contended, "revolutionary" (1978, 110)—that is, it would have destroyed the crop lien system as the basic social relation in cotton production. Beyond that, it may have provided the investment potential for building a truly strong cooperative economy. Lack of capital had been the basic weakness of previous cooperative ventures. But it was sectional strife within the Alliance movement that damaged its chances for success. Those states not engaged in cotton production objected to the limitation of the plan to nonperishable (e.g., cotton) commodities. When the cotton states refused to strike the "nonperishable" restriction the northern states refused to endorse it (Mitchell 1987). Macune's "patient explanations were rarely printed and almost never given a fair hearing"; the plan was "attacked relentlessly, generally without intelligence" by its opponents (Goodwyn 1978, 330).

Education. The Alliance, especially in the South, struggled for better education. Low levels of literacy and numeracy contributed to the powerlessness of both black and white farmers at the ballot box and in negotiation with creditors, landlords, and merchants. Under Macune's direction many suballiances developed adult education programs in which children and literate adults helped teach Alliance men and women. The mathematics curriculum was grounded in the computation of interest rates, crop shares, and such figures as the per capita wealth of the nation (the latter providing a basis for comparison of elite wealth versus their own wealth). Reading and writing focused on studying forms of exploitation around the globe, unified by the "warning" that the "centralization of wealth and power, a reciprocal process, always leads to repression by the rich and powerful of the poor and powerless" (Mitchell 1987, 114). Macune sought to develop the farmers "identity as workers and their opposition to organized capital" (1987, 119). Formal lessons were interspersed with practice in oral presentation and debate of various issues raised by the lessons. Macune published a curriculum—a fascinating series of formal lessons in the National Economist on topics such as "American Government," "Political Economy," and the "History of Land." Mitchell writes that Macune's lessons challenged dominant notions of progress, contending that history was only a "progressive degradation of the masses" (1987, 108). This "morality play in reverse" (1987, 108) hinged on the "moral value assigned to labor and challenged the right of capitalists to a share of the product produced by labor (1987, 117). In short, "the Alliance curriculum was based on the premise that American society was divided into two great classes, those who produced wealth with their labor, and those who extracted wealth from the labor of others" (Mitchell 1987, 118).

Needless to say, such education encountered opposition from local elites who benefited from farmers' illiteracy and innumeracy. Indeed, many planters opposed schooling for farm youth because it took them out of the fields. Perhaps even more threatening were the ideological challenge to the right of nonproducers to a share of the product of labor and the political challenge to the domination of government by that same elite. Struggle over the local school meant division around the most important symbol of rural communities, since school buildings served not only as schools but as meeting halls, churches, and places for social events. Eventually the Alliance educational project faded with the demise of the Alliance. Ironically, its emphasis on education was soon appropriated by progressive reformers and used to legitimize a curriculum and education that was quite contrary to the democratic politics and ideology of the Alliance. The Alliance saw education as a means of "liberation and empowerment," while progressive reformers often "saw schooling as a means of social control" (Mitchell 1987, 177).

The Decline of Populism

Just as the Alliance grew from many sources, its demise had several causes. The defeat of the cooperatives by the merchant-banker coalition encouraged the Southern Alliance to move, along with the Northern Alliance, toward politics. This tendency was also facilitated by the increasing oligarchy that developed from initial inclusion of "farmers" of various social strata in the South and the wide-open membership of the northern Alliance. As the strength of the cooperatives diminished, the lecturer system collapsed. This was to some extent replaced by the reform press, but unlike the lecturer-organizer the press did not engage in public debate with the rank and file. This medium constituted more of a one-way "quasi-interaction" (Thompson 1990). The consequence was an increasing separation of leadership from the members—a fact that may have both led to and reinforced the movement toward party politics. The turn to third-party politics, especially at the national level, drained energy and resources from local economic development. Regional differences—some specifically related to agriculture but also related to race and party loyalty—proved insurmountable at this time.

Defeat in the economic sphere led to action in the political sphere. Success in one sphere or another was needed to establish confidence, morale, and a material base for expansion to other spheres. The failure of the economic cooperatives—owing to unequal capital resources and a countermobilization in the form of a boycott by bankers—led to an attempt to muster more equally distributed political (one-man, one-vote) resources. Again the dominant class exerted its power by changing the rules of the electoral game. Barnes (1989) has described the 1896 election as "critical." This campaign marked a transformation that was to benefit the "moneyed interests" over the masses (Goodwyn 1978). The Alliances themselves should have anticipated just such a countermeasure by capital, and their failure to do so and act accordingly reveals how detached their leaders were from their grass roots by 1896.

In a series of conventions from 1889 to 1892 the Alliances developed a political party known as the People's party or the Populist party. A relatively standard set of issues composed the platform of the party, although as time went on the silver issue tended to predominate in the rhetoric of the office seekers. The thrust of many Populist demands clearly indicates that this movement was an attempt to resist the consolidation of monopoly capital.[3] Populists saw the role of government as ensuring an environment in which competitive capitalism could thrive. Thus "natural monopolies" such as transportation, communication, or utilities should be publicly owned. If manufacturers of certain products gained monopolistic advantage, the Populists advocated state or cooperative ownership of similar plants to provide competition to the private-sector monopoly. Demands for the nationalization of the railroads followed from the long history of attempts, dating back to the Grange, to regulate freight rates, end the railroads' discriminatory practices that favored larger farmers, and sever connections between railroad and grain companies.

At another level this opposition to monopoly capital combined with a producer ideology to oppose "absentee ownership". Farm land, it was argued, should be owned by the family that works on it. Fear of monopoly control over agricultural markets led to opposition to futures trading in agricultural commodities. Other strategies intended to create a more competitive environment for capitalism were advocated. The Populists pushed for an end to "class-biased taxation," which meant a move toward less regressive taxes, such as a progressive income tax. An assault on the domination of finance capital was to be made by the abolition of national banks as well as by creating enough inflation to free the indebted from their burdens. The latter came to involve increasing the money supply by the coinage of silver. The Populists wanted the government to circulate enough currency for business to be transacted in cash and thus end credit dependency (Taylor 1953).

While a more competitive capitalism was equated with democracy, the Populists also advocated the secret ballot and the direct, popular election of U.S. Senators. Finally, the working class ties led to demands for an eight-hour day for wage workers (a condition that few farmers could hope to achieve for themselves). While much of the rural component of the Populist movement pushed for women's suffrage and temperance, these demands were compromised by their fusion with the Democratic party, which depended on the urban, ethnic, working-class vote. McNall (1988) contends that when the Populists did stand up for women's suffrage, they lost Democratic votes. Other issues that led to deep divisions within the movement involved regional differences over the subtreasury plan and, of course, the race issue. The fusion of Populists with the Democrats also meant compromise with the party of white supremacy in the South.

Whether a state-level alliance originated as a political organization or as an alternative economic institution, by 1890 the push toward a more explicitly political resolution to farmers' grievances was well under way. In many states Populists fused with the local minority party to capture state and local offices. Kansas represented the strength of the Alliance as a political entity. In the 1890 election the People's party of Kansas won 90 seats in the lower house while the Democrats and Republicans together won only 35. Holdovers kept the state's Senate in the hands of Republicans, who won the governorship as well as seven of nine district judgeships. The Populists also sent five of seven congressman and one senator to Washington. Throughout the Midwest, Great Plains, and the South, the Alliances demonstrated electoral power at state and especially local levels that seemed to catch the two major parties by surprise. Even at the national level "about 44 Congressmen and U.S. Senators elected in 1890 were claimed as Alliance supporters" (Taylor 1953, 293).

This success pushed the dominant parties to increase their efforts at cooptation through fusion with state Alliances or incorporating certain issues in their own platforms. Thus the People's party often fused with Republicans in the South and Democrats in the North. In 1892 the People's party won five more seats in the U.S. Senate and 10 more congressional seats. Taylor (1953) estimates that the party also captured 50 state-level offices and more than 1,500 county-level offices and state legislative positions.

By 1894, however, the turn to electoral politics at the expense of neglecting the Alliance's economic base began to show its negative effects. In most states, especially in the South, the cooperative movement and the exchanges provided a network for the early political success. This basis for providing more immediate and concrete answers to the farmers' problems was eroding, however, and the more distant promises of office seekers for legislative action were greeted with less enthusiasm in 1894. The opposition, too, had by now regrouped, responding with tactics ranging from cooptation to economic reprisals to electoral fraud.

By 1896 the People's party had become quite independent of Alliance control. Mobilization was increasingly geared toward national rather than local politics, draining the resources and morale of the rank and file. The Populist party joined with the Democrats in nominating William Jennings Bryan for president but refused to accept the Democrats choice of Arthur Sewell as the vice presidential nominee because he was "president of a bank, director in railroads and other corporations, and a wealthy employer of labor" (Taylor 1953, 305). The Populists nominated Tom Watson of Georgia for vice president instead. The campaign marked a transformation in electoral politics. The Republican acquisition of campaign funds reached new heights under the direction of Mark Hanna. Bryan's candidacy is primarily remembered for his obsession with the "silver issue" to the detriment of other substantive concerns around which the movement had also developed. William McKinley won "primarily because of the nationwide increase of 2 million Republican voters . . . primarily from New York, Pennsylvania, and New England, which Bryan had conceded" (McNall 1988, 288). The resources that poured into the Bryan presidential campaign, the turn of the campaign away from agrarian issues, and the fusion with Democrats lent to losses of many local and regional offices that had been obtained in the earlier 1890s. Defeated in economic struggle, the remnants of the agrarian movement were now defeated in political struggle.

While analysts often view this defeat as "the end" of the movement, there was no such complete closure. Indeed, within a few years the cooperative movement got back on its collective feet. And this time—under quite different economic conditions (i.e., relative prosperity)—they were far more successful.

Chapter 3

Prosperity and Depression, 1900–1939

The history of farmer movements raises some interesting questions for theorists of social movements. Up to 1900 farmer movements tended to develop in reaction to the relative deprivation of farmers with respect to other segments of society or with respect to their own previous status. In the first two decades of the twentieth century, however, strong farmer movements developed in the context of relative prosperity. Many of these movements shared political, ideological, and economic objectives with the Grange and National Farmers' Alliance, which rose in the crises of the late nineteenth century. Perhaps the most important difference between the farmer movements in these two eras involves their perseverance. Three of the farmer movements born in the early twentieth century are still with us today. Two of these are currently the largest and most powerful farmer organizations in our society. This development lends support to an alternative set of theoretical explanations to social movements, collectively referred to as "resource mobilization."

Early twentieth-century farmers continued to have the same basic interests as they had in the late nineteenth century, but with increasing prosperity they had more resources with which to wage their struggle. The lack of capital was a basic cause of prior failures to develop alternative cooperative institutions. This relatively long run of good farm prices provided the capital needed to organize such cooperation. Furthermore, the nature of the opposition changed somewhat as well. First, under conditions of general prosperity the dominant class had more flexibility to grant concessions. That is, the proverbial "pie" was simply bigger and capital could serve a bigger slice. Second, these concessions were not simply forthcoming from the goodness of the capitalist collective heart but were an attempt to preempt or coopt the increasing strength of the socialist movement in the American countryside as well as in the cities. On one hand, cooperatives were to become a sort of compromise with the agrarian socialist movement. On the other hand, they were also to become a means of capturing the farmers themselves as a resource to be used for far more conservative interests. Danbom (1979, 68) found that many urban reformers favored agricultural cooperative development because it would stabilize farmers' political behavior, making them more conservative, conformist, deferential, and obedient. The firm institutionalization of cooperation in the first two decades of the twentieth century created a qualitatively different political context for dealing with the arrival of the next agricultural crisis in the early 1920s.

The American Society of Equity

Only a few years after the collapse of the Populist party the American Society of Equity was born. Its primary organizer was James A. Everitt, of Indianapolis, Indiana, the publisher of *Up-to-Date Farming and Gardening* and owner of a feed and seed business. Everitt was, however, quickly deposed as this organization's leader by a faction that claimed his ideas were borrowed from others, especially from W. L. Hearron of Carlinville, Illinois. Initially, the basic idea of the Equity was for farmers to collectively control the marketing of their production, distributing it more evenly across the year so as to avoid the price fluctuations that came with harvest. Associations of producers of specific commodities would meet each year to agree on a minimum "equitable" price, below which they would not sell.

In its first five years the organization was highly centralized under Everitt's control, and subscription to his publication was tantamount to membership. Farm women were admitted without dues as were farm people younger than 21 or over 75. Some of the early leadership came from veterans of the Alliance and the Populist movements. Focusing primarily on wheat and tobacco, the Equity first attained its greatest strength in Kentucky, Wisconsin, Minnesota, the Dakotas, and Montana (Saloutos and Hicks 1951).

The networks created by Everitt's organization soon developed into a somewhat independent means of organizing commodity producers within specific locales. The most important of these concerned tobacco producers in Kentucky, Tennessee, and Wisconsin. The Equity raised the hopes of tobacco producers to rise above the poverty that they felt was imposed on them by the "tobacco trust." Because many tobacco farmers were also tenant farmers, their poverty was not simply an effect of the tobacco market structure. In 1906 an organizing campaign obtained farmers' pledges that 58 percent of the tobacco crop would not be sold at prices offered, but would be collectively sold by the newly formed Burley Tobacco Society. In 1907 this organization claimed to have 103,000 acres out of 135,000 acres planted so pledged and planned to eliminate the 1908 crop. Indeed, according to Saloutos and Hicks (1951), the 1908 burley crop was only 18 percent of normal production. This control came only with a great deal of violence against the "independent" farmer who sought a "free ride" to better prices on the backs of those farmers who had committed to collective action. The "night riders" of the Burley Tobacco Society subjected these free riders, as well as tobacco buyers, to personal violence. Unpledged tobacco acreage was often destroyed as a last resort to assuring production control. In late 1908 the American Tobacco Company bought the 1906 and 1907 crop from the Burley Tobacco Society for 17 cents per pound and about 20 cents per pound, respectively (Saloutos and Hicks 1951). The average price paid for tobacco in 1908 was 10.2 cents per pound, which was itself an increase of 3.5 cents over the 1903 price (USDA 1967, 124).

In the meantime, the Equity was undergoing an internal upheaval. After Everitt's overthrow the Equity was transformed into a "highly decentralized" body composed of "an unwieldy collection of state and commodity organizations" that were bound only by a "common name and common enemies," with "local interests" dictating action rather than a general agricultural program (Saloutos and Hicks 1951, 121).

The Equity developed a strong base in Wisconsin in its early years among both tobacco and wheat producers. Later it became involved in the organization of cooperative cheese production associations as well as cooperative livestock shipping associations. The Equity promoted the progressive politics that arose in Wisconsin in the early twentieth century, advocating state life insurance, income tax, limitations on the labor of women and children, workmen's compensation, and a state-owned binder-twine plant. The Equity attacked the College of

Agriculture, criticizing its devotion of resources to increasing productivity in agriculture. The Equity saw increased production as the problem, rather than the solution. This criticism led a state commission to recommend in 1915 that the College of Agriculture be more responsive to the needs of farmers. To this day the land-grant college complex continues to receive this sort of criticism from some farm groups. The success of Equity's cooperative ventures in the wheat-growing areas coincided with the progressive politics of wheat producers (often of Scandinavian descent) in Minnesota, the Dakotas, and Montana. The border states, too, were influenced by the relative success of Canadian wheat farmers in obtaining financial and legislative assistance from their government for the creation of cooperative elevators.

In 1908 the Equity Cooperative Exchange grew out of the American Society of Equity as a means of marketing spring wheat in these northern states. A primary political objective was to obtain assistance from the Minnesota and North Dakota state legislatures in the construction of cooperative elevators to compete with the private grain companies. Leading the opposition against this project was the Minneapolis Chamber of Commerce, an organization that had only several years earlier destroyed the Minnesota Farmers' Exchange by denying it membership to the chamber. This struggle for public assistance in building cooperative elevators would also outlive the peak years of successful mobilization by the Equity, providing a source of continuity to the new organizations that gradually usurped or absorbed the Equity. Though the Equity was often accused of being communist, their opposition also came from the Left. An attempted merger of farmers and organized labor was subverted by the Milwaukee Socialist party. Curiously, this attack hinged, in part, on the movement's appropriation of the Socialist platform as a means of pulling the two groups together (Saloutos and Hicks 1951).

The demise of the Equity, like that of many of its forerunners, seems to have been caused by enthusiastic overexpansion—an expansion based on temporary economic conditions. Also like earlier cooperative movements, the political agenda sapped much of its resources. Given its decentralized character, the Equity met somewhat different fates in various locales. Many of the Equity members and often entire local organizations simply merged with the Farmers Union or the Nonpartisan League. Some local organizations survived to the contemporary era.

The National Farmers' Educational and Cooperative Union

If there is an heir to the tradition established by the Granger and Alliance movements, it is the National Farmers' Educational and Cooperative Union, or the National Farmers' Union (NFU). The NFU's ideology and analysis of farmers' problems, its emphasis on economic cooperation, and its political objectives are a twentieth-century adaptation of the more progressive elements of nineteenth-century agrarian populism. Indeed, a history of the Farmers' Union (Barrett 1909) shows, through biographical sketches of its early leaders, that such leadership drew heavily on farmers who were once members of the Grange or the Alliance, or both.

The founder of the Farmers' Union was in fact an ex-Alliance member from Rains County, Texas. Isaac Newton Gresham was also a tenant farmer and newspaper man who suffered the same poverty that pervaded most of Texas cotton country. Gresham begged for credit to feed his family while he began his organizing campaign, promising his creditor the business of his constituency once the organization was established. A Texas state charter was issued in 1902 that created the Farmers' Educational and Cooperative Union of America "to organize and charter subordinate Unions . . . in Texas and the U.S., to assist them in marketing and obtaining better prices for their products, for fraternal purposes, and to cooperate with them in the protection of their interest, to initiate members, and collect a fee therefore" (quoted in Taylor 1953, 339).

There were 10 original members: three Populists, one Socialist, one Independent, and five Democrats. The organization spread rather quickly within Texas and then eastward across the South. The membership fee was a dollar and monthly dues were five cents. Organizers were financially rewarded for their work by receiving $12.50 of the first $15 collected for a local union. Gresham's poor bookkeeping eventually led to accusations of mismanagement of funds, and most of the original members were soon replaced as leaders (Taylor 1953, 340). By 1905 the Farmers' Union claimed 200,000 members and had a significant presence not only in Texas but in Indian Territory, Oklahoma Territory, Louisiana, Georgia, and Alabama. The Farmers' Union was beginning to make inroads in Mississippi, Missouri, Tennessee, South Carolina, North Carolina, and Kentucky. All the officers, however, were still Texans, and in late 1905 the Farmers' Union was reorganized to provide broader representation. Gresham's death in 1906 coincided with the election of C. S. Barrett, the well-educated son of a prosperous Georgia farmer, as the NFU's new president. Under Barrett the NFU made remarkable strides over the next 22 years. Ironically, this Georgian would see the movement shift from his native South to the western Midwest.

By 1912 the Farmers' Union had reached its peak in the South. The 12 cotton states contributed 77 percent of the NFU's receipts. The substance of the organization primarily revolved around cooperative marketing of cotton. In support of this practice, the Farmers' Union bought or built more than 1,500 cotton warehouses and sold cotton directly to U.S. and British textile mills. There were also attempts in the early years to secure voluntary pledges to reduce the acreage planted to cotton as a means of raising cotton prices. In various regions the NFU experimented with a diversity of cooperative projects—fertilizer plants, coal mining, banking, insurance, gas stations, and so forth—but the main success was in the area of cooperative purchasing and marketing. Taylor contends that, with the possible exception of the Equity, the Farmers' Union probably "contributed more by way of successful enterprises than any other farmers' organization" (1953, 355).

The social stratification that derived from the land tenure and crop lien system blocked the development of the Farmers' Union in the South. The Farmers' Union turned northward into the Great Plains and western Midwest, where it gained a stronghold that persists to the present. Kansas provided the first major inroad into this region. The Farmers' Union had recruited 8,000 Kansas farmers by 1908 and 120,000 by 1920 (Saloutos and Hicks 1951, 224–25). In many northern states the Farmers' Union attracted large numbers of Equity members as that organization fell into decay. Attempts at formal merger with segments of Equity took place with some success between 1910 and 1927, and the Farmers' Union sometimes acquired Equity property, but more significant was its simple recruitment of former Equity members.

The Farmers' Union was particularly successful in its cooperative business ventures in Nebraska. Along with this success, however, the Nebraska Farmers' Union took a unique turn toward a more conservative political posture than the Farmers' Union held elsewhere. This more laissez-faire attitude toward the role of government in agriculture was only relaxed by the Nebraska Farmers' Union during the Great Depression. The Nebraska Farmers' Union emphasized cooperation rather than government intervention as a means of restricting the power of private capital; that is, it advocated competing effectively against such capital through formal economic cooperation.

By the 1920s the Farmers' Union was an important economic and political organization in Kansas, Nebraska, the Dakotas, Colorado, California, Missouri, Iowa, Oklahoma, Minnesota, and Wisconsin. The organization had shifted from a strength in the cotton states to a very significant role in the Wheat Belt and to considerable influence in the western Corn Belt. Furthermore, the Farmers' Union was beginning to develop a base in the dairy region that would become a future stronghold.

Perhaps the politics of the Farmers' Union are as important as its cooperative economic enterprises. In fact, the two elements are difficult to separate. First, the success of the cooperatives provided selective economic incentives that facilitated recruitment to NFU politics and ideology. Even if its members were not so deeply committed to NFU ideology, politicians paid attention to membership figures of any large, well-organized group of farmers. At the same time, the NFU's economic success lent credibility to its political stance. Second, the economic practice of cooperation corresponded with a political philosophy that was often centered on an anti-capitalist ideology and provided a practical and positive alternative to complement the group's critique of the status quo.

This anti-capitalist ideology is evident in the membership restrictions that developed in the division between farmers and nonfarmers—or, more exactly, certain nonfarmers. According to Crampton, only farmers or "persons felt to have a real stake in the rural community's welfare" were eligible for membership (1965, 11). Bankers, merchants, lawyers, or those that speculate on agricultural products or otherwise injure agricultural interests were excluded. Country mechanics, teachers, doctors, ministers, and socially committed newspaper editors were eligible. This attitude is particularly understandable, given the Farmers' Union's origins in the South, where elite families often controlled local commercial and financial capital as well as the law. This same social structure had given rise to the earlier radical Populist critique of capitalism in the Alliance movement. The ideology also resonated in the North, where banks and absentee landlords exercised more control and influence than popular American mythology generally acknowledges. The railroads, monopoly capital, speculators, and middlemen in general had long been suspect, even by the so-called independent farmers of the Midwest and Great Plains.

While the Farmers' Union inherited this ideology as the substance of its politics, it also inherited a distaste for the form of political participation represented by the negative experience of the Alliance's absorption and subsequent demise in party politics. Thus the Farmers' Union was from the start curiously—though perhaps pragmatically—reluctant to engage in partisan politics. Gresham's introduction to the NFU's first constitution strongly insisted that the organization was not a political party, and the constitution was amended in 1905 to "absolutely forbid any member of the Union from even discussing politics at a Union meeting" (Taylor 1953, 358). The National Farmers' Union would selectively invoke this rule by censoring certain local political activities. Such limitation prompted the North Carolina Farmers' Union to withdraw from the NFU in 1919 to pursue more direct and militant politics. Still, the Farmers' Union generally became involved in politics. Barrett himself was very active politically. He served as a member of the Country Life Commission and as a representative of U.S. farm organizations at the post–World War I Paris Peace Conference. Saloutos and Hicks write that "almost every president from Roosevelt to Hoover honored him with an appointment of one kind or another" (1951, 221).

Under Barrett's leadership the Farmers' Union distinguished between "politics" and "partisanry." Acknowledging that the "ballot is the deadliest weapon known to modern history," the NFU focused on influencing candidates, conventions, and platforms rather than fielding Farmers' Union members as candidates for office (Barrett 1909, 47–48). Given the two-party system and the position of farmers in the class structure, this form of participation may have functioned to make the parties more dependent on the Farmers' Union instead of the farmer being dependent on the party. The Farmers' Union approach was to develop a political program reflecting its interests and expect politicians to pick up these ideas as part of their campaign in the hopes of attracting the farm vote. The Colorado Farmers' Union developed the practice of surveying candidates on issues as well as reporting legislative votes by current officeholders.

Crampton (1965) identifies four basic aspects of the ideology that informed the Farmers' Union political position. First, a sense of "disadvantage" portrays the farmer as victim of both nature and the political economy of capitalism. This aspect of the Farmers' Union ideology is often reflected in analyses of the farmers' exploitation by agents of capital. This approaches a form of class consciousness that encouraged the traditional Farmers' Union sympathy and alliance with organized labor. Second, a pacifism sees war as tied to the interests of the wealthy. This pacificism was expressed by the Farmers' Union through its advocacy of both extreme isolationism (especially prior to World War II) and world government (especially shortly after World War II). Third is cooperativism, which as an economic principle was meant to combat capitalism by replacing the "profit system" with a "cooperative commonwealth" in which "all business is cooperatively owned" (Saloutos and Hicks 1951, 231). As a moral principle, this supported pacifism and the threats that competitive economic and social relations of capitalism posed for the application of "The Golden Rule." Fourth is the family farm ideal, which was related to the other elements, especially to the sense of disadvantage and to cooperativism. While cooperativism was the economic means of defending the family farm, the ideal of the family farm, grounded in Jeffersonian democratic ideology, was the basis on which political appeals were made as a means of defending this ideological objective.

The NFU's important and influential agenda primarily revolved around policies that would enhance cooperative economic development on one hand and restrict the concentration of monopoly capital on the other. At times these positions appeared as distinct camps within the Farmers' Union, but they were in fact not inherently in conflict with each other. This led to advocacy of government extension of credit without private banks, restrictions on ownership of large amounts of land, and even government ownership or control of many natural resources and natural monopolies such as transportation networks and energy production and transmission facilities.

The agricultural colleges of the land-grant system were also the target of Farmers' Union attacks. The assumed goals of increasing productivity were questioned by the NFU, which believed that it was foolish to spend tax dollars to increase farm productivity when surplus agricultural production was the farmers' primary problem. Milo Reno, who later led the Farmers' Holiday Association, was particularly strident in his attacks on the elitism of the agricultural college faculty, the irrelevance of the research, and the alliance of the land-grant system with agribusiness interests against the farmer. Even more explicitly, the Farm Bureau, with its ties to the land-grant system, became the avowed opponent of the Farmers' Union.

Saloutos and Hicks write, "In spite of its rather considerable successes, the Farmers' Union itself was never a well-integrated body" (1951, 252). Perhaps some of that success was because of its loose federation rather than "in spite" of it. The lack of centralization may have encouraged local participation and allowed the NFU adaptability to specific local variations in class structure, political culture, commodity specialization, competing organizations, and so forth. The Farmers' Union continues to be a major farm organization today through its cooperatives and its political influence. Thus the Farmers' Union plays a role in several other farm organizations we will now discuss.

The Nonpartisan League

In the late 1800s an important segment of North Dakota agriculture was characterized by large-scale enterprises in which capitalist (primarily absentee) entrepreneurs hired large numbers of workers to produce grain. These "bonanza farms" were, however, for the most part eliminated by the turn of century and replaced by smaller family-sized farms (Friedmann 1978). In the early twentieth century the American Society of Equity enjoyed considerable success in organizing North Dakota farmers. Many North Dakota farmers were either foreign-born (27 percent in 1910, primarily from Northern Europe and Russia) or former wage workers from the collapsed bonanza farms who were struggling to establish independent ownership of their land. Collective bargaining and cooperativist ideologies resonated with both the class history and ethnic cultural background of these farmers. These practices were ever more attractive given the fluctuating world grain markets and the apparent domination of that market by "big business" interests.

By 1914 the Society of Equity and the Farmers' Union had made the construction of a state-owned terminal elevator a major issue in North Dakota politics. Such a project was ratified in referendum by a 3 to 1 majority in 1914 (Taylor 1953). The state administration, however, spent the legislated money on a feasibility study that argued against the elevator. In 1915 the legislature voted against construction of the elevator. This failure to represent the clearly expressed will of the people provided a powerful symbol and a focal point for the development of a movement that extended far beyond the issue of the elevator. Credit for this "frame extension" (Snow et al. 1986) and the organization around it is usually attributed to Arthur C. Townley, as founder of the Nonpartisan League.

Townley was raised on a farm in northwestern Minnesota and had been a school teacher before migrating to western North Dakota in 1904 with his brother. Working closely with the land speculators who controlled this region, the Townley bothers also organized innovations such as a neighborhood collective to purchase the implements necessary for other production innovations in large-scale wheat farming. After a year spent wandering to the West Coast, Townley returned, now on his own, to North Dakota to begin flax production. Within four years Townley was being promoted as the "flax king of the Northwest" by the railroad land agents, speculators, bankers, implement dealers, and seed salesmen who backed him. In 1912, however, an early frost in North Dakota and the decline of flax prices from $3 a bushel to less than $1 drove Townley into an $80,000 debt and bankruptcy (Morlan 1955). Townley vowed revenge on the forces that broke him and joined the Socialist party.

The North Dakota socialists had a record of electoral success in some communities. Their agrarian platform, borrowed primarily from the Alliance and Populists, advocated state provision of rural credit, state-owned mills and elevators, state crop insurance, and unemployment insurance. This program was quite popular with the farm population, although few farmers wished to actually join the party. Recognizing this discrepancy between the popularity of the platform and the popularity of the party, the Socialists hired Townley to initiate a new "department" that would permit farmers to join the party without having to sign the "red card." Townley's success outstripped the Socialist party's political capacity to organizationally and ideologically deal with the newfound allies. The next year the Socialists discontinued the project, pointing out that the new department had as many members as the party itself.

The traditional dogmatism of American Socialist party politics impeded the North Dakota Socialist party's ability to accept the adaptations required of the doctrine in application to what Davis (1980) has called "propertied laborers"—that is, independent farmers and those tenants and debtors who aspired to such status. Many Socialists saw the interests of farmers as being opposed to the interests of urban and rural wage workers. This uncompromising definition of the "working class" whose emancipation was the Socialist party's "historic mission" (Saloutos and Hicks 1951, 206) was only one example of many in the history of U.S. farmer movements in which dogmatism would suppress the opportunity for a farmer-labor alliance. Saloutos and Hicks suggest that this failure to accept the farmers lack of education "on the subject of socialism" and the Socialist tendency to blame the farmers themselves for their predicament, obstructed potential expansion of a socialist constituency (1951, 156–57).

Townley, apparently following the advice of A. E. Bowen, a fellow Socialist organizer, left the party while retaining its basic program. Townley attended an Equity and a Farmers' Union meeting in early 1915 concerning the construction of the state-owned elevator. He saw the opportunity that the issue provided for moving farmers to this larger agenda. Perhaps as important as the substance of Townley's emergent movement are the recruitment tactics and the nonpartisan political strategy introduced by the Farmers' Nonpartisan Political League of North Dakota. Saloutos and Hicks describe the mobilization process: "In short, the tricks of the accomplished salesman and the orator were put into full swing by an ably trained group of radicals advocating a Socialist program" (1951, 162).

In organizing a community the Nonpartisan League would identify sympathetic local residents. This might be done, for example, through existing Equity or Farmers' Union networks, or through farmers who attended a meeting elsewhere or contacted the Nonpartisan League after reading its literature. These local sympathizers would then introduce a trained Nonpartisan League organizer and a Nonpartisan League lecturer to other local farmers (Taylor 1953, 433–34). When organizers talked agrarian politics and economics, they repeated a few themes, mostly attacking the farmers long-standing enemies (i.e., the chamber of commerce, the railroads, the banks). Organizers were apparently instructed to "agree with everything the farmers said and to condemn everything he disliked" (Saloutos and Hicks 1951, 161). Townley believed that if they could get the farmers to invest $6 in a membership they would develop a loyalty to the organization. He reportedly instructed organizers to "make the rubes pay their goddamn money to join and they'll stick—stick 'til hell freezes over" (quoted in Saloutos and Hicks 1951, 162).

Membership was to remain secret until the local organizing drive was complete. This was intended to prevent early intervention in the campaign by opposing forces such as merchants, bankers, the press, or law-enforcement agents. Once the drive was well under way and the word was out, however, the Nonpartisan League would set up a public picnic or schoolhouse meeting at which Townley and the League's other best speakers would stage something "reminiscent of a Billy Sunday revival or one of the early Populist gatherings" (Taylor 1953, 434). By this time the opposition of local merchants could be countered by the local Nonpartisan League organization. Taylor writes that "many a small- town businessman lived to regret bitterly his opposition to the League when an organized farmer boycott eventually forced him out of business" (1953, 435). Membership grew quickly enough to establish the League's own newspaper, the *Nonpartisan Leader*, by September 1915. This served as a means of countering local press opposition by addressing charges made against the League, showing opposition to be "the interests" against "the farmers," and sometimes turning their opposition's ridicule into a means of solidifying membership. For instance, one politician's alleged suggestion that Nonpartisan League activists "go home and slop the hogs" became a rallying cry for the movement.

The emphasis on strong local organization was related to the political strategy of the Nonpartisan League. Townley and the Nonpartisan League believed that elections were won at the precinct level and that third-party politics could not be successful. Instead, the direct primary, a recent reform, could be used to capture the majority party. The Nonpartisan League argued that the two major parties differed only at the national level and that, at the state and local level, partisanship only served to divide farmers against themselves. Thus the Nonpartisan League worked in early 1916 to nominate its own candidates for state offices, focusing on the Republican primary. Only farmer members had votes in the convention that endorsed the Nonpartisan League's candidates, and League officials and organizers were not permitted to accept nomination. County and national offices were not sought. The Nonpartisan League was simply seeking to take control of North Dakota's legislative, judicial, and executive branches. Every Nonpartisan League candidate won in the primary, and in the general election they captured every elective office in the executive branch with the exception of treasurer, where they had run a Democratic candidate. Furthermore, the Nonpartisan League elected three state Supreme Court justices and gained control of 85 percent of state House seats. In the Senate the Nonpartisan League won 18 of 24 contested seats. Twenty-four holdover senators who were not up for reelection, however, kept the Nonpartisan League from full control of the Senate.

Passage of the Nonpartisan League program required amending the state constitution. This was particularly important with respect to the development of state ownership, but it also involved changes in electoral processes. The Nonpartisan League easily pushed this legislation through the House, but it failed to pass the Senate. Nevertheless, the League did achieve some of its other objectives in this first legislative session. A state inspector of grains, weights, and measures was authorized; some tax exemption was granted to farm improvements; railroads were increasingly regulated and were restricted from discriminating against cooperative elevators; limited women's suffrage was passed with an amendment calling for complete women's suffrage; a public welfare commission was established to look into woman and child labor; a nine-hour day for (employed) women was passed; education funding was tripled; night schools were created for adult education; and inheritance taxes on large fortunes were increased.

The Nonpartisan League's opposition began to regroup in 1917. Led by the press and banking interests, local merchants and other business interests sought to discredit Nonpartisan League leaders and the Nonpartisan League program. The Nonpartisan League leadership was charged with being everything from Socialists to confidence men to anarchists. America's entry into World War I provided an opportunity to attack them as pro-German traitors, while the Russian Revolution provided opportunity to label them conspirators in world revolution. The opposition also attempted to coopt the movement with an inadequate elevator bill that would serve to discredit state ownership. Similarly, as the League moved into Minnesota, cooptation was attempted in the form of a rival "Nonpartisan League of Minnesota" organized by wealthy urban businesspeople.

In Minnesota there was increasing contact with organized labor, laying the basis for the development of the Farmer-Labor party (Morlan 1955). In Wisconsin the Nonpartisan League had an uneasy relationship with Robert La Follette's Progressive movement that involved a sharing of many objectives but an apparent fear on the part of La Follette's followers that the Nonpartisan League would usurp its own organization of the progressive constituency. At the same time La Follette's presidential ambitions encouraged a positive relationship with the Nonpartisan League outside of Wisconsin. The Nonpartisan

League also quickly developed some presence in Montana, South Dakota, Nebraska, Kansas, Iowa, Idaho, Colorado, Washington, Oklahoma, and Texas. By 1920 the *Nonpartisan Leader* claimed a million readers and the League claimed nearly 250,000 members.

The 1918 election in North Dakota secured Nonpartisan League control over state government, including the Senate. While political inexperience was a public relations asset in the Nonpartisan League campaign to replace incumbents with a "farmer regime," office-holding demanded the acquisition of skills needed to fulfill the requisite tasks of governance. This included not only learning the legislative process but also for many Nonpartisan League representatives improving their reading, writing, and speaking in English. To accomplish this the 1918 Nonpartisan League legislators all stayed in one hotel, and each night a secret caucus was held in which a rehearsal of the next day's legislation would be carried out. The "training school" was effective not only in passing Nonpartisan League legislation and training new legislators but also in completing the session in record time and reducing the cost of the session by $50,000 over the preceding session (Taylor 1953).

The 1918 legislation provided for an industrial commission to administer state-owned industries and enterprises; the Bank of North Dakota to finance those industries; the construction of a state-owned elevator, warehouse, and flour-mill system; a home-building association; state hail insurance; an experimental creamery; a graduated income tax that distinguished between earned and unearned incomes; workmen's compensation; absentee voting (with special privileges for farm women); and further assistance to cooperatives (Saloutos and Hicks 1951; Taylor 1953). The opposition now escalated its attacks on the Nonpartisan League and increasingly attracted resources from outside the state. Capital recognized the threat that the Nonpartisan League posed to its interests in North Dakota and elsewhere. But opposition to the Nonpartisan League program also began to emerge from within the organization as well.

In drawing up the League program a split had developed between forces that wished to establish state-owned and -directed programs and those who advocated socialism based on cooperatives with greater autonomy from the state. The latter position was derived from the ideas of Frederick C. Howe and was advocated within the League by the leadership of Arthur LeSeuer. Howe wrote that the development of a "producers' commonwealth" should "be worked out along quasi-cooperative rather than state-socialistic lines in order that the program will not be jeopardized with every election" (quoted in Saloutos and Hicks 1951, 191). The actual program enacted in 1918 took the opposite course.

LeSeuer and others who left the League criticized the "instability" of the program, pointing out that a fickle electorate could erode League power and "put the entire program in the hands of its enemies" who could quickly undermine it (Saloutos and Hicks 1951, 194). Socialist economic development, these forces argued, required longer time frames than permitted by biennial elections. This perspective was particularly strong among those League elements drawn from the America Society of Equity and the Farmers' Union. Their prior interest in the cooperative movement originally led to support of the League in hopes of obtaining the political means for supporting cooperative economic development. This dissension not only caused problems within the League, but such arguments were also capitalized on by the League's outright opponents.

The external forces of opposition to the organization enjoyed more and more advantages after 1918. World War I and the Russian Revolution facilitated a nationwide conservative reaction to the progressive tendencies of the early twentieth century. Charges of treason, either pro-German or pro-Bolshevik, became commonplace, and Townley was in fact jailed on charges of disloyalty for allegedly "conspiring to discourage enlistments" (Morlan 1955, 336). Such charges were couched in the context of the large German and Russian ethnic populations living in the region. The radicalism of the U.S. farm population led the federal government, the chamber of commerce, and other agribusiness interests to use the Extension Service to organize the American Farm Bureau Federation as a conservative countermeasure. When courtroom challenges to the Nonpartisan League program largely failed, legal harassment was used against individual leaders. In addition to the disloyalty charge, Townley, for example, was also charged with illegal financial manipulations, though he was never convicted of the latter. On the other side, the leadership of the Socialist party was increasingly critical of the Nonpartisan League, claiming, "The Social Revolution, not political office, is the end and aim of the Socialist Party. No Compromise, No Political Trading" (quoted in Morlan 1955, 355).

Although the Nonpartisan League gubernatorial candidate, Lynn Frazier, won reelection in 1920, the League lost ground in the state legislature. There were numerous reasons for this. Independent Democrats and Republicans temporarily buried their differences and organized the Independent Voters Association (IVA) as a means of defeating the Nonpartisan League. Many Republicans pledged support of cooperatives, effectively drawing away an element of the Nonpartisan League constituency. Indeed, "having failed to devise an original and alternative program," the IVA adopted a "platform that approved the principles of the League" promising only to make it "workable and efficient" and to drive League officials "from the public crib" (Saloutos and Hicks 1951, 201). Despite such promises, the IVA rather cynically planned to "emasculate the industrial program" (1951, 201). The failure of farm women to vote in proportion to their more conservative urban counterparts also hurt the Nonpartisan League in the 1920 election.

The electoral campaign as well as the organization itself was also significantly effected by the beginning of the postwar farm depression. The state flour mills lost money as wheat prices fell. Cooperative stores, in turn, began to fail with the farm economy. Farmers were increasingly unable to pay their dues, and the postdated checks collected for memberships were often voided. Under these conditions the dismantling of the Nonpartisan League program began in 1921, facilitated by an effective recall and replacement of Governor Frazier and the Industrial Commission by IVA personnel. Nevertheless, the Nonpartisan League did not simply disappear. In 1924 it again won control of the North Dakota House. Nonpartisan League governors were elected again in 1924, 1926, 1932, and 1936. The Nonpartisan League successfully supported candidates for the U.S. House and Senate throughout the 1920s and 1930s, reflecting the shift of attention by agricultural interests away from state politics and toward Washington, D.C. Morlan (1955) notes numerous long-standing achievements of the League: bringing formerly "radical" ideas into accepted public practices such as greater regulation of elevators and railroads, progressive taxation, state-sponsored and cheaper credit, political support of cooperative development, developing the basis for modern midwestern liberalism with its highly independent-minded electorate, and the birth of Minnesota's Farmer-Labor party, the forerunner to today's influential Democratic Farmer Labor party in that state.

In retrospect, however, it also appears that the dissenters within the Nonpartisan League may have been correct about the need to maintain greater autonomy from the state. In a moment of comparative weakness, the Nonpartisan League's enemies mustered resources from within and without the state, used legitimate criticism as well as falsehoods, and borrowed from the Nonpartisan League agenda that had won the hearts of farmers and then either diluted that platform or simply reneged, recapturing enough of the state apparatus to dismantle many hard-won gains. Aside from the National Farmers' Organization, this lesson, however, was taken by few other organizations in the following decades. The New Deal ushered in an era of increasing dependence on and incorporation into the polity. It is only in the 1980s that we begin to see a new awareness of this reluctance to invest organizational resources into the public sphere, in the form of rural manifestations of the "new social movements" that begin to suggest organizing independently of the state.

American Farm Bureau Federation

America's progressive reform movement of the early twentieth century had both urban and rural manifestations. The rural agenda is perhaps best epitomized by the work of Theodore Roosevelt's Country Life Commission and its interest in imposing the "organization and efficiency" of modern industrial society on rural America (Danbom 1979, 46). Prior to the rise of the Farm Bureau, this broad movement inspired two other attempts at the federation of the many independent farm groups into one large organization. The Farmers' National Headquarters was founded in 1910 but retained much of the leftist populism of farm organizations that still relied on the attitudes of farmers themselves as the basis of policy advocacy. Thus direct election of U.S. senators, a federal farm loan program, and public ownership of transportation and basic natural resources were part of a political stance that stood in opposition to what would become the political program of the Farm Bureau. In 1917 a more conservative federation, the National Board of Farm Organizations, was created "after the fashion of the U.S. Chamber of Commerce" (Saloutos and Hicks 1951, 257). The rise of post–World War I conservatism, however, coalesced with the elitist tendencies of progressivism to eclipse these attempts at federation. The American Farm Bureau Federation simultaneously embodied both the conservative reaction to the cooperative socialism of the early twentieth century as well as the "top-down" organizational character derived from progressivism. Thus the Farm Bureau opportunistically appropriated a portion of the ideology and economics of the cooperative movement but replaced the populism and socialism with a far more conservative political agenda. Furthermore, this was accomplished in an increasingly bureaucratic rather than democratic organizational framework.

Just as the Farmers' Union was in practice often less radical than its leftist rhetoric, so too the Farm Bureau, at least in its early years, was not as conservative as its resource base and leadership might suggest. The emphasis on cooperation alone was enough to pose some threat to certain sectors of private capital. Early flirtations with a form of collective bargaining or voluntary production control and demands for increased government credit programs steered the organization away from the more purely conservative ideology often espoused by some early leadership and for which the Farm Bureau is known today. The Great Depression also impeded the full development of an extremely conservative agenda. Following World War II and especially after McCarthyism's purge of leftist political ideology in policy debate, however, that conservatism dominated the Farm Bureau, which became the dominant voice for agriculture in the world of politics. Here we will consider only the pre–World War II era (Chapter 5 takes up the Farm Bureau's post–World War II history).

The second decade of this century witnessed a tremendous upsurge in socialist political influence in the United States. This was hardly confined to urban areas. The Socialist party candidate in the 1912 presidential election received surprisingly strong support in many rural areas, especially in Oklahoma, Texas, Louisiana, Kansas, and Arkansas (Green 1978). The Nonpartisan League, with its Socialist-minded agenda, proved to be very strong in North Dakota. These political tendencies, coupled with the Russian Revolution and increasing threats of alliance between farmers and workers, stimulated a wave of repression of leftist political activity as well as the facilitation of reformist measures to coopt or preempt the more radical leftist politics. The Farm Bureau was born of this reaction.

The basic infrastructure for the emergence of the Farm Bureau was being laid nearly a decade before the Farm Bureau became an official organization. In 1911, stimulated in part by the Country Life Commission Report, the Chamber of Commerce in Binghamton, New York, along with the Delaware, Lackawanna, and Western Railroad, hired a county agent to educate farmers in modern ways of agriculture. The chamber called this their "Farm Bureau" (McConnell 1953,

47). At this time the county agent was simply an employee of the county, or perhaps even of the local chamber of commerce, whose salary depended on local fundraising. The county-agent system derived from a program established in Texas to combat the Mexican boll weevil in the late nineteenth century. At this point the relationship between the county agent and the state college of agriculture was quite informal. At least in the northern states, the agent usually had some college education, and the college often provided technical advice but no financial assistance (Baker 1939). In many parts of the United States the Binghamton model was copied. Often county funds were made available once a certain level of local funds were raised privately. The latter funding came primarily from the local business community. As this Farm Bureau movement developed, huge contributions came from businesses like Sears, Roebuck, and Company and International Harvester, as well as the Chicago Board of Trade.

The financing of such work by railroads, bankers, and local merchants was already suspect, but the involvement of such large retailers, manufacturers, and speculators raised questions about the nature of the Farm Bureau that have never been laid to rest. These were, after all, the very groups that most previous farm organizations had seen as their opponents, not their allies. In 1914, however, the federal government began to finance the county-agent system through the Smith-Lever Act. By 1917 nearly every state had an extension program that was now closely tied to the state college of agriculture. World War I, with its drain on both the rural labor force and world food supplies, reinforced the productivist obsession with increasing mechanization and capital intensification that was inherent in the county-agent system but had been seriously questioned by many prior agrarian Populist movements. The expansion of the county-agent movement with federal funding and assistance created both the apparent need as well as the means for coordination of these independent county Farm Bureaus.

Missouri organized the first statewide Farm Bureau in 1915. By 1918 there were more than 10 state Farm Bureaus. In 1919, delegates from 36 states met in Chicago to officially found the American Farm Bureau Federation (Saloutos and Hicks 1951). Midwestern interests tended to dominate this first convention and thus the direction of the Farm Bureau. Kile (1948) writes that the eastern, southern, and western states wanted the movement to remain strictly educational and to exclude political lobbying and the development of cooperatives. Kile furthermore contends that "the full declaration of purposes was intentionally avoided by the assembly, but in every official action the strife between the two elements was evident" (1948, 51). The structure of representation, the means of financing, even the name of the organization all reflected this schism. The Illinois delegation, representing the Illinois Agricultural Association, had by far the strongest representation, followed by Iowa and Indiana. This central Corn Belt region has been the center of the Farm Bureau from the start.

This first convention also reflected the conservatism as well as the bureaucratic impulses of the movement. Harvey J. Sconce, president of the Illinois Agricultural Association, distanced this farm organization from the Populist lineage with an opening keynote address that attacked organized labor's politics and blamed labor for inflation. Sconce claimed, "It is our duty in creating this organization to avoid any policy that will align organized farmers with the radicals of other organizations" (quoted in Kile 1948, 50). Similarly, the man chosen as the Farm Bureau's first President, J. R. Howard of Iowa, declared that he stood as a "rock against radicalism." Resolutions were passed at this convention that attacked organized labor, declared the Farm Bureau to be "unqualifiedly in sympathy with the governments determination to suppress radicalism" and offered assistance to "rid the country of Bolshevism and other anarchistic tendencies" (quoted in Saloutos and Hicks 1951, 259). Henry C. Wallace, editor and future secretary of agriculture, foretold the bureaucratic—perhaps even technocratic—future of the Farm Bureau when he called on the federation to "get to work at once on a real business program. . . . That doesn't mean turning the work over to committees of farmers, either. Every line of work must be in charge of experts" (quoted in Kile 1948, 56). Most previous farmer movements had sought to keep the work in the hands of farmers, who tended to distrust "experts."

A resolution passed that contained a more traditional plea for "cost of production" in farm prices. The calculation of such cost even referred to the loss of "unrestored fertility taken from the soil" and noted the "unpaid labor of women and children" (Saloutos and Hicks 1951, 268). This demand, however, was dropped from the resolutions the very next year. Immediately the Farm Bureau created a bureaucratic structure. A public relations department had distinct divisions that provided press releases, two news weeklies, a service that provided information to editors, an in-house publishing department, and a film production service. Another department was primarily concerned with the study of cooperation both domestically and internationally. This was subdivided by commodity groups, though the goal was to "unite the local commodity cooperatives into a national marketing program" (Saloutos and Hicks 1951, 271). There was also a legal department, a transportation department, a financial department, and a very important legislative department that did extensive lobbying.

The strong financial grounding of the Farm Bureau also distanced it from other farm organizations. Support from agribusiness, the high dues charged for membership, the effective governmental subsidization of its organizing through the Extension Service and of its expertise through the agricultural colleges all lent to a powerful resource base that permitted the Farm Bureau to hire the experts recommended by Wallace. Saloutos and Hicks note that the "salaries paid to the officials and the budget appropriations made" were "far more typical of large business than of the general run of farm organizations" (1951, 272). Critics and opponents of the Farm Bureau have often contended that it is an organization of and for large farmers. Such a charge may be more valid if directed at the Farm Bureau leadership.

The Farm Bureau also attracted farmers of every strata. Its organizational efficiency, economic incentives, and early political program were enough to recruit many farmers who perhaps aspired to be bigger farmers or perhaps only to make a better living. This sort of charge seems to misunderstand the nature of the Farm Bureau and to evaluate it on criteria applicable to democratic rather than bureaucratic organizations. When the Farm Bureau is understood as a bureaucracy, created and financed by the state and agribusiness, it is not surprising that there is such a distance between its leadership and constituency, as so many critics have noted. That distance is only a cost if the goal was to build a democratic organization. We have seen, however, that the initial claims were, on the contrary, to build an efficient business and educational organization.

The Farm Bureau's success along those lines is hard to refute. More problematic has been its political role. The bureaucratic structure lends to the possibility that the organization may lobby for the interests of particular factions of farmers, or perhaps even for the interests of themselves as bureaucrats. The organization may seek to legitimize this political role by pointing to a vast constituency. If that constituency, however, has been recruited by the organization's economic incentives, the claim of political representation is suspect. Indeed, following a brief period of political success in pushing through legislation that was essentially derived from other groups, the Farm Bureau moved into a crisis period in the late 1920s in which its political position was unclear. McConnell writes, "One obstacle to the formulation of the necessary program was that the Farm Bureau Federation had not been formed around an idea but around a bureaucracy. Neither leadership nor membership was committed to any central core of doctrine" (1953, 59). In this sense, the Farm Bureau at this time provides an excellent example of an organization that is guided by what Weber (1978) would call a formal rather than a substantive rationality. The bureaucratic form provided a vehicle of efficiency that meshed well with the bureaucratic organization of the U.S. Department of Agriculture (USDA) as well as with agribusiness, but that form itself was without substance. Thus it was readily captured by particular interests who could control the top levels of the bureaucracy. Those interests, not surprisingly, were primarily associated with agribusiness and the USDA.

In the 1920s the Farm Bureau worked closely with a bipartisan group of senators often referred to as the "farm bloc." Regulation of grain exchanges, stockyards, and packers; agricultural export credit; tariffs on farm products; and the legalization of cooperatives with the Capper-Volstead Act were among the legislative successes for which the Farm Bureau could claim some credit. In the mid-1920s, however, a split developed between those advocating an emphasis on the development of cooperatives and those who wanted to build a primarily political organization that would be the "voice of American agriculture." The latter group won out with the election of E. A. O'Neal of Alabama as Farm Bureau president. This Farm Bureau position led to an erosion of its influence and membership. Throwing support to the unsuccessful McNary-Haugen plan to protect domestic farm prices with tariffs and export surplus at world market prices, and then collaborating with Herbert Hoover's disastrous Federal Farm Board, the Farm Bureau entered the depths of the Great Depression desperately in need of rebirth.

The organization of 14 farm organizations into the National Agricultural Conference in 1933 was the first step of the Farm Bureau on the road to recovery. The Farmers' Union was the only other major organization that might have contended for a strong share of political influence. The crisis tended to awaken the latent radicalism within the Farmers' Union, however, moving them to the left and even toward direct actions, such as Milo Reno's Farmers' Holiday Association, and left them somewhat outside the sphere of influence held by the more conservative Conference. In this organizational vacuum the Farm Bureau helped to construct a New Deal farm program that would effectively rebuild the organization around its existing resource base.

The production quota schemes for acreage reduction in the Agricultural Adjustment Act (AAA) required a great deal of administrative oversight at the local level. The USDA contended that the Extension Service was the only institution that could readily carry out such a task. An infusion of federal funds went into the Extension Service comparable only to the World War I period that had laid the basis for the creation of the Farm Bureau in the first place. Now the federal government was again providing the resource base for resurrecting the Farm Bureau since the traditional closeness of the Farm Bureau with the Extension Service gave the Farm Bureau effective control of the administration of the AAA. McConnell writes, "When the AAA was first set up, the Farm Bureau sent word to the state federations to decide whom they wanted to administer the act in their own states. In many communities the local farm bureaus 'literally took over' the task of organizing the AAA committees" (1953, 75). This act, as well as its successors, not only provided an identification of the Farm Bureau with this aspect of New Deal farm policy but also benefited the larger farmers that the Farm Bureau had always been accused of favoring.

Especially in the South, the administration of the AAA by local elites provided very disproportionate benefits, sometimes enhanced by outright fraudulent enforcement. This resulted in both stimulating the development of the Southern Tenant Farmers' Union as well as a tremendous outmigration of sharecroppers from the rural South. Many of these former sharecroppers moved west to become hired farm workers. Revision of the AAA in 1936 consolidated the local AAA groups at the county level. This further benefited the Farm Bureau by generalizing the administration across commodity lines in a structure that exactly paralleled Farm Bureau organization and was more readily directed by county agents (McConnell 1953, 78). The Farm Bureau emerged from the depression with a stronger resource base in the agricultural colleges and extension than ever before. This position would enhance their power in the postdepression era when they would seek to dismantle those aspects of New Deal policy that were not to their liking.

Farmers' Holiday Association

Depression set root in rural America in the summer of 1920. Prices received by farmers were cut in half by the summer of 1921. Some recovery was made in the mid-1920s, but in 1929 the arrival of the Great Depression created desperate conditions for most U.S. farmers (Cochrane 1979). Iowa was among the places particularly hard hit: "In 1930, a bushel of Iowa corn dropped from 90 cents to 56 cents; a year later, it was 28 cents; by the summer of 1932, it was 12 cents or lower" (Dyson 1986, 84). The mechanization of corn production prepared the ground for such a catastrophe. Tractors were purchased on credit terms that increased the debt load already suffering from the effects of speculative landholding. Furthermore, as tractors replaced horses, more pastureland became available for corn production while the new costs of production for fertilizers, gas, oil, and the hybrid seeds increased. Taxes, too, had increased considerably as farmers financed educational development and road construction. Dyson (1986) writes that by 1930 schools and roads absorbed 60 percent of Iowa's taxes and that property taxes had doubled since 1915. In this more commercialized production system, farmers were ever more caught up in a web of economic interdependencies, while retaining an image of themselves as independent and an aspiration toward autonomy. Nevertheless, the increased costs of production and the declining returns put Corn Belt farmers in a "cost-price squeeze" that led to more and more foreclosures that threatened hopes of independent ownership. These were the conditions that gave rise to the Iowa-based Farmers' Holiday Association.

Leadership of the Farmers' Holiday Association is generally attributed to Milo Reno, president of the Iowa Farmers' Union from 1921 until 1930 but a dominant figure in that organization until his death in 1936. Born in Iowa in 1866, Reno followed his parents in associating with many of the protest movements that had come and gone over the more than 50 years before his assuming the presidency of the Iowa Farmers' Union, which he had joined in 1918. Reno's analysis of the farm problem led to advocacy of two related solutions. Reflecting the experience of his younger days, Reno claimed to "have been a Greenbacker for over half a century" (Shover 1965, 26). Thus Reno advocated inflationary policy, blaming the deflationary policy of the Federal Reserve Board for decimating the farmers' asset base and precluding their ability to meet mortgages undertaken in a period of higher land prices.

Reno's other fundamental demand was for the guarantee of "cost of production" to farmers. The notion of "cost of production" for Reno included the actual average expenditures for inputs, a wage for the farmers' labor, a 5 percent return on investment in land, and a depreciation allowance (Shover 1965, 38). Reno's preference was for the government to guarantee farm prices at this level. In 1927, however, he had already submitted a resolution to a coalition of midwestern farm organizations, the Corn Belt Committee, suggesting that legislative inaction would mean that "the time will have arrived when no other course remains than organized refusal to deliver the products of the farm at less than production costs" (quoted in Shover 1965, 27).

The failure of both protectionism in the McNary-Haugen legislation of the 1920s and of the voluntary production restriction in Hoover's Farm Board in the early 1930s eventually led Reno to advocate just such a strategy. The National Farmers' Union had been split over the Farm Board issue, but in 1930 the anti–Farm Board forces gained ascendency. The Iowa Farmers' Union and Reno had been among the strongest critics of Hoover's policy, while the Farm Bureau, in which the Iowa Farm Bureau was the dominant state faction, supported Hoover. This polarization impeded political and ideological moderation in a state whose recent relative prosperity was now being rapidly erased by the depression. The stage was nearly set for the Farmers' Holiday Association's "farm strike."

An episode often known as the "cow war" is significant in understanding the farm strike, insofar as it created a climate of hostile and physical confrontation between farmers and authorities as well as the opportunity to develop networks and tactics for rapid physical mobilization of farmers to a particular place. In 1917 Iowa began testing cows for tuberculosis on a voluntary basis. In 1923 this became compulsory in some counties. In 1929, however, such testing was mandated for the entire state. This regulation not only involved costs and risks on the part of farmers but was seen by some farmers as a violation of privacy. By 1931 the strains of depression combined with these sentiments, with a negative attitude by Reno and others toward government and agricultural college "experts" and the taxes that paid their salaries, and with hostility toward the meatpackers, who obtained "millions of pounds of good meat at condemned prices" (Saloutos and Hicks 1951, 439). The result was a movement to resist the testing. While radio played a novel role in this mobilization, in the counties of greatest resistance committees were organized by telephone lines. The arrival of testing agents quickly brought neighboring farmers to the objector's farm. The veterinarians would usually simply leave peacefully, although force was sometimes used.

Enforcement of the testing law in the Tipton area of Iowa required a declaration of martial law following a violent confrontation of "armed agents" with some 400 farmers. Two thousand soldiers occupied five Iowa counties for two months to complete the testing (Shover 1965, 32). A somewhat embarrassing situation for the government arose when cows were condemned that happened to belong to the parents of the girl judged by the federal government to be the healthiest girl in the United States, and she attributed her health to drinking milk every day. Her father, however, actually supported the program, reflecting the fact that this "cow war" incident did not involve or even have the support of most Iowa farmers. Their interest was focused on broader issues of the overall economy and talk of a farm strike by Reno and the Iowa Farmers' Union leadership. Nevertheless, a climate of hostility had been created and some mobilization tactics learned.

In 1931 the Iowa Farmers' Union passed resolutions calling for inflation, increased graduated income and inheritance taxes, confiscation of wealth in wartime, and "a farmers' buying, selling and tax-paying strike" unless government assistance was provided (Saloutos and Hicks 1951, 442). In the spring of 1932 local mass meetings were held across Iowa. A general convention held in Des Moines declared the intention to call a farmers' strike or "holiday" on 4 July. The name "holiday" mimicked the term used by bankers who closed their banks to prevent withdrawals in the depression. The agrarian fundamentalism inherent in the movement's analysis is reflected in the strategy itself as well as in a portion of a poem published in the *Iowa Union Farmer:*

> Let's call a Farmers' Holiday
> A Holiday let's hold
> We'll eat our wheat and ham and eggs
> And let them eat their gold.

The farmers believed that by staying home, buying nothing, and selling nothing they could make government and business recognize their fundamental role in the economy.

The idea spread beyond Iowa into Minnesota, South Dakota, North Dakota, Nebraska, Illinois, Wisconsin, Missouri, and Montana but consisted mostly of local and regional organizations with only loose affiliation with the official Farmers' Holiday Association. This led to a very uneven enforcement of the strike. Though Reno had long advocated the strike, it quickly grew beyond his control. Iowa Farmers' Union and Farmers' Holiday Association policy soon simply followed or endorsed the strikers rather than leading them. Considering the violence that accompanied such actions, this lack of centralized leadership may have functioned to protect Reno and his closest followers from legal responsibilities. As we have seen, holding actions conflict not only with the farmers' ideology of independence but also contain the structural problem of the free rider. Control of this problem requires the ability to negatively sanction or apply a "cost" to breaches of solidarity. In the absence of moral or normative commitment by nearly all constituents, physical coercion is usually a necessity.

Sioux City, Iowa, became the first major battleground of the Holiday movement. Dairy farmers led the blockade of this major meat-packing center. Dyson describes the blockade as taking "the form of a military siege" and that "within a few days, the supply of milk was almost dried up" (1986, 86). Picket camps began to spring up around both large and small trading centers. Violence at the barricades rapidly escalated from fist fights to the use of gunfire as a means of intimidating would-be violators of the strike. The Farmer-Labor party governor of Minnesota actually called on his fellow governors to use the state militia to enforce the strike until prices rose to cost of production. Other governors, however, were more likely to use their police force to break the farmers' picket lines. Local successes with the dairy holding action encouraged grain and livestock producers, but these less perishable products were much more difficult to effectively withhold. Livestock shipments simply rose in Chicago as they slowed in Iowa. Things settled down in the fall of 1932 as harvesting occupied farmers and the presidential election provided some hope.

Franklin D. Roosevelt's farm policy was still being drawn up when the farmer's patience began to wear thin. Now, however, the strike action was all but forsaken as farmers organized locally against the wave of foreclosures. Tactical innovations derived from the "cow wars" and the strike were used to disrupt auctions of farm land, homes, and equipment. Calling for a legislative moratorium on foreclosure, the movement spread even farther from its Farmers' Holiday Association roots, although its more violent manifestations took place in the association's strongholds. In LeMars, Iowa, some 600 people took over a courtroom, demanding that the judge agree not to process foreclosures. On his refusal he was blindfolded, taken from the courtroom, severely beaten, and threatened with death. The county was placed under martial law (Saloutos and Hicks 1951). In Denison, Iowa, 800 farmers physically overpowered 50 law-enforcement officials in stopping a farm sale. This county, too, was placed under martial law and also occupied by state militia as arrests were made. A tactic that usually carried an implicit threat of violence was the "penny auction" in which local farmers would see to it that bids for the farmer's repossessed property never rose to more than a few dollars. The property was then donated back to the original owners. More typical but less dramatic and newsworthy action involved local "councils of defense" privately working out compromises with creditors with the threat of force being, again, only implicit.

Dyson claims that the Farmers' Holiday Association built a parallel local state that "effectively bypassed law enforcement bodies and the whole legal system" (1986, 83). The political system had failed, so they "laid it aside and operated through a sort of rough grass roots democracy" (1986, 88). Opponents of the Farmers' Holiday Association labeled the same behavior vigilantism. Nevertheless, the New Deal farm program sapped the strength of the Farmers' Holiday Association. Reno's distrust of the federal government, his longstanding antagonism with Secretary of Agriculture Wallace, and his hostility toward the Farm Bureau, "the professors," and the land-grant complex must have made for a bitter death in 1936 as these forces forged a new agricultural policy that would only serve to strengthen their own future role in structuring U.S. agriculture.

Affirming Gamson's (1990) contention that the unruly are often successful, however, the Farmers' Holiday Association's actions surely had some influence on the urgency of passing New Deal farm legislation, if only to preempt further action of this sort. Federally supported production control was an innovation that had been considered quite radical only a short time before. Furthermore, the general strategy of the strike or holding action would rise again in the 1950s and 1960s with the National Farmers' Organization and in the 1970s with the American Agricultural Movement, while the "farm gate defenses" and penny auction would be studied again in the 1980s by a new generation of farmers facing what seemed to them to be strikingly similar difficulties.

The Southern Tenant Farmers' Union

The production control payments and commodity loans of the New Deal that helped bring an end to the Farmers' Holiday Association in the Midwest had a different impact in the South. The class structure, grounded in sharecropping and tenancy, led to unequal access to government relief, massive outmigration, and the rise of a protest movement. The primary organizational form of the protest was constituted by the Southern Tenant Farmers' Union (STFU). The New Deal cotton program required farmers in 1933 to plow under every third row of cotton and then reduce planting in 1934 by 40 percent. In exchange, the government supported a base price and issued checks to producers that subsidized the market price. Initially, such payments were to go to tenants and landowners in proportion to their share of the crop. In 1934 "the benefit-distribution ratio was changed in the landlords' favor" (Grubbs 1971, 19). Tenants and sharecroppers were, however, still to receive a portion of the payment. These producers, who constituted more than three-fourths of the farmers in the Delta cotton region, began to complain that they were not receiving their fair share of the subsidy, if anything at all. Many were being evicted for such complaints. Landlords reduced others to wage labor status to avoid sharing the subsidy.

The southern sharecropper was at a serious disadvantage in this conflict. The Agricultural Adjustment Administration (AAA) was set up at the county level, and this permitted local elites in a highly inegalitarian social structure to implement the program in their own interest. The tenants suffered from decades of impoverishment, undereducation, illiteracy, lack of organization, and a tradition of deferential interaction with an elite who held power and authority in nearly every sphere of southern rural culture. Black tenants and croppers faced the additional burden of racial oppression. The relative poverty of resources vis-à-vis the landowners necessitated that the tenants take the struggle beyond the local power structure. This need to seek solutions beyond the locale contained the irony that the federal government was pumping money into the hands of the elite. To make matters worse, that capital was being used to acquire previously unaffordable machinery to substitute for sharecropper labor.

Appeals to the larger society took the form of an increasing number of journalistic exposés on the poverty of the sharecropper that sometimes described the unfair and unscrupulous administration of the AAA in the region. Coincidentally, appeals also began to reach Washington through political and academic channels. A USDA-commissioned study by a Duke University professor, for instance, clearly exposed the problems with the program itself and with the cheating that was taking place. Such reports, however, tended to fall into the chasm of a split between liberal USDA reformers like Rexford Tugwell, Gardner (Pat) Jackson, and Jerome Frank and more conservative AAA personnel like AAA head Chester Davis and Cully Cobb, head of the AAA's cotton section. Responding to a private, internal memorandum in 1934, Davis publicly claimed that "only a tiny minority of landlords would ever exploit their tenants" and that such practices could not be prevented because "no . . . cotton adjustment program can change human nature" (quoted in Grubbs 1971, 33). Nevertheless, Cobb sent an investigator, E. A. Miller, to the Arkansas Delta. Miller, however, refused to examine evidence collected by Clay East, an emerging leader of the tenants. Instead, Miller interviewed landowners and told another of the leaders, H. L. Mitchell, that they should abandon the tenant's cause since "the landlords are all your friends and these sharecroppers are a shiftless lot. There is no use of being concerned about them as they don't really count. They are here today and gone tomorrow" (quoted in Grubbs 1971, 34). The problem, of course, did not go away so easily.

Secretary of Agriculture Wallace was initially content to turn investigations of such complaints over to local AAAs under the leadership of the Extension Service. Grubbs contends that the county agents effectively functioned as "defense attorneys" for the landlords and that such a policy meant that "the planters were investigating themselves" (1971, 39). The first showdown came in Tyronza, Arkansas, and revolved around the legal issue of whether or not the landlords were required to keep the same tenants or simply the same number of tenants. Given the massive displacement of tenants that had already taken place, the increasing mechanization, the high levels of depression-era unemployment, and the reduced acreage objectives of the AAA, the latter policy would effectively strip most tenants of any claim to AAA benefits as they renegotiated cropping arrangements with new landlords in an environment in which the labor supply far exceeded demand.

Tyronza was the home of two young Socialist businessmen whose occupations provided intimate knowledge of local political culture: Clay East, a gas station owner, and H. L. Mitchell, a dry cleaner. Tyronza was also the home of Hiram Norcross, a planter whose ruthlessness drove many of his tenants into the fledgling sharecroppers' union that East and Mitchell envisioned and were organizing with the encouragement of the Socialist leader, Norman Thomas.

Mitchell and East had already achieved some success in obtaining aid for particularly needy local people, though their goal had been to democratize control of the more general New Deal relief and works programs that were also dominated by the planter class. They obtained Socialist party support for a survey of tenant conditions and published the results in a booklet titled *The Plight of the Sharecropper*. Such successful and sympathetic actions helped legitimize their leadership in the eyes of a farm population given to suspicion of help from nonfarmers.

In early 1935 Mitchell and three other tenant leaders drove to Washington, D.C., to meet with Secretary of Agriculture Wallace to discuss the situation in general and the Norcross situation in particular. The meeting was arranged through their friendship with Dr. William Amberson, a socialist professor of physiology in Memphis with ties to influential reformist liberals within the USDA. According to Grubbs (1971), Wallace, though polite and sympathetic, never quite seemed to grasp the impossibility of the local AAA committees functioning in a democratic manner in the cotton South. Perhaps Wallace, a native Iowan and familiar with an entirely different form of tenancy, never understood the totalitarian character of the southern plantation system. He did, however, promise an investigation and sent Mary Conner Myers, a Boston lawyer with expertise in administrative law, to the Delta. Her telegrams back to Washington indicated shock at the conditions of the tenants and admiration for their fortitude and courtesy under such trying conditions. Her official report, however, was suppressed by Chester Davis and is still missing from the National Archives (Grubbs 1971, 51).

Nevertheless, the liberals in the Legal Section of the AAA, led by General Counsel Jerome Frank, began to pursue the Norcross case, knowing that it represented hundreds of similar scenarios across the

Cotton Belt. Norcross was illegally evicting tenants for joining the STFU. Furthermore, because he was chair of the local AAA committee, the impossibility of justice at the local level was made clear. Unfortunately for the croppers, the local power structure reached all the way to Washington. Frank and others in AAA who had pursued the interest of the tenants were fired by Davis in one of many purges of liberals that USDA would see in the next two decades. Regardless of the question of his naïveté on questions of southern social structure, Wallace apparently buckled to higher pressures to shelter not only the AAA but the broader New Deal program. Roosevelt needed the support of key southern congressmen such as Senate Majority Leader Joseph Robinson of Arkansas and Senate Finance Committee Chair Pat Harrison of Mississippi. In the end the USDA held that landowners were not bound to keep the same tenants in place in order to receive government subsidies for cotton production.

Meanwhile, back in the Delta, Mitchell, East, and others were making strides in organizing the STFU. Always looking for tenant leaders, they tended first to rely on nonfarmers affiliated with the Socialist party. J. R. Butler, for instance, primary author of the STFU constitution, was a rural Arkansas school teacher and fellow Socialist. His ideology and analysis represented a "mish-mash" drawn from "Populist, Wobbly, and other midwestern radical sources" (Grubbs 1971, 63). Rural ministers were also a source of leadership, especially for organizing the black tenants. Indeed, the black church left a strong mark on the STFU. The equation of the Bible's Pharaoh with the landlords, the style of oration and hymn singing (the famous "We Shall Not Be Moved" and "Roll the Union On" among others, are products of the STFU meetings), and lessons in the need for strong solidarity were all influences drawn heavily from black religious tradition.

In smaller communities the STFU often formed one integrated local. Around larger towns and plantations, where white and black tenants were less familiar with one another, separate locals were formed. In many cases, however, both groups met together, and the leadership pushed the idea that it was still one union, fighting for the same thing (Grubbs 1971, 68). Integration of this sort was, of course, in violation of southern traditions and even southern law. Meetings were often broken up by law officers in both official and unofficial capacity. Ward Rogers, a white minister, was arrested and charged with, among other things, introducing a black leader as "Mister" (Mitchell 1987, 27). Unofficial violence against the STFU also increased as the organization spread. Leaders and followers were subjected to beatings, death threats, and their homes were subject to gunfire. Law-enforcement agents, when not personally involved, looked the other way at violence that defended the status quo. In one case a lone witness to a violent attack on a union meeting was murdered after refusing to retract an accusation of the deputies involved (Grubbs 1971).

The tasks of organizing, providing legal defenses, and simply providing the means of survival for evicted croppers required money. The tenants, who lived not only in poverty but in a largely noncash economy, had none. Only a small percentage of dues was ever able to be collected. Financial assistance came primarily from the North—from the American Civil Liberties Union and the National Association for the Advancement of Colored People, but mostly from relief funds associated with Socialist and Communist party groups and from churches. The former affiliation rather quickly became troublesome as Communist party dogma interfered with STFU objectives of building "one big union" that would help "replace tenancy with occupant-ownership" (Grubbs 1971, 64).

The Communists wanted to create two unions—one for managers and owners and one for tenants and workers. As with midwestern debtors, adherence to Communist party doctrine blinded them to the reality of tenants' aspiration to property ownership. The Communist role in Alabama, for example, further frustrated STFU leader Mitchell, who saw the party's divide by tenure policy as "an effort to put the screws on the STFU" and to geographically block the STFU's more practical and grass roots organization (Grubbs 1971, 83). To the west, a Cherokee leader by the name of Odis Sweeden organized several STFU locals around the specificities of the Oklahoma situation. This expansion, however, was never fully integrated into the STFU. Indeed, when asked to help black and white tenants obtain land, a Choctaw chief simply told Mitchell, "When the white man and the black man get ready to take back the land, just let the Indian know. We will get our guns, and we will come, too. We do not need a union. We are already organized" (Mitchell 1979, 80).

The major step toward expansion followed from a strike against the picking of cotton that was called in 1935. Rather than actively picket the plantation, workers tended to complain of illness, report fear of retaliation for scabbing, or express a need to go fishing. By the end of the year pay scales were raised, though not quite to the level demanded by the union. Regardless, the STFU claimed victory and new locals rapidly emerged. In the Missouri boot heel one plantation owner, Thad Snow, even invited the STFU to organize his plantation and sought to convince his neighbors of the benefits of unionism. The success of the strike encouraged the STFU to seek support of the American Federation of Labor (AFL) in the fall of 1935. While the AFL passed a resolution that effectively recognized the STFU, not much more was forthcoming from this "money-conscious and dues-conscious rather than class conscious" organization (Grubbs 1971, 87).

In 1936 the STFU's three basic strategic choices—collective bargaining, public relations, and political appeals—tended to merge. In a public relations ploy, Mitchell organized about 100 evicted tenants into a roadside tent colony. Their landlord had been considering an STFU contract when he succumbed to peer pressure from the local elite. Not only was the tent colony subject to a dynamiting, but planters across the Delta retaliated by increasing the eviction of STFU tenants. Washington responded with promises of targeting evicted tenants for Resettlement Administration assistance. The STFU voted to strike again. This time the planters were prepared to counter. National Guardsmen were dispatched while police arrested strikers and shipped them off to private prison farms, "often without formalities such as judges, juries, warrants or attorneys adding red tape to the process" (Grubbs 1971, 103). Outsiders, organizers, and the press were also subject to arrest and harassment. The tenants introduced a picketing technique in which pickets would "march" in a long single file that appeared to enhance their numbers while calling on workers to leave the fields. The tactic, however, rendered strikers vulnerable to attack, and blacks especially were subject to assault.

As the strike continued, the terror campaign against the STFU escalated until a white minister and a sympathetic white woman were beaten by planters' thugs in Arkansas, and a shocked public forced the government to act. Roosevelt could not act too conspicuously as he was campaigning for the reelection of Arkansas's Senator Joseph Robinson. He did, however, shift the investigation of complaints from the USDA to the Department of Justice. As it happened, Attorney General Homer Cummings had heard firsthand from his Yale classmate and YMCA official Dr. Sherwood Eddy of the "legalized slavery" system embodied in the private prison farm business. As the election approached, Cummings obtained a grand jury indictment against a particularly notorious Arkansas deputy for "aiding and abetting and holding in slavery" (Grubbs 1971, 117). Not only was the STFU's fundraising strongly enhanced by this success, but the private prison farms themselves were eliminated in Arkansas within the next few years.

Governors began to call commissions to study the tenant problem, and the STFU was often but reluctantly represented. The STFU questioned the basic landlord-tenant relationship, contending that it was the source of the other problems. More practically, they demanded regulation of plantation stores; enforcement of the maximum 8 percent interest rate, child labor, and eviction laws; tenant compensation for farm improvements; rights of free speech and assemblage; a minimum wage law; abolition of private prison farms and the poll tax; and cooperative farms to replace the large plantations (Grubbs 1971, 121). The Arkansas commission did declare tenancy to be a "serious menace to American institutions" and blamed monoculture, speculation, high interest rates, and marketing inefficiencies for the situation. The commission's stated policy objectives included enabling tenants to own their own homes, restricting corporate acquisition of farm land, improvement in health and educational systems, and the standardization of written leases (Grubbs 1971, 123).

The question of farm tenancy became a major public issue. A Gallup poll found that more than eight of 10 Americans favored government loans to enable tenants to buy their farms. The public debate clarified some of the racism and paternalism characteristic of the tenant problem, especially in the South. A North Carolina agricultural economist wrote in an academic journal that black sharecroppers could not "be given on an extensive scale, the status of owner . . . the Negro is, for a number of reasons, an indifferent individual. He cannot be characterized as an ambitious person" (Forster 1936, 91). Governor Junius Marion Futrell of Arkansas contended that the average tenant "has the mentality of a 12 year old child and should be subject to compulsory birth control or sterilization" (quoted in Grubbs 1971, 126). The public response of advocating independent ownership was also not particularly well-received by the more Socialist-minded leadership of the STFU. Perhaps owing to the Communist party's fetish with large-scale and collectivized production, they envisioned instead cooperatively owned plantations with expert management and a highly developed division of labor.

At the federal level, Roosevelt also commissioned an influential study of farm tenancy that had STFU representation. This study deepened Roosevelt's and Wallace's sympathy with the STFU cooperative farm vision. An attempt to directly legislate such experiments failed, but through legislation that allowed Roosevelt to convert the Resettlement Administration into the Farm Security Administration (FSA) such experiments were undertaken with some promise as Wallace even came to see the advantages of collective ownership of expensive machinery and land by small farmers. In general, however, Washington was not prepared to advocate cooperative production, only cooperative organization of individual purchasing and marketing. Before long the Farm Bureau led the assault that eliminated what McConnell has described as "the greatest innovation in agricultural policy" since the Homestead Act and the "greatest attempt to cope with the problem of rural poverty" in the nation's history (1953, 96, 112).

In 1937 the STFU sought membership in the Congress of Industrial Organizations (CIO), which only exacerbated existing tensions within STFU leadership concerning the potential loss of autonomy under such an affiliation. Direct membership in the CIO was possible but not very pleasing to the more radical elements of STFU, who had little enthusiasm for John L. Lewis's authority. Indirect membership through the United Cannery, Agricultural, Packing and Allied Workers of America (UCAPAWA) was also possible. This organization, however, was dominated by Don Henderson, the STFU's old Communist antagonist in Alabama. His promise of autonomy to the STFU proved persuasive, and the STFU went into the CIO through membership in UCAPAWA. Immediately problems arose. The dogmatic class analysis and the subsequent "divide by tenure" policy of the Communists failed to appreciate the common problems of small cotton farmers. Payment of dues by the cash-poor tenants were now made mandatory, were five times the amount of the old dues, and went to Washington rather than Memphis. Some STFU leaders also contended that the Communists were encouraging a black separatist movement in an attempt to wrest control from the existing leadership. Expulsions based on charges of using divisive tactics to fragment the union led to vengeful criticisms by former members that led to even more division.

In January 1939, in the midst of the infighting, a dramatic new protest emerged in the Missouri boot heel. Led by Owen H. Whitfield, a black STFU organizer with UCAPAWA sympathies, more than 1,000 evicted sharecroppers camped along U.S. Highway 61 in a public display and protest that Cantor (1969) contends anticipated certain qualities of the protest forms in the civil rights movement some 15 to 20 years later. The scene again riveted public attention on the plight of the sharecropper. Promises, threats, and excuses flowed from Washington while the landlords retaliated with charges of Communist agitation and used the event to attack the Farm Security Administration cooperative experiments, one of which was home to Whitfield. Law officers eventually destroyed the efficacy of the protest by forcing the croppers off the highway and into the adjacent swamps. The event did not prove to be an opportunity for reconciliation of the leaders but rather revealed the depth of the schism within the organization. When UCAPAWA renewed its determination to collect dues, STFU leaders were expelled for demanding that dues be sent to Memphis, not Washington. At this point the STFU voted to secede from UCAPAWA and the CIO. Key black leaders stayed with the CIO, however. These disputes led to a decline in external support and increasingly confused and demoralized the rank and file. UCAPAWA moved toward organizing cannery workers.

The tremendous changes that came with the 1940s led to the continued decline of the STFU (just as it did to farm labor unionization efforts in California). World War II brought further mechanization of cotton production and the deployment of a practical mechanical cotton picker (Daniels 1985). Croppers and farm workers moved to the cities for industrial employment or went into military service. Postwar anti-Communist hysteria spelled the demise of men like Henderson in the labor movement. Mitchell helped tenants find better-paying farm jobs in the East and later became involved in farm worker strikes in California and Louisiana, after which he worked for the AFL-CIO organizing fishermen and tractor drivers on sugar-cane plantations. The STFU cooperative production vision ended as FSA was dismantled and became the ever more conservative Farmers' Home Administration.

In the end, the struggles of the STFU may have had greater effect in facilitating the transformation of tenants into indebted "owners" outside the South. The class position of the southern tenant and sharecropper was always closer to that of the wage laborer than the midwestern or Great Plains tenant who was more able to capitalize on legislation (mostly easier credit) meant to relieve the problems of tenancy. It would be decades before the agricultural wage worker would achieve comparable gains politically or economically. At the same time, it is difficult not to recognize the lessons learned in organization and protest by STFU members if one looks ahead to the civil rights movement, when a recently and rapidly urbanized black population adapted aspects of the culture and tactical innovation of the tenants' struggles to a situation that may have had more similarities than is commonly acknowledged.

The New Deal and World War II altered the structure of American agriculture, and thereafter farmer movements took a considerably different shape. Although those farm organizations firmly entrenched in strong cooperative economic enterprises provided some linkage to the most recent era, cold war political repression and the demographic demise of the rural population altered or suppressed much of agrarianism's ideological inheritance and transformed the character of farmers' political participation as the United States moved simultaneously toward a postindustrial and permanent war economy.

Chapter 4

After World War II

World War II ended depression-level prices for farm products. According to Cochrane (1979), prices received by farmers increased 138 percent between 1940 and 1946. Furthermore, net farm income increased by 236 percent in the same time span. The typical postwar collapse of farm prices was delayed by an extension of price supports (farmers had accepted price ceilings during the war) and by massive food relief aid programs to Europe and Asia. By 1951, however, the prosperity associated with the war had ended. The reduction of federal price-support levels and the adoption of backlogged technology stimulated a long-term erosion of the farm population. New technologies had become both affordable with the wartime prosperity and necessary with the war's drain on labor. In 1950 there were 5.4 million farms in the United States. By 1959 there were 3.7 million. The number of farms dropped to 2.7 million by 1969 and to 2.3 million in 1978. The 1987 Census of Agriculture showed 2.1 million farms. These demographics provide the basic structural context in which post–World War II farmer movements operated.

The end of the war found the Farm Bureau as the dominant voice in Washington with respect to farm policy. The National Farmers' Union (NFU) and the Grange also represented substantial numbers of farmers. The Grange, however, was increasingly relegated to less agriculturally dependent regions and was not very aggressive politically. The NFU, on the other hand, continued to struggle against the Farm Bureau's increasingly conservative political ideology and influence. In the immediate postwar years the NFU seems to have rejuvenated their left-populist political agitation. Some NFU publications equated cooperativism with economic democracy and monopoly capitalism with fascism (e.g., Vogt 1948). NFU demands for state intervention carried strong egalitarian impulses that sought to improve life for working people both on and off the farm. There was also an eagerness to bring cooperative economics to the city, especially in the area of health care and food consumption. The NFU worked closely with organized labor for policy that would keep farmers on the farm and out of the labor market. The NFU and labor advocated strong price supports for agriculture, but the NFU also pushed for federal housing programs, public television, integration of labor union–based consumer cooperatives with farmer cooperatives, food stamps, free college education, and so forth. Some state affiliates pushed for a graduated property tax on land, inclusion of farm workers in minimum-wage legislation, and the drafting of capital as well as men in wartime.

The defeat of the NFU-supported Brannan Plan in 1949 and 1950 reflects the Farmers' Union's loss of influence in Washington. The Brannan Plan would have replaced price supports based on volume of production with direct but limited income supports. When the NFU's progressive agenda became a target of McCarthyist attacks in the early 1950s, the organization began to shrink away from the sort of demands that derived from their left-populist roots. Instead, it moved toward mainstream Democratic party politics that tended to focus on sustaining cooperativism and certain elements of New Deal agricultural policy, such as higher price supports for agricultural commodities. The impact of McCarthyism on the NFU's political agenda was wideranging. The Iowa Farmers' Union provides an interesting example of these effects. This example also demonstrates the important notion of "abeyance" processes developed by Taylor to refer to the qualities that particular organizations adopt to "sustain themselves in non-receptive political environments and provide continuity from one stage of mobilization to another" (1989, 770). These qualities include an intense, long-term commitment to the organization's goals and tactics; the exclusion of the less committed; a highly centralized structure; and a rich political culture.

The Iowa Farmers' Union had, under Milo Reno's leadership, given birth to the Farmers' Holiday Association in the 1930s. After Reno's death in 1936 the Iowa Farmers' Union had declined in membership and moved to the right (Dyson 1986), but this shift was reversed in

1944 with the ascendance of Fred Stover and his supporters. The NFU had for a long time been outspoken in favor of a world government and was thus a strong supporter of the newly formed United Nations, as well as an opponent of the North Atlantic Treaty Organization (NATO). When the United Nations intervened in Korea, the Iowa Farmers' Union under Stover's leadership refused to support the intervention, denouncing it as both imperialist and in violation of the NFU's long-standing anti-militarism. The incident accelerated a process in which the left-wing elements were being purged from the NFU. The Iowa Farmers' Union was expelled from the national organization and was forced to relinquish the "Farmers' Union" title, becoming first the Iowa Farmers' Association and then the U.S. Farmers' Association (USFA). Stover and his colleagues became victims of McCarthyist attacks. Membership dwindled to the resolute, and the USFA went into an "abeyance process" (Taylor 1989).

Stover and the USFA regularly published a newspaper and annually convened with an increasingly aging membership. In the 1960s and early 1970s the USFA was heavily involved in the antiwar movement, working with Students for a Democratic Society (SDS) chapters and routinely denouncing yet another imperialist war. The USFA continued to publish its analysis of the "farm problem," though this was often subordinated to its peace and anti-imperialism agenda. In one attack on both the war and the narrow vision of the National Farmers' Organization (NFO) attempts at collective bargaining, Stover advocated "another kind of holding action"—that America's "most precious crop" was its boys being taken away "to carry on an illegal war. . . . A farmer who lets the military-industrial complex take his son away for nothing, hardly deserves more than $19 for his hogs" (Stover 1968, 15).

Taylor contends that "the most important consequences of abeyance structures for future mobilization around persistent discontents" are the provision of activist networks, repertoires of goals and tactics, and collective identity (1989, 770). This is precisely what the USFA provided in the more receptive political climate of the 1980s farm crisis (we will return to the role of USFA later in this chapter).

The narrowing of the range of options in political debate over farm policy by McCarthyism and Farm Bureau hegemony, the continued erosion of farm price-support levels under the Eisenhower administration (with the Farm Bureau's advocacy), and the declining power of the farm vote with decreasing farm numbers set the stage for a solution to the farm problem that did not depend on Washington. Not surprisingly, given the political imbalance created by the demise of the Farmers' Union in Iowa and its history as a center of the Farmers' Holiday Association, a new movement for collective bargaining emerged in Iowa in the mid-1950s.

The National Farmers' Organization (NFO)

The conditions we have just described coincided with a severe drought and the collapse of hog prices to give birth to the National Farmers' Organization (NFO) in 1955. The movement emerged in southern Iowa and northern Missouri under the powerful oratorical skills of Oren Lee Staley, a Missouri farmer who served as president of NFO for most of its first quarter century of existence (1956–79). Staley helped transform the NFO from a protest group that simply threatened another farm strike as a means of sending a message to Washington to a serious collective bargaining organization that used the "holding action" tactic as leverage to bargain with buyers and processors of farm production.

At its first meeting in 1955 the NFO officially committed to nonpartisanship and to being a nonpolitical organization. While relying primarily on an economic strategy (i.e., collective bargaining) rather than a political or governmental one, the NFO has also maintained lobbying efforts aimed at increasing price supports and has engaged in a strong and steady critique of monopolistic tendencies in agricultural marketing as well as an offensive against the Farm Bureau and its (mis)representation of farmers in favor of agribusiness. In these ways the NFO and the NFU have increasingly been found as allies in national politics.

The extent to which widespread collective bargaining would effectively restructure the agricultural marketing system is indicated by the internal turmoil and external opposition that plagued the NFO from the start. Early supporters and even some officials abandoned the NFO in 1957 when the organization received a $3,000 grant from the United Auto Workers (Wood 1961). More supporters fled after a failed merger with the NFU. When the NFO began a series of "test" holding actions in 1959, others shied away at the costs of withholding, and the radical character of this tactic was challenged by most other farm organizations, politicians, and the media. The cooperative economic base of other primary farm organizations was threatened by the NFO, since it challenged these cooperatives to provide cost of production plus profit. The NFO often mobilized cooperative members to use their cooperative membership to make just such demands. The irony of farmers striking or withholding from their own cooperatives was an embarrassing indication of how farmers had lost control of their cooperatives. Such action revealed cooperative management's tendency to respond in the same manner as the private, for-profit sector.

While the media editorially denounced the NFO, it also appreciated the drama of the NFO's holding actions. Mass slaughters of livestock, the dumping of milk, and the violence associated with "scab" marketing all provided great copy for selling newspapers and wonderful visual representation of the farmers' plight on the newest form of mass communication: television. The NFO also relied heavily on another technology that had been less common in farm households during depression-era mobilizations: the telephone. The NFO developed a "minute man" system based on telephone networks that allowed them to mobilize large numbers of a county's farmers to a meeting or a picket line in less than two hours (Rowell 1984).

The basic goal of NFO was to win contracts with processors that would guarantee "cost of production and a reasonable profit"—the old Farmers' Holiday Association cause (Dyson 1986, 207). The NFO, however, formally recruited members to contractual obligations to market their production through the NFO. Holding actions designed to pressure processors into signing contracts with the NFO often lifted market prices enough to encourage nonmembers and less committed members to try to market their goods. As in similar events of the past, violence and intimidation were common means of dealing with this free-rider problem. Shotgun blasts at farm trucks, tire slashings, dynamiting of barns and buying stations, fence cuttings, and other forms of vandalism were decried by the media and NFO opponents.

Social movement scholars should not be surprised at this tactical means of addressing the extreme free-rider problem given by such a situation (see, for example, Gamson 1990). Any success in the holding action cannot be distributed selectively to participants but instead becomes a public good (i.e., higher market prices). This is often the only form of social control available to constrain a free rider that is actually raising the challengers' costs and threatening the very success of the holding action. Much like a labor strike, the costs of "free riding" or scabbing must be increased. For organizations with otherwise scarce resources and no ability to restrict the distribution of benefits won by the organization, violence and intimidation are often the only means available. Besides the opposition of media, other farm organizations, and processors, the problem of enforcing holding actions was also complicated by the de facto control over farm marketing exercised by bankers and landlords. Here the appearance of the farmers' freedom and independence is revealed as more aspiration than reality. Access to credit or land could be terminated by credit institutions and landlords when the latter groups tended to oppose the NFO approach and its potential threat to local and regional elites and power structures.

Membership figures are hard to obtain for the NFO. They were kept secret for strategic reasons. The first meeting in October 1955 brought representatives from 16 Iowa and eight Missouri counties. A second national meeting included representatives from Nebraska, Colorado, and Montana. By March 1956 Staley was claiming 180,000 members in 13 states, with Arkansas and Oklahoma becoming stronger. NFO recruitment was based on a system that provided limited economic incentives to organizers. An organizer received $7.50 for every new member recruited, but only a maximum of $15 per day. If no new members were recruited in a day, the recruiter received nothing for his efforts. This scheme was designed to build on local networks in which each new member would bring in a few additional new members rather than depend on a centralized staff of professional recruiters (Rowell 1984).

When better prices and the end of the drought began to erode enthusiasm in the late 1950s, the NFO embarked on a series of "test" holding actions to sustain the collective bargaining concept. Holding actions were expected to generate media attention as well as reveal the farmers' opponents. Improving market conditions tended to obscure the farmers' fundamental antagonists. Like crises, holding actions tend to clarify such underlying antagonisms. The first holding actions were on hogs and were regionally confined to Iowa, Nebraska, Missouri, and Kansas. Some of these generated "wildcat" actions in other states. Certain communities in Wisconsin and Minnesota, in particular, appropriated the tactic and began to push the strategy in the dairy sector, which had a strong cooperative tradition. The violence associated with each holding action came to a climax in Bonduel, Wisconsin, in 1964, when a gun-wielding farmer with a truckload of livestock ran over and killed two NFO pickets. This event captured national media attention (e.g., *Time* magazine carried photographs of the dead farmers). The NFO retreated until a dairy holding action was called in 1967 (Walters 1968). This action also brought violence. The perishable quality of milk lent power to the producers and spectacle to the action. Milk dumpings were held for media benefit, an approach that sought to display the desperation of farmers but tended to backfire with the general public. The NFO was accused of being callous to the needs of the hungry or simply as working against the interests of the public as consumers.

The ability to quickly deplete perishable milk supplies was threatening enough that the federal government intervened with a series of legal harassments. These have undermined the organization's ability to operate with full efficacy. The suits tended to focus on anti-trust violations (i.e., seeking to monopolize the sale of milk). Ironically, in one such case the NFO turned around and charged the same crime against the two largest dairy cooperatives—Associated Milk Producers, Inc. (AMPI), and Mid-America Dairymen, Inc. (Dyson 1986). After a decade of legal expenses, no convictions were made. While AMPI went on to earn implications of scandalous "lobbying" with the Nixon administration, the NFO went on to make the famous Nixon White House Enemies List, a matter that is usually described in boast more than shame by NFO members. In 1973 Nixon's Securities and Exchange Commission charged the NFO with violating federal law when it borrowed money from members to alleviate the disastrous effects of Nixon's 1972 Soviet grain deal. When grain prices skyrocketed, the NFO was caught with presale priced contracts with the big grain companies (who reportedly did enjoy advance warning of the sale [Morgan 1979]). Many NFO members reneged on their contracts, and the NFO was left with a huge debt.

These legal problems took a great toll on Staley and the NFO. In 1979 Staley resigned and was replaced by DeVon Woodland from Idaho. The NFO continues to bargain collectively, though more quietly, and has had some considerable success in marketing milk and livestock in certain regions and especially in regional specialty markets, such as sunflowers and walnuts. Dyson (1986) reports NFO claims of $1 billion in annual sales.

The NFO's critique of monopoly market conditions and expressed concern that monopoly capital will eventually control the land continues a long populist tradition. NFO local networks and tactical innovations such as its "Minute Man" system, as well as the legacy of an activist protest culture, were influential in the American Agricultural Movement mobilization in the late 1970s and in defenses against foreclosures in the 1980s. Similarly, the NFO has always lobbied for higher price supports from Washington though there has also been an inherent lack of confidence in such a solution. Government programs, as implemented, are seen to coincide with the decline of the farm population and increasing debt loads as farmers expand to reap advantages of policies that favor large producers (Rowell 1984). This distrust anticipates certain sentiments of some of the "new social movements" that arose in rural America in the 1980s farm crisis. While the NFO's overall turn away from farmer dependence on governmental solutions is realistic given the increasingly small voting power of farmers, the NFO solution requires that farmers themselves also be more realistic about the levels of independence they actually retain. In many ways their reluctance to obligate themselves contractually to collective bargaining derives from a sense of autonomy that is more apparent than real, given the very oligopolistic and regionally monopolistic marketing conditions of modern agriculture that they oppose.

Rural America

The nature of post–World War II agricultural policy formulation facilitated the increasing influence of specialized commodity associations compared with the general farm organizations (Bonnen 1973). This is because agricultural policy tends to be built around specialized commodity programs that simply adjust the basic New Deal framework every few years. Organizations such as the National Cattlemen's Association or the National Corn Growers are more effective in advocating a highly focused pursuit of narrow policy goals than general organizations that seek to represent a plurality of often conflicting interests. The long-term consequence of such a piecemeal approach to policymaking, however, is a neglect of the well-being of the farm sector as a whole. To the extent that agricultural policy is assumed to be rural policy and insofar as other policy that affects rural life is often constructed in a similarly narrow-minded manner, it is no surprise that by the 1970s many farm and rural people were seeing that the very fabric of rural economy and society was deteriorating.

Several other developments facilitated the emergence of a social movement in the mid-1970s that sought to focus political attention on the whole of rural society and not just the agricultural sector. The trend toward the farm sector's reliance on nonfarm sources of income solidified during the 1970s. The Soviet grain deal of 1972 increased farm prices enough to temporarily make farm income more than one-half of total farm family income, but as these prices fell again rural Americans became increasingly aware of their dependence on non-farm income. This perspective was surely reinforced by a "population turnaround" in the 1970s that saw the population of nonmetropolitan places increase at a rate of 16 percent, compared with rates of 3 percent in the 1950s and 4 percent in the 1960s. Furthermore, the population growth in specifically rural places (outside of places with more than 2,499 people) was 20 percent in the 1970s compared to –2 percent in the 1950s and 3 percent in the 1960s (Lichter, Fuguitt, and Heaton 1985).

A politically significant component of this population turnaround involved a cohort of young people—college-educated in the late 1960s and early 1970s—who, in returning to rural areas or escaping urban life, brought with them an activism, political experience, and a commitment to a broad range of social issues. This group gave a boost to a prior generation of activists grounded in general farm organizations (especially the NFU and the NFO), cooperatives, churches, and labor unions. Many government officials who struggled to serve the rural public in the face of Washington's neglect or incompetence also became involved in organizations concerned with social and political change.

The energy, enthusiasm, and idealism of the younger activists joined with the experience and resources of the existing groups to create an organization called Rural America in 1975. Through a series of conferences Rural America developed a platform of policy demands on a broad range of social issues pertaining to rural life. Regional field offices and state affiliates were organized as well as national-level programs around specific issues. An early membership application form (Rural America 1977) contends that Rural America's mandate was to "carry out action-oriented research," monitor governmental programs, testify on pending legislation, provide technical assistance, and act as a clearinghouse of information. Much of this mission was elaborated in a monthly newspaper, *Rural America: A Voice for Small Town and Rural People*, published in Washington, D.C., where Rural America maintained an active lobbying effort.

An interesting aspect of Rural America that anticipates divergent directions by some of the organizations that would eventually spring from it involves a tension between Rural America's calls for local control of rural communities and the primary placement of those calls to Washington, D.C. Clearly, the interest in radical, grass-roots democracy by the more youthful element found some fertile ground in similar, more established concerns voiced primarily by certain cooperatives, the NFU and other descendants of left populism. Nevertheless, it is a reflection of the extent to which the rural United States had become dependent on federal policy that appeals for local self-government were made to the White House and Congress. In the 1980s some of Rural America's offspring broke away from this particular political and ideological limitation and grew toward more full-fledged manifestations of what are known as the "new social movements."[4] Substantively, the concerns of Rural America were very much those described as the concerns of "new social movements." Rural America called for participatory democratic mobilization around farm issues, including land ownership and agricultural labor, but it also addressed issues of poverty, environment, rural housing, health care, education, energy, transportation, legal assistance needs, civil rights, the special needs of rural youth and elderly, and women and minorities.

Alongside these other interests Rural America made a number of policy recommendations specifically for agriculture. Rural America demanded a democratization of the USDA, the land-grant college system, and the Extension Service that would remove these institutions from agribusiness control and become more representative of the interests of family farmers, farm workers, minorities, consumers, and environmentalists. Policies were advocated that would encourage organic farming and target small and beginning farmers for special technical and economic assistance. Rural America wanted to ban larger than family corporations from engaging in agricultural production or farmland ownership and to enforce antitrust laws against concentration in the food-processing sector. Price-support programs were not to be tied to volume of production but rather to stabilize, along with an "ever-normal granary," farm prices and to support family income. Rural America argued against tax policy that encouraged speculative investment in farmland, against inheritance tax policy that tended to interfere with the intergenerational transfer of intact family farms, and against tax policy that encouraged the advertising of food (contending that advertising was consuming too much of the public's food dollar). Rural America wanted the USDA to invest more in facilitating the development of cooperatives for both farmers and consumers. In an apparent reference to government harassment of the NFO, Rural

America demanded that farmers have the right to organize and to strike as a means of securing economic justice. Rural America also demanded that hired farm workers have the same rights and protections that are guaranteed to workers in other occupations.

The Carter administration's secretary of agriculture, Bob Bergland of Minnesota, provided as sympathetic an ear to such demands as any secretary of agriculture had for some time. In January 1981 Bergland's USDA published *A Time to Choose,* a document that supported many of Rural America's claims with official data. This amounted to little more than a "parting shot," however, since the Reagan administration would choose a completely opposite direction, leading toward the most severe economic crisis that rural America had faced in decades.

The farm crisis in the 1980s drew on key leaders who had developed skills with Rural America in the 1970s. Activists within Rural America with particular interests in agricultural matters often went on to organize more specifically around the farm problem, although most maintained a concern for the larger patterns of rural life. This was often expressed in the form of an agrarian fundamentalism that saw agriculture as the linchpin of the rural economy. The Iowa Farm Unity Coalition and Prairiefire Rural Action, Inc., were two influential 1980s farm groups that grew directly out of the Rural Iowa affiliate of Rural America. Rev. David Ostendorf served as director of the Midwest Office of Rural America in Des Moines and then as director of Prairiefire without changing addresses. Ostendorf (personal interview 1989) notes that Rural America was "getting in a much, much more serious financial crunch all the time. . . . It was in their interest and ours for us to spin off. And so we did become independent then. We incorporated as Prairiefire Rural Action in 1985 and we really didn't miss a day in terms of the work."

This personnel depletion process meant, however, that Rural America itself spent less time with agricultural issues at a moment when a farm crisis was clearly pressing rural Americans in ways that made the agrarian fundamentalist message of the farm-oriented groups most credible. Browne reports that "Rural America's staff was not following or even much aware of the current status of the farm bill in 1985," working instead to maintain the organization "by contracting to do technical work on housing and transportation problems for local rural governments" (1988, 39). Nevertheless, Rural America had already played a vital role in developing a core leadership network who used their political and organizational experience in the agricultural crisis of the 1980s. Some of the state affiliates of Rural America have now become members of the National Family Farm Coalition (NFFC). Rural America's linkage of agriculture to certain other rural issues facilitated similar extensions by progressive groups in the 1980s. Perhaps nowhere was this extension more significant than in the positing of high-input, chemically dependent agriculture as contrary to the interests of family farming. This particular position began to erode the traditional political animosity between environmentalists and agriculture as a whole. The contention that only a certain type of agriculture was environmentally unsound laid the basis for potential alliance between environmentalists and family farmers. Before Rural America transmitted this legacy to the movements of the 1980s, another farmer movement emerged in the Great Plains that would also contribute to the shape of farmer movements in the 1980s.

The American Agriculture Movement (AAM)

In the 1970s farm income took a roller coaster ride, falling drastically from 1973 heights, leveling in the election year of 1976, climbing sharply between 1977 and 1979, then falling again in 1979–80 (USDA 1982). Throughout this period the price of farm land in America's most significant agricultural regions continued to climb. Promises of continued exports led to competition among farmers for land in expansionary drives associated with high grain prices. Government policy that encouraged wealthy nonfarm people to invest in farm land as a tax shelter further inflated farmland prices. In order to meet the higher prices of farmland and expand production, farmers borrowed heavily in both real estate and non–real estate credit markets. Thus throughout the 1970s assets and debt rose together. Many agricultural economists and most financial institutions encouraged the continued expansion and borrowing that fueled this inflation.

The first major indication that something was wrong came from farmers, who began to feel the effects of grain price instability in the context of huge debt loads. Interest rates did not change with grain prices from year to year. Interest payments still had to be met each year. The summer of 1977 came on the heels of the most recent decline in net farm income and a large negative gap between prices paid by farmers (for inputs, taxes, and interest) and prices received by farmers (USDA 1980, 1982). In this context the American Agriculture Movement (AAM) emerged out of café discussions among frustrated farmers in Campo, Colorado. The objective of the AAM was to push the federal government toward ensuring 100 percent parity levels for farm goods, as opposed to the low support levels contained in the 1977 Farm Bill. The pressure for such government action was to be created by a farm strike that would prove the significance of agriculture to the nation's economy and regain the farmer's political power. Unlike Rural America's broader ideological framework, the AAM's ideology was saturated with a much stronger agrarian fundamentalism. This so colored the AAM's diagnosis that other rural problems were effectively neglected under the assumption that 100 percent parity would resurrect rural American communities and regions.

The AAM mobilized quickly. The first meeting of 40 farmers on 6 September 1977 grew to 700 farmers on 13 September and then to 2,000 farmers, including the U.S. secretary of agriculture and television coverage on 27 September. The simplicity of the AAM's demand for 100 percent parity obscured regional and specific commodity interests. By January 1978 the AAM claimed 1,100 local offices in 40 states (Browne and Lundgren 1988). In the beginning the AAM used television wisely, with a dramatic if well-rehearsed protest style that readily attracted news coverage. A mass rally with strident speeches would be followed by a "tractorcade" or parade of farm machinery and the intentional use of "broad-shouldered and heavy-set farmers, strategically placed at visible locations," to distribute AAM literature, recruit members, and pose an implied threat of disruption or unruliness (Browne and Dinse 1985). All of this captured media attention and widely publicized the AAM in a highly cost-effective manner. One AAM leader was quoted as saying, "We may be stupid, but at least we're smart enough not to buy TV time" (Cigler and Hanson 1983, 106).

Reflecting farmers' frustration with general farm-organization representation, a study of the Kansas chapter of the AAM found that 35 percent of Kansas Farm Bureau members identified themselves as AAM members while another 27 percent claimed to be sympathizers (Michie and Jagger 1980). Similarly, 54 percent of Kansas Farmers' Union members joined the AAM, and 66 percent of Kansas NFO members joined the AAM. The latter two findings are not surprising since the Farmers' Union and the NFO always shared the policy goal of high price supports and NFO members had experience with the strike tactic. The high percentage of Farm Bureau membership in the AAM is significant, however, insofar as the Farm Bureau is, as critics often charge, embarrassingly revealed to be lobbying against the interests (in high price supports) of a substantial portion of its own membership.

According to Browne and Dinse (1985), the AAM quickly moved in two directions. On one hand, it expanded toward a system of locals that came to be coordinated at state levels with considerable variation between state affiliates as well as between locals within state organizations. This variability primarily coincided with local leadership, sympathy from local bankers and businesspeople, and regional commodity specialization. On the other hand, the AAM also moved toward a more centralized organization in Washington, D.C., that sought to bridge local differences, especially those emerging between commodity-specific or regional interests, and to present a united front to Congress and the White House.

In this case the role of the locals essentially became one of recruiting members, staging protests, and enforcing the threatened strike. The strike, however, was a near impossibility, and there is little indication that anyone, including most AAM officials, really believed that farmers would refuse to plant the 1978 crop. First, the debt load that instigated the political mobilization precluded such a tactic insofar as it would be an invitation to foreclosure. Second, net farm income had already begun to rise again (USDA, 1982). Thus one of the primary functions of the locals was essentially already abandoned by the AAM in the spring of 1978. The locals supported the Washington focus by producing the AAM's largest rally and tractorcade on the nation's capitol in January 1978. AAM farmers lobbied and protested throughout the spring. A common joke among the 1980s movement leaders is that one AAM farmer called home from Washington to say that they "were going to straighten this thing out if it took all week." In the end, President Carter's resistance to AAM demands (on budgetary and food price inflation grounds) led to the Emergency Assistance Act, which increased price supports by 11 percent (Browne and Dinse 1985).

Given that the AAM's singular goal was 100 percent parity, this gain was seen by many AAM leaders as a loss. The result was to reinforce the AAM's tendency to view the farm problem (less than parity prices) as the consequence of a conspiracy of multinational agribusiness and financial capital orchestrated through the Trilateral Commission. The Carter administration's close links with the Trilateral Commission were further evidence of the conspiracy. Conspiratorial explanations of the farm problem are, of course, hardly novel. Similarly, the identification of politicians, multinational grain companies, and banks as the villains is at least as old as the late nineteenth century and even the eighteenth century (in the rhetoric of the American Revolution and its aftermath). But perhaps never before has the argument held such experiential credibility as at this time. Farm commodity, food-processing, and retail markets had become increasingly monopolized (Zwerdling 1980). So, too, had farmers' inputs become increasingly monopolistic, especially in the area of farm equipment and petrochemical products. A subsequent Trilateral Commission report did in fact claim that the elimination of "nearly all protection for farm products" should be the "objective of U.S. farm policy" (Johnson et al. 1985, 46). The Trilateral Commission report recommended the elimination of import restrictions on beef and dairy products so that U.S. farmers would compete with "unsubsidized" agricultural production in other (mostly Third World) nations.[5] Furthermore, credit was also increasingly dependent on centralized sources and seen as subject to singular control from Washington through the Federal Reserve Board. Finally, federal policy was seen as setting the parameters within which the agricultural economy operated.

Ironically, the AAM drew from both New Left and ultra-Right literature to validate its specific version of the conspiracy or "master swindle" (Kohl 1979). At times, as in the publication *Acres, USA*, the agrarian fundamentalism and critique of the "corporate" interests merged with an environmental interest that argued for an "eco-agriculture" that abandoned the dependency on credit and the agribusinesses that came with the dependency on chemicals (Browne and Lundgren 1988, 65). The AAM also drew on a traditional agrarian fundamentalism that was elaborated and revitalized by the National Organization for Raw Materials (NORM), whose officials often spoke at AAM meetings and influenced AAM literature. NORM contended that raw materials production (agriculture, forestry, mining, and fishing) was the basis of all new wealth and that parity prices for such production was essential to economic health and a just society. A NORM publication contended that these producers of new wealth were the "roots" of the economy. "Cut off the roots" and the "rest of the economy dies." Parity pricing for raw materials "will restore the economy to its proper balance and this balance will bring us true prosperity. It's that simple" (NORM pamphlet, n.d.).

The conspiracy, then, was to deprive these producers of just prices as a means of enriching a parasitic elite whose power was based on their possession of paper (money) and control of financial institutions that managed that paper but whose interest was also in control of land and food production. This adaptation of a Marxist labor theory of value and ruling-class theory was blended with right-wing literature that contained anti-Semitism and saw the conspirators as interested in eroding democracy, family, individualism, and patriotism (as in their "no-win" Vietnam policy) so as to facilitate the emergence of a world government that would be their more effective servant (Kohl 1979). The Trilateral Commission was seen—again borrowing from both right- and left-wing thought—as a precursor of such an institution, whose power would be solidified in the coming depression that their policies were creating.

As the less committed fell away from the AAM, this sort of analysis gained more and more centrality; it was a process that fed upon itself by driving away farmers who saw such analyses as extremist. At the same time, the dramatic protests and flamboyant speeches that the AAM had depended on for media coverage began to increasingly reflect not only this extremist position but also the frustration of AAM leaders and an anger that began to turn Washington and the media against the AAM. Television lost interest as AAM events became "routine," and the media began to either neglect the AAM or to focus negatively on its unruliness (tying up Washington traffic, disrupting the political process, threatening politicians, fighting with police, etc.) while ignoring its substantive political demands. Ironically, then, the mass media that had helped propel the AAM to national prominence also helped to bring about its demise once the AAM became worth less as a commodity for news consumption. Such a problem is not, of course, unique to the AAM. Any social movement that depends on media for publicizing its case will face the problem of continuously innovating the drama and appearance of spontaneity that the media demands without crossing over into the realm of "extremism" that the media tends, in a sort of self-fulfilling prophecy, to discount as unimportant and without influence.

By 1980 the AAM had become much more like the other general farm-organization lobbies that it had only recently challenged as ineffective voices (Browne and Dinse 1985). The AAM began to take up the advocacy of gasohol (gasoline derived from grain) as a solution to both farm and energy problems. In 1982 the original split was formalized into two organizations: AAM, Inc., and Grassroots AAM. Under the influence of a public relations firm's guidance, the former organization moved toward a more mainstream Washington lobby structure and formal organization and away from protest-style political activism.

Grassroots AAM remained a more informal, decentralized organization that retained the option of protest. This grass-roots activist approach was bolstered by the AAM's disappointment with the 1980 election. President Jimmy Carter had already earned the wrath of the AAM. His embargo of grain sales to the Soviet Union pushed the AAM leadership to support Ronald Reagan in 1980. Reagan's campaign promise to balance the federal budget was, of course, also very attractive to the AAM and many other farmers hoping for relief from rising interest rates (Sigelman 1983). On election, however, Reagan took a stronger free-market position than Carter had ever held, moving toward the Trilateral Commission recommendations that were more vigorously pursued by the Bush administration through the General Agreement on Trade and Tariffs (GATT) negotiations. This alone flatly contradicted AAM demands for 100 percent parity, and, of course, Reagan's balanced budget promise turned into the greatest escalation of the federal deficit in the nation's history. Thus Grassroots AAM's local activism may have rendered it less visible as such, but, more importantly, the group kept a core of activists in touch with local conditions as U.S. agriculture moved into the 1980s and the most serious crisis to face family farming since the 1930s. In this way the AAM, especially its Grassroots form, provided leadership, political experience, and networks for new organizations that emerged in response to the farm crisis of the 1980s.

Farmer Movements in the 1980s

Numerous factors combined to create the 1980s agricultural crisis (Mooney 1986; Petrulis et al. 1987; Strange 1988). The most immediate, concrete manifestation of the crisis to farmers, however, was the increase in farm foreclosures carried out by credit institutions and enforced by local law-enforcement personnel. Given the high visibility of certain federal government actions such as Carter's grain embargo and rising interest rates, government and credit institutions became the target of protest when farmland prices dropped by more than 50 percent in some areas. While commercial banks and life insurance companies were subject to protest, the public (Farmers' Home Administration) and quasi-public (Federal Land Banks and Production Credit Associations) lenders took the brunt of the farmers' protests, "farm gate defenses" (the name often given to the 1980s version of the 1930s penny auction), and general ill will. These latter lending institutions did, in fact, play a central role in facilitating the overcapitalization of U.S. agriculture (Amols and Kaiser 1984; Mooney 1986, 1988).

The crisis was most directly confronted by a new generation of rural activists that began with the mild mannered Rural America and then grew up with the rough protest culture of the AAM's single-minded vision. The crisis struck hard at this particular cohort of farmers. These young men and women had to borrow heavily to begin farming in the 1970s as the price of land rapidly escalated beyond its productive value. In 1981 those land prices began to fall. Both beginning farmers as well as farmers who expanded in the 1970s were caught in an escalation in the ratio of their debts to assets. This debt/asset ratio is a basic indicator of the health or solvency of a farm, at least from the creditor's point of view. Declining land values diminished the asset base, thus altering the ratio. For a time, rising interest rates further negatively effected the debt/asset ratio. The result was that those credit institutions that had been so eager to loan money in the 1970s began to enforce a wave of foreclosures unseen since the Great Depression. Furthermore, the Reagan administration directed the Farmers' Home Administration (FmHA) to eliminate or foreclose on thousands of family farmers. The clientele of the FmHA tends to be young, low-net-worth, and beginning farmers. The irony of Reagan's action is that the FmHA is the current form of the Resettlement Administration and the Farm Security Administration. These institutions emerged from depression-era legislation to help just such farmers deal with that crisis. To many, it seemed that the AAM prophecy was being fulfilled. Land was being taken away by the banks, and rural communities were suffering increasing unemployment and the loss of businesses. Thus both the conspiracy theory and the agrarian fundamentalism were being validated by the events of the early 1980s.

The magnitude and characteristics of the crisis tended to vary by region, largely by state borders. Because banking laws vary from state to state, the relative dominance of different lenders also varied. This fact, as well as individual state's jurisdiction over foreclosure, lent to the need to develop intrastate organizations that could provide legal counseling and services to that state's farmers in their struggles vis-à-vis the various institutional lenders. Furthermore, local commercial banks (especially in states that impede branch banking) and FmHA, PCA, and FLB offices also varied within each state.

Morris's notion of "local movement centers" is useful in understanding the farmer movements of the 1980s. He describes the origins of the civil rights movement as "dozens of local movements with their own organizations, activists, interorganizational relationships, boundaries and funding bases" rather than "one homogeneous civil rights movement" (1984, 40). The civil rights movement needed mechanisms that could transmit knowledge of local struggles, successes, and failures across the nation. So, too, did the farmer mobilizations of the 1980s, since the geographic variation in the crisis generated a plurality of mobilizations bounded by state and locale. According to Morris, the black church and certain educational institutions provided an important means of diffusing and coordinating the struggle for civil rights among these local movement centers.

To some extent religious groups provided such a resource for agrarian protest. The National Catholic Rural Life Conference (NCRLC) and other ecumenical organizations facilitated communication within and between religious groups that exist among the U.S. farm population. Nevertheless, given the variable concern expressed by particular bishops and pastors, churches also functioned to enhance the local and regional specificity of mobilization. Furthermore, the role of churches was crosscut by conflicting interests. More often than not, local lending institution officials and distressed farmers were members of the same church.

Given the concentration of farm youth in land-grant institutions and the conservative character of the colleges of agriculture, it is hardly surprising that educational institutions played little direct role in the mobilization. There were exceptions. Larger meetings and conferences were often held in university buildings. Across the nation a few sympathetic faculty in various colleges and universities provided what help they could offer, though often in a clandestine manner. Overall, however, the campuses were rather quiet with respect to the whole crisis.

Perhaps the greater contribution of education actually occurred some 10 to 20 years earlier. Many leaders of the local movement centers had been in college in the 1960s. They brought a wealth of experience with collective action as well as strong elements of anti-militarism, democratic egalitarianism, feminism, and environmentalism that became part of the popular ideology among a segment of this generation who had migrated or returned to rural communities in the 1970s. While such an analysis was relatively impotent in the prosperous 1970s, its resonance increased rapidly with the coming of crisis in the 1980s. Armed with this analysis and a zealous commitment to the provision of financial and legal counseling or, failing that, collective protest action to impede foreclosure proceedings, these young leaders gained more and more legitimacy among both older and younger farmers in their communities. This legitimation was facilitated by the relative inability of the existing dominant farm organizations to provide such an analysis or such services.

Clearly the largest U.S. "farm" organization, the Farm Bureau, was incapable of any progressive response to the crisis. Indeed, the crisis itself was in part the outcome of Farm Bureau's hegemonic alliance with agribusiness in the making of agricultural policy since World War II. The Farm Bureau's analytical framework could only interpret the crisis as the inevitable weeding out of poor managers, a process that was perhaps seen as unfortunate but also as a necessary price for progress and as a positive development in the long run. Such an analysis became less and less potent and increasingly cost the Farm Bureau credibility as the crisis began to show cohort-specific effects and to threaten farmers whose neighbors knew them to be good, hard-working managers. The National Farmers' Organization's collective bargaining focus was far too narrow a framework for dealing with a crisis grounded in credit-based production relations. While more sympathetic, its response also tended to blame farmers for not having worked with NFO prior to the crisis, implying that a "good manager" would have joined a collective bargaining association.

The most obvious candidate for coordinating these local movements was the National Farmers' Union. To some extent the NFU facilitated movement toward mainstream and instrumental political action. It also channeled resources toward organizations that provided legal-financial counseling and that became involved in confrontational protests. Along with the churches, however, the NFU's primary emphasis reflected its traditional faith in the federal government as a potential defender of the family farm, and its resources have been directed toward legislative politics. This was one of two types of movements that developed in response to the crisis. These movement types are related in some ways and even overlap in membership. But they can also be distinguished from each other. Although both types exhibit certain new social movements characteristics, we will refer to the first as "mainstream" and the second as "left-populist."

The more mainstream 1980s farmer movement developed the incentives to sustaining organizational activity that were lacking in the

AAM. The immediacy and duration of the crisis lent to the need for collective action at the local level to deal with the wave of foreclosures. An unsympathetic administration in Washington pushed certain groups to provide financial and legal consulting services with respect to foreclosure and bankruptcy proceedings. Support groups were also organized to help deal with the emotional stress associated with the possible loss of one's farm.

Legal and financial counseling services were provided by telephone hot lines. These hot lines derived from earlier AAM efforts but were elaborated on and more highly developed in the 1980s. The organizations tended to increasingly use farmers who had been through such struggles over foreclosure to serve as counselors. Efforts were made to match those farmers experienced with particular types of lenders (e.g., private banks, Federal Land Banks) with those clients who faced the same institutional lenders (Browne and Lundgren 1988). The organizations' limitations by state borders within which their legal expertise was effective also functioned to turn the attention of these organizations away from Washington and toward state government. Browne and Lundgren (1988) contend that the nature of these services kept the new organizations in touch with the latest developments in the countryside. In this way, these movements gained legitimacy and the respect of the farm population as they surpassed the more general farm organizations in helping farmers deal with the crisis. Resources were drawn heavily from rural churches but also from universities, foundations, organized labor, individual contributions, and community groups (Browne and Lundgren 1988; Ostendorf personal communication 1989). The new organizations often retained strong local autonomy insofar as they were actually coalitions of local or regional organizations operating within a state.

Browne and Lundgren point to the Iowa Farm Unity Coalition as "typical" of such organizations, although it "assembled one of the most comprehensive sets of services" (1988, 73). This organization is described as a "loosely knit, locally controlled network of farm activists" whose board of directors "has been unable, and perhaps unwilling, to impose rigid discipline on the rank and file" (Browne and Lundgren 1988, 73). The specific success of the Iowa Farm Unity Coalition is in large part due to its close affiliation with and resource support from Prairiefire, Inc., the organization that grew directly out of the Iowa affiliate of Rural America. In many other states, Rural America had more indirect influences on these mainstream organizations. Rural America not only played an important networking function, but the 1980s groups also borrowed much of the substantive political ideology, the broader range of social issues, and the Rural America resource base. The environmentalism, the feminist influences, and the anti-militarism blended with a populism that was reinforced by the intimate ties of groups to distinct locales. This intimacy derived from both an ideological commitment to grass-roots participation and the financial and legal counseling that held these groups together. These ideological positions transformed the analysis of the farm problem posed by the traditional farm organizations. This analysis became increasingly legitimate in the context of the organizations' very practical immediate service in a time of crisis.

These organizations also transcended the Rural America framework by adapting the protest culture of the AAM as well as the AAM's use of the media. The new organizations demonstrated that they had learned from the mistakes of their predecessor. They took the protests not only to state legislatures but also to local banks and individual farms. These organizations tacitly and symbolically recalled the depression-era protests of their members' grandparents. This functioned to legitimize the protest by romanticizing it and distancing it from a similar activism that had more recently been negatively associated with the AAM. Such organizations also improved their use of media. Dramatic protests and farm gate defenses explicitly sought (not always successfully) to restrain tempers and violence. The clergy were often cast as spokespersons, and religious symbols were appropriated. Crosses, for example, were placed on courthouse lawns to represent each local farm foreclosure. The new organizations seemed to understand that the television news does not provide the time for serious discussion of the complex political and economic problems of the crisis. Perhaps this fact escaped the AAM, since it in fact posited a solution simple enough to be conveyed in a brief sound bite. Given this fact, these groups tended to point the media in the direction of the drama of destroyed personal lives or to the ironies of the crisis, such as the increased need of farm families for food stamps.

The efficient use of media attention led Hollywood to produce several motion pictures detailing the personal drama of the loss of family farming.[6] By 1985 the actresses Jane Fonda, Jessica Lange, and Sissy Spacek were testifying in Washington and appeared on the evening news speaking in favor of legislation to preserve family farming. "Farm

Aid" concerts, ironically modeled after the "Live Aid" concerts for famine relief in Africa, were being produced to benefit these organizations and their farm relief projects.

In 1986 many of these groups came together in the form of the National Family Farm Coalition (NFFC).[7] This development redirected attention toward Washington and federal policy in the 1990 Farm Bill. This filled the vacuum created by Rural America's demise and the demand for immediate attention to local conditions in the earlier 1980s. Nevertheless, the NFFC is still primarily grounded in its local organizations, many of which are themselves coalitions within states or regions. The attempt to effectively represent such diffuse regions and commodity interests on specific agricultural policy issues is, of course, as much a dilemma for NFFC as it has been for previous farm organizations. The effect of this may be, however, to elevate the more universal (and new social movements) elements of these organizations.

Many of these groups have sponsored conferences, such as an annual Farm Women's Conference, specifically designed to focus on issues facing farm women. These attract widespread participation by public officials and urban women associated with organized labor. The environmentalist ethic of the newer groups has been reinforced by various churches' apparent rediscovery of the Christian notion of "stewardship." Furthermore, the environmentalism has evolved into an analysis that sees stewardship as only possible under conditions of smaller family-farm production. This reinforces the emergent alliance between a segment of the farm population and the environmental movement.

Another coalition of 1980s local movement centers, the North American Farm Alliance (NAFA), represented a more left-populist tradition with stronger elements characteristic of the new social movements.[8] NAFA also stood out with respect to a self-conscious reflection on its role as a "prefigurative" (Boggs 1986) movement that anticipates the future. This means that NAFA's goals tended to be seen as inseparable from its political strategy. Where a bureaucratic or hierarchical structure may be more effective in dealing with parallel organizational structures in the state or corporate sector, any departure from democratic process and structure to meet immediate goals is seen as ultimately self-defeating. Thus NAFA tended to work outside of what Boggs calls the "bourgeois public sphere" (1986, 47). The new society is considered to be in embryo, or prefigured, in the movement itself.

Personal associations developed between the younger activists and older veterans of farmers' mobilizations, especially the Farmers' Holiday Association of the 1930s. Past farmers' struggles were seen as a source of wisdom, but the most significant lesson learned from the past seemed to be NAFA's reluctance to place blind faith in the state as a potential defender of agrarian (or any producer "class") interests. Contrary to the other agrarian movements' tendency to become immersed in mainstream political participation, NAFA appeared in the periphery of the political arena in which U.S. agricultural and rural policy is formulated. This marginality was due in part to an uncompromising commitment to an ideology that recognized and opposed multiple but interrelated forms of domination.

NAFA's analysis of the farm crisis portrayed the defense industry as the primary competitor of the family farm for government support; rural America as an "internal colony" subjected to similar forms of exploitation perpetrated on "third world" rural peoples by multinational corporations; the inequalities both within rural communities and between working people and "profit-seekers" as a threat to democracy; the reproduction of patriarchal family relations as a process imposed on farm people by state agencies, corporate bureaucracies, and an environment of chronic economic crisis; and, similarly, an externalization of blame for the ecologically destructive character of most U.S. agriculture as a consequence of constraints imposed by federal agricultural policy that is seen as oriented more to the interests of the oil, chemical, farm equipment, and grain trade lobbies than to the interests of land stewardship and family-farm production.

The mainstream groups exemplify a parallel analysis that contains feminism, environmentalism, democratic egalitarianism, and to some extent anti-militarism but in a more tempered language and less integrated way than does the NAFA framework. This makes mainstream organizations currently more politically effective on particular issues. This is due in part to the lesser strength of a unifying principle that in turn permits the compromise necessary for "success" in the political arena. The unity of the NAFA analysis, on the other hand, negates such compromise. Each issue is tied to the other, implying that, in the end, only the termination of monopoly capitalism can free farmers, laborers, women and men, ethnic minorities, and the earth from the multiple forms of domination that derive from monopoly capital's alliance with the state. Touraine calls this a "non-negotiable sphere" (1988, 134).

NAFA's nonnegotiable claims and prefigurative identity goes against the grain of the political system. Like other new social movements, however, such opposition may prevent NAFA from being devoured by that system. Thus the new social movements are said to "express themselves at the political level, while keeping their autonomy as social forces" (Touraine 1988, 134). The conscious effort to ensure internal democracy increases its lack of compatibility with mainstream forms of political organization. While the lack of integration with the polity may be seen by some observers as a problem of ineffectiveness, it may also be seen as an opportunity to emancipate rural society from dependence on the state. There is an almost intuitive recognition that relations of domination are as deeply embedded in the state as in capital, though there are residual inclinations toward participation in the mainstream political culture. Thus NAFA has tended toward a characteristic that Boggs attributes to the "new social movements"—that is, a resistance to establishing a "center of gravity" in the "normal corridors of power" (1986, 47).

These tendencies toward nonnegotiable positions and resistance to dependence on a subordinated integration with the existing political system are not derived simply from the New Left/counterculture elements within NAFA. This quality is also grounded in NAFA's roots in an "abeyance process" (Taylor 1989)—a process that by its nature encourages the development of a political culture around nonnegotiable objectives. Specifically, this concerns its relationship with the United States Farmers' Association (USFA).

NAFA was officially formed on 8 April 1983 in Des Moines, Iowa, by farm activists from 23 states and two Canadian provinces. Merle Hansen, current president of NAFA, stressed unity in his keynote address: "not only unity of farmers but with other groups in this country and abroad, who are also common victims" (quoted in Ritchie 1985, 252). Hansen's father had been active in one of the more progressive mobilizations of the Farmers' Holiday Association in the 1930s, and Hansen spent his youth listening to regional activists discuss agrarian politics and economics at his family's home (personal communication 1990). Hansen was, at the time of the founding of NAFA, also vice president of the USFA. The USFA not only convened the meeting that organized NAFA but played a major role in events leading up to its founding.

As a fragment of the New Left/counterculture migrated to rural areas in a quest for community and an environmentally sound existence, the USFA continued to promote its analysis. The group changed the masthead slogan of its newspaper from "Peace and Parity" to "Peace, Parity and Power to the People," reflecting the influence of the New Left. The derivation of NAFA's "Farms Not Arms" slogan is clearly not far removed from the USFA's emphasis on using the state to sustain family farming rather than the military. It is also, significantly, not far removed from the biblical injunction to beat swords into plowshares.

In the 1970s the USFA actively recruited to membership and to its board of directors the young men and women emerging as promising local rural leaders who shared USFA's philosophy. The USFA played a key role in networking these highly educated, progressive young farm men and women around an anti-militarist agenda that also provided an identification with the long-term struggle for an agrarian democracy. A key event in this process was a USFA-sponsored symposium in Ames, Iowa, in March 1980. The conference brought together the emerging young rural leaders influenced by New Left and countercultural thought with veterans of agrarian mobilization since the 1920s. At the time, falling land prices were only beginning to be reported in specific areas. The prophetic analysis of veteran NFU activist Art Thompson was shared, however, by other "old-timers" and was soon legitimized for the younger generation:

If farm land prices are actually falling. . . . This downward spiral will ultimately threaten the survival of large numbers of family farmers, plus many of the banks, businesses and rural communities that serve them. A wholesale economic crisis is quite likely which will spark a whole new round of farmers' protests against the foreclosures and low prices, much like the movements of the 1930s. (quoted in Ritchie 1985, 244)

At this point the analysis was still predominantly contained by the USFA's New Deal roots and thus focused on a political diagnosis and remedy. The problem was seen as being a consequence of government policy in the service of monopoly capital or the "large corporations." The deepening of this crisis in the early 1980s continued to stress political action. The state was called on to forsake its alliance with "agribusiness" and provide a defense of the family farm in the form of higher (parity-level) price supports, foreclosure moratoria, restrictions on "corporate" farming and absentee land ownership, beginning farmer assistance programs, and so forth. All of this was to be funded by shifting money from the military. The traditional anti-militarism of farmer movements carried a special weight in the 1980s insofar as the farm crisis paralleled a tremendous increase in military spending.

The emergent analysis contained an agrarian fundamentalism, derived from AAM and NORM influences, as NAFA effectively "colonized" portions of the AAM by attracting some of its key young leaders to NAFA's more coherent analysis (Allison personal interview 1990; Quinn personal interview 1989; Ringer 1990). This agrarian fundamentalism blended with the agrarian New Left's belief that the development of its cultural objectives—community and democracy in a sustainable environment—had greater potential in less densely populated areas, where the anonymity of city life could be escaped and personal identity could be more easily established. The more traditional analysis seems to have readily absorbed the environmentalist and feminist elements contained in the New Left agenda. NAFA's first executive director was a feminist woman, Carol Hodne (personal interview 1989). Hodne served in this capacity from 1983 to 1989 and edited NAFA's paper for a period of time. Interviews with leaders indicate a conscious effort not only to resist patriarchal relations within the organization but also to attack the institutional bases of patriarchy in rural society. NAFA meetings and conferences not only included sessions devoted specifically to women's issues but reflected a sensitivity to efforts to remove gender bias in the process.

The inclusion of environmental interests was also apparently readily received by the more traditional elements. Of course, the latter's economic analysis hinged on an awareness that overproduction is a key problem. To the extent that resolution of most of the environmental problems posed by "modern" agriculture would at the same time reduce production, regulation of agriculture in the interest of the environment would, if applied to all producers, effectively contribute to supply management as well as play to the interests of smaller, less capital-intensive farms. Again, this reflects the continued erosion of the ideology that pitted farmers against environmentalists. Like the more mainstream groups, environmentalists tend to be seen as an ally against large-scale agribusiness forms of production. Here the urban "new class" provides a natural alliance as the primary market for locally grown, organic foods. Thus the class base of the new social movements shares an opposition to the technocratic domination of agriculture. Perhaps the current struggle against bovine growth hormone (BGH) is a condensation of many of these issues.

In the midst of massive overproduction of milk, the agro-scientific complex has introduced an expensive means of producing even more milk. The new social movements' critique of this technology is directed at its specific social implications—it threatens to further concentrate dairy production. The technocratic response of the pharmaceutical industry has relied on the old productivist ideology contending that more production is the measure of progress. Consumers, concerned about the quality of such milk, have largely joined in the opposition to BGH, and several major grocery chains have refused to purchase such milk. This struggle is only the first test of a wave of new biotechnologies. Significantly, these groups have not rejected science and technology per se but have challenged its specific social uses. More socially appropriate technologies are sought as goals for scientific-technical research and development, rather than simple service of agribusiness profit. In this, both mainstream and left-populist groups have renewed the century-old agrarian critique of the land-grant college systems' domination by agribusiness to the neglect of family farming.

Feminism and environmentalism within the new agrarian social movements also encouraged a reluctance to depend on government. The state is seen as a primary culprit in the reproduction of patriarchy as well as maintaining a farm policy that coerces producers to produce in an ecologically irrational manner. Feminist tendencies recognize the need to erode patriarchal social relations within the households, but they also recognize the significant obstacles that state institutions pose in that familial struggle. Inheritance laws, tax laws, census definitions of "farm," voting rights within government, and quasi-government and cooperative agencies are among various ways in which the state reaches into the household to reproduce patriarchal relations regardless of—or even against the will of—the male partner. Many of these activists share the view that the state effectively prevents sustainable agriculture—that "sustainable agriculture is illegal" (O'Connor 1990).

The point these movements stress is that the nature of state intervention is such as to preclude the transition to an environmentally sound agricultural production. To change production practices under present policy is an invitation to foreclosure. Thus agrarian social movements must open up spaces in which new agricultural practices can take root. Given the view of the state as a facilitator, if not an embodiment, of patriarchal, racist, and productivist relations of domination, NAFA organizations in particular tended toward a search for opening "free spaces" apart from the reach of the state where new social relations and forms of production can develop. A more advanced example of the attempt to break from any dependency on the state is found in the Wisconsin Farmland Conservancy, an offshoot of Wisconsin Farm Unity, the NAFA organization in that state.

The Wisconsin Farmland Conservancy is seeking to organize land trusts in which entire farm communities would remove their farm land from the market place. This regional decommodification of land is seen as an opportunity to create a free space or autonomous region in which sustainable agriculture can develop outside the reach of federal policy or the private interests of landed and financial capital. The Wisconsin Farmland Conservancy grew out of the struggle against creditors to stop foreclosures. Certain members of Wisconsin Farm Unity began to question the need to own land as individuals and redirected resources toward the prior objectives of democracy, community, and stewardship. The land trust was seen to be a means by which these people would, according to Tom Saunders, set about "not to create intentional communities, but to create communities, intentionally" (quoted in Theorin 1990). Darrell Ringer (1990), a NAFA leader in Kansas, has also advocated the land trust model. Like the Wisconsin Farmland Conservancy, Ringer's preference seems to be a form that exists outside the state and is organized at the local level.

As the economic "crisis" moved toward "stagnation," these environmental and feminist elements, as well as other cultural issues, especially those pertaining to minorities (e.g., black land loss, Native American rights, better conditions for migratory workers, etc.), seemed to be superseding traditional agrarian political and economic interests. NAFA now seems more likely to find itself functioning as an abeyance organization. Like the USFA that facilitated the birth of NAFA itself, NAFA's most important role may be to provide the base of support and networks for future organizations.

A new social movement "tends to oscillate between an ethics based on conviction" and "a logic of efficacy," which leads toward immersion in the official political arena (Touraine 1988, 136). NAFA's tendency toward maintenance of a sphere of autonomy in a nonnegotiable ethical conviction may actually be enhanced, or even enabled, by the presence of more mainstream organizations that share similar substantive values but lean toward an emphasis on a "logic of efficacy." Perhaps the two complement each other more than they realize (their competition for a similar membership and resource base suggests an antagonism) in forming a symbiotic relationship in the political and social environment. Together they might "walk on two legs" (Boggs 1986, 178) or struggle on two fronts—the public and private spheres.

Feminism and environmentalism seem to represent not only a particularly significant qualitative shift from the more traditional farmer movements but also provide a common ground between the mainstream and left-populist tendencies of the 1980s movements. Perhaps the 1990s will see these elements serve as the basis of stronger alliances between progressive movements in urban and rural America. There is no doubt that the traditional and even the most conservative farm organizations will have to deal with redefined roles for farm women as well as a new emphasis on environmentally sustainable agricultural production. Their adaptation or resistance to broader societal change will, in part, be influenced by farm and rural economic conditions. Those conditions are ever more likely to be global in character. This is why the General Agreement on Trade and Tariffs (GATT) and the North American Free Trade Agreement (NAFTA) have received so much attention from farm organizations. While North American agriculture has always been shaped by world markets, the new globalization of capital demands that farm organizations that can "think globally and act locally" may obtain advantages in both the political and economic marketplace.

FARM WORKER MOVEMENTS

Chapter 5

The Depression Era

Farm worker movements have developed relatively late in U.S. history, the most significant ones during the twentieth century. Farm labor organizing corresponded to the development of agriculture organized around a food-for-profit system. It took place in the context of large-scale agricultural operations that employed hundreds and even thousands of workers and were based on a primarily capitalist agriculture, as distinct from a system of commodity producing small farmers. Since this process has occurred unevenly throughout the United States, farm worker movements have been concentrated in those areas where the development of what is sometimes called "corporate agriculture" has been the most prominent, primarily in the West and particularly in California, where one-quarter of all hired farm labor in the country is employed, mostly in labor-intensive fruit, vegetable, and horticulture production.

Certain characteristics of large-scale agricultural production have contributed to generating social movements among farm workers. First, these large enterprises have possessed considerable financial resources, making possible significant concessions without endangering their economic viability. Second, they have required a large labor force, especially for harvesting activities. While nationally farmers do 65 percent of the farm work, during the past decade in California more than 75 percent was done by hired workers. In some cases even the mechanization of harvesting has created different jobs or led to an expansion of production rather than reduce a harvest-time labor force. For example, fruit and vegetable production doubled from 1950 to

1980 owing to expansion of acreage and increased yields. Reflecting this, the average agricultural employment in California increased slightly between 1950 and 1980, from 218,000 to 224,000 (Martin et al. 1988, 2–5).

Also, the tasks farm workers perform have tended to be more similar than different, at least compared with employee specialization in some industries. The result has been fewer differences in skill and pay. This rough equality of job status among farm workers has facilitated feelings of collective identification and solidarity.

Third, a significant gap has persisted between the income and working conditions of agricultural labor and those prevailing in most working-class urban occupations. This has been due in part to the exclusion of farm workers from most federal labor legislation, most significantly the National Labor Relations Act. One interpretation of farm worker movements is that they represent attempts to "catch up" to the level of urban, industrial workers. Although this is certainly one goal, we will argue that they signify more than that.

Finally, the agricultural labor force has been overwhelmingly composed of racial and ethnic minorities and recent immigrants. The latter includes both temporary and permanent residents. Agribusiness operations have generally preferred such a labor force because of their low cost and perceived passiveness.

Social movements in agriculture have most frequently taken the form of attempts at unionization. The context for these periods of protests was the consolidation of California's agriculture into a form resembling that of industry. Agricultural land ownership has been markedly concentrated, and a relatively small number of agribusiness operations have dominated production for a number of crops. One result of concentration is that by 1982, 10.6 percent of California agricultural operations accounted for almost 90 percent of its agricultural sales. These "farm factories" are large family or nonfamily corporations that borrow substantial capital, frequently expand production by purchasing or renting additional land, hire production managers along with large numbers of seasonal workers, and establish subsidiaries for packing and transporting their produce.

Prelude to Depression-Era Protests

While ownership of agricultural land in California and several other southwestern states had been heavily concentrated from the outset, during several decades prior to the unrest of the 1930s industrial agriculture in California assumed the overall characteristics that persist today. By 1930 one-third of all large-scale farms—those having a gross output of more than $30,000 annually—were located in California. Within California, these large-scale farms represented only 2 percent of the total number of farms but produced 29 percent of the state's agricultural output. Also, the largest 10 percent of California farms controlled 80 percent of its farmland and produced more than 50 percent of its agricultural output (La Follette Committee Hearings 1940, pt. 47, 17217; pt. 54, 19861).

During the 1920s Mexican immigrants became the dominant source of agricultural labor in California, supplemented by a substantial number of Filipino immigrants. These two groups largely replaced Japanese, Asian Indians, and Anglo Americans in the fields. The original impetus for an expansion of Mexican immigration was U.S. involvement in World War I. Before, Mexican nationals had been primarily used in railroad construction and mining in the Southwest. Those engaged in agriculture tended to be concentrated around the U.S.-Mexican border region.

Before 1917 Mexican nationals entered the United States with little difficulty. When the Immigration Act was passed in February 1917, however, a literacy requirement and an $8 "head tax" were placed on prospective immigrants over age 16. Immediately after passage of the law, the U.S. Department of Labor was besieged with stories about the shortage of labor for southwestern growers. The impending U.S. entry into World War I dictated that the federal government forestall any situations that might inhibit the war effort. In this context, grower pleas were sympathetically received. In May most of the restrictions for Mexican immigrants were lifted, including the literacy test and head tax. A year later Mexican immigrants were granted the right to stay for prolonged periods.

In any case, the enforcement of the law was quite lax, and for over a decade southwestern growers had access to what seemed a virtually unlimited supply of low-cost Mexican labor. The comprehensive Immigration Act of 1924 that stipulated strict quotas for the number of immigrants allowed from most nations exempted Mexico from this quota system. Combined with substantial illegal entries that most likely exceeded legal immigration, these measures ensured a vast supply of inexpensive—and for a time passive and unorganized—Mexican workers for southwestern agriculture. The 200,000 low-paid, largely

Mexican farm workers in California during the 1920s made possible a significant expansion of labor-intensive crops. Most notable was a 400 percent increase in the production of cotton, a crop that became the site for militant, large-scale strikes in 1933 and 1939.

The only significant threat to this arrangement was the introduction of two bills in Congress in 1925 and 1926. The Box Bill and Harris Bill, named after Texas representative John Box and Georgia senator William Harris, would have placed Mexican immigration on a strict quota basis with an allotment of only 1,575 immigrants a year. The rationale was that the easy access to low-cost Mexican labor placed small farmers and other growers at a competitive disadvantage, especially the southern cotton growers whom both Box and Harris represented. The American Federation of Labor (AFL) also supported these bills on both racial and economic grounds (Reisler 1976, 207, 173). Ultimately, neither of these bills made it out of committee, and a similar Box-Harris Bill introduced in 1928 was also unsuccessful.

These legislative attempts nevertheless stimulated grower recruitment of Filipino laborers during the late 1920s as potential replacements should their access to Mexican immigrants be severely restricted. Most of the initial Filipino immigrants came from the Hawaiian Islands where many had been employed on sugar cane plantations. Nearly all were males and most were under the age of 30 (Lasker 1931, 23). Filipinos did have one notable advantage over Mexicans for the growers, at least initially. Since the Philippine Islands were then a possession of the United States, Filipinos could not be subject to immigration laws and thus their immigration could not be legally restricted.

Although Filipinos were supplementary to Mexican workers, their presence did serve two functions for the growers. First, it created an even greater oversupply of farm labor, contributing a slack agricultural labor market that helped ensure continued low labor costs for the growers. Also, competition and animosity between Mexican and Filipino immigrants quickly developed, setting both groups against each other for agricultural jobs. Together, these features helped divide the farm labor force and inhibited their organization.

Although the depression years witnessed the kinds of labor organizing and unionization campaigns that growers feared, many of these tended to be along ethnic lines with only limited success in integrating diverse ethnic groups within the same organization. Not surprisingly, the more successful attempts were those that consciously included workers from a variety of ethnic and national backgrounds. Also, these unionization efforts could draw on institutional resources of national organizations, such as a cadre of dedicated organizers or funds supporting unionization efforts.

The Rise of Farm Labor Insurgency

The initial attempt at agricultural labor organization came when a number of local Mexican unions combined to establish the Confederacion de Uniones Obreras Mexicanas (Confederation of Mexican Labor Unions). For farm workers, the Confederacion called for better wages, an end to exploitation by labor contractors, and the elimination of employment agencies. They were not, however, directly involved in the several agricultural labor strikes during the late 1920s that included a spontaneous and quite militant strike by workers in Imperial Valley's canteloupe industry in the spring of 1928 (Daniel 1981, 108–109).

The farm labor movement of the depression years produced a series of strikes and unionization attempts that occurred under the leadership of several different labor unions, including one affiliated with the CIO. These efforts also precipitated increasingly coordinated efforts among growers and between growers and local law-enforcement agencies to put down labor strikes and arrest farm worker leaders. What is particularly notable about the farm labor movement of the 1930s, however, was that it eventually led to attempts by both the federal and California governments to ameliorate some of the harsher conditions associated with migratory agricultural work and also to provide limited support for agricultural unionization. Although temporary in duration, these reform efforts represented the first time that the strong alliance between large-scale agricultural landowners and government agencies and officials had been ruptured. These circumstances appear to be a prerequisite to genuine agricultural labor reforms and were not to recur until another farm labor movement gained sufficient momentum during the 1960s and 1970s.

The union that led most of the successful strikes during the early 1930s was the Cannery and Agricultural Workers Industrial Union (CAWIU), an outgrowth of the Communist party's Agricultural Workers Industrial League (AWIL) formed in 1929. AWIL filled a void created by the reluctance of the American Federation of Labor (AFL) to become involved in a serious way in agricultural field work.

CAWIU contained dedicated organizers, and its policy of nondiscrimination according to race or nationality had the potential of bringing together Mexican, Filipino, Japanese, and Anglo farm workers. Although affiliated with the Communist party, CAWIU was not successful in converting many farm workers to its ideology, but its leadership of various strikes was far more effective in winning concessions than other strikes during the same period that did not utilize its expertise. CAWIU developed a comprehensive list of strike issues: a basic wage of $2.50 for an eight-hour day with time and a half for overtime, union recognition, preferential hiring through the union as an intermediary, election of rank-and-file worker committees to negotiate with employers, and hiring without discrimination according to race, color, union affiliation, or strike participation. If universally instituted, these demands would have essentially eliminated a labor contractor system in agriculture that has been subject to repeated charges of exploitation and abuses of farm workers (Jamieson 1945, 85).

During 1930–32 California experienced 10 major strikes by agricultural workers, three involving more than a thousand workers. In what was to become a pattern for the next several years, an April 1930 strike by 5,000 Mexican, Filipino, and Japanese farm workers in Imperial Valley resulted in eight union leaders being convicted under California's criminal syndicalist law. CAWIU provided leadership to all the larger strikes. These protests were a prelude to the enormous eruption of strike and organizational activity during 1933, which included a series of cropwide walkouts, beginning during the spring and continuing over the length of the harvest season. Crops included peas, berries, peaches, and grapes. For example, a strike involving 6,000 peach pickers spread to seven counties in the upper San Joaquin and lower Sacramento valleys and resulted in major wage gains. By August CAWIU membership had increased to 8,000.

The culmination of this series of protests was a strike in cotton involving 18,000 workers. Each year wages were set at a meeting of cotton growers under the auspices of the San Joaquin Valley Agricultural Labor Bureau. The context of the strike was the decline in wages by more than 50 percent for cotton choppers and pickers since 1930. The strike began in early October in southern San Joaquin Valley, where most of the cotton was grown, but soon spread to encompass much of the length of the valley. Mobile groups of picketers covered a 114-mile stretch from Bakersfield to Merced and urged workers to join them in the strike. CAWIU demands included a substantial raise in wages, the abolition of labor contractors, the hiring of union members without discrimination, and union recognition. Growers retaliated by evicting strikers from company-owned housing, and local police and the highway patrol conducted mass arrests of strikers. In the most violent incident, a group of armed vigilantes opened fire without warning on unarmed workers at a union meeting in Pixley, leaving two dead. Although 11 ranchers were arrested and positively identified by those on the scene, all were acquitted.

The Roosevelt administration at first was reluctant to get involved in the dispute, but it eventually sent a mediator, who was refused entrance to a tent camp of strikers. A U.S. Labor Department official was also unsuccessful. Resolution was reached through intervention by a fact-finding committee appointed by California governor James Rolph and led by University of California labor historian Ira B. Cross. The committee condemned the conduct of growers and the massive violation of civil liberties of farm workers. It recommended a compromise wage rate which was accepted by both sides. The cotton strike lasted 24 days and was the largest agricultural labor strike to that point in U.S. history.

During 1933 a total of 48,000 farm workers participated in 37 strikes involving 14 different crops. CAWIU led 24 of the strikes, including most of the largest, and 21 of these registered gains for the strikers (Jamieson 1945, 427). According to several CAWIU organizers, including Dorothy Ray Healey and Caroline Decker Gladstein, the union encouraged worker committees to develop a list of grievances and demands. Most of these included abolition of the labor contractor system, adequate fresh drinking water, improvement of labor camp housing and sanitation, and wage raises. Worker committee meetings were also important in planning and coordinating strike activities (Healey 1976).

Some analysts pointed to the Communist orientation of CAWIU as a severe shortcoming that would prevent the union from reaching many farm workers and becoming established (P. Taylor personal communication 1975; Meister and Loftis 1977, 37–38). While having some validity, this criticism appears to have been greatly exaggerated. CAWIU organizers were under pressure from the national Communist party to inject more anticapitalist analysis into their meetings with striking workers. Also, the union never satisfactorily resolved the tension typical of radical political organizations between the ultimate goal of social transformation and the achievement of concrete concessions won through negotiations and compromise. Nevertheless, the union did not appear to stand in the way of accepting compromise solutions. Most of its leaders understood that the union's support among farm workers was directly related to its ability to use collective action as a means of bettering the economic situation of field labor and deemphasized ideological arguments (Daniel 1981, 141–42). In fact, during its short life it was by far the most effective of any agricultural labor organization at that time in mobilizing farm workers for protests and leading and sustaining strikes. While only an estimated 5 percent of its 20,000 members at the end of 1933 were committed to its ideology (Mini 1935, 226), most farm workers welcomed its leadership and ability to mount an effective strike and unionization campaign. For example, CAWIU would sometimes enter spontaneous strikes and walkouts and attempt to provide leadership. Sometimes its intrusion was resented, but in most cases its assistance was appreciated.

The primary shortcoming of CAWIU as an organization was that it did not originate from farm worker experience. Its two most prominent organizers were Pat Chambers, a 31-year-old construction worker, and 20-year-old Caroline Decker, who had already been involved in a Kentucky coal miners' strike. Like most CAWIU organizers, neither was familiar with agriculture. The union hoped to counter this weakness by providing an institutional framework for the development of leadership talent among the farm worker population. When working with farm workers in a particular region, CAWIU sought to incorporate the most militant workers into their organization. In fact, given the successful role of the American Left in socializing activists and nurturing grass-roots activism (Flacks 1988), it is quite plausible that some of the mostly Mexican farm workers who initially began to assume leadership and organizational roles in CAWIU-led protests went on to become involved in other strikes and unionization campaigns during the remainder of the decade.

Still, CAWIU's affiliation with the Communist party did help mobilize growers' efforts against it, often with the help of local officials. Grower opposition to the union nevertheless was virtually identical to its opposition to the numerous other agricultural labor organizations that have attempted to better the conditions for its constituency, from the early IWW and Japanese efforts to the UFW's unionization campaigns of the past several decades. Instead, the Communist issue could be used selectively by the growers for their own purposes. In a 1934 report prepared by a conciliator for the U.S. Department of

Labor, retired army Brigadier General Pelham D. Glassford, an Arizona farmer, wrote,

Apparently, a small group of growers and shippers who have set themselves up to rule Imperial Valley desire only to fog the issue with their doctrines of violence, intimidation, and suppression of the workers. . . . After more than two months of observation and investigation . . . it is my conviction that a group of growers have exploited a "communist" hysteria for the advancement of their own interests; that they have welcomed labor agitation, which they could brand as "Red," as a means of sustaining supremacy by mob rule, thereby preserving what is essential to their profits, cheap labor; that they have succeeded in drawing into their conspiracy certain county officials who have become the principal tools of their machine. (Jamieson 1945, 109; Daniel 1981, 248–49)

This statement was particularly significant coming from a person who was known to be anti-Communist and anti-union.

The end to CAWIU's presence in the fields, and largely to the organization itself, was the result of a campaign of extraordinary harassment, intimidation, and legal prosecution by local and state officials and vigilante groups. The agricultural labor strikes continued into mid-1934, beginning with Imperial Valley's lettuce and pea farms early in the year. The official response to these first two strikes representing over 4,000 workers signaled what was to come. Strike leaders were arrested; union meetings were tear-gassed; union-sponsored caravans and rallies were violently broken up; and Mexican residential areas and labor camps were raided in search of union supporters. Picketing struck fields was effectively prohibited by mass arrests, even without the existence of an anti-picketing order. For example, an auto and truck caravan of hundreds of strikers in Brawley that intended to join a strike meeting in El Centro was prevented from leaving when attacked with tear gas and clubs by dozens of city police, sheriff's deputies, highway patrolmen, and American Legionnaires. Even a lawyer for the American Civil Liberties Union was kidnapped, robbed, threatened, beaten, and left in the desert by a vigilante mob (Daniel 1981, 228–30). Strikes in other areas of the state met similar responses.

On 20 July, the second day of a general strike in San Francisco that had been called in support of a strike by maritime workers, the Sacramento headquarters of CAWIU was raided by police with the assistance of a group of vigilantes. Eighteen leaders were arrested, including Pat Chambers and Caroline Decker. Sixteen CAWIU members, including 15 arrested in the raid, were charged under the terms of California's criminal syndicalism law. The law specifically covers "crime, sabotage, violence, or unlawful methods of terrorism with the intent to approve, advocate, or further the doctrine of criminal syndicalism." The law was sufficiently vague, however, as to what constituted a violation to allow for the prosecution of anyone advocating worker protests of any kind. After a five-month trial, eight of the defendants, including Chambers and Decker, were found guilty and began serving time. The verdicts were immediately appealed, and in 1937 the State Court of Appeals overturned their convictions. Years later the law itself was ruled unconstitutional.

The raid on CAWIU headquarters stimulated more general attacks against farm workers throughout the state. Meetings were raided, individuals beaten up and kidnapped, and leaders arrested. Similar actions occurred in waterfront areas in the state in response to the maritime strike. The 29 August issue of the *Nation* carried a two-and-a-half-page list of acts of violence by police and vigilantes directed against both urban and agrarian workers throughout California during the summer of 1934 (Levenson 1934, 243–45). In March 1935 CAWIU was dissolved, and farm worker unionization activities declined for several years. Without a statewide, inclusive organization like CAWIU, unionization efforts were carried on sporadically by a number of small, local unions, most based on a single ethnic constituency. Before the next major effort to organize California's agricultural work force began in 1937, the large agricultural growers had solidified their opposition by the formation of an organization explicitly devoted to combatting farm labor unions. Also, a transition in the agricultural labor force was rapidly taking place as white dust bowl migrants were replacing Mexicans and Filipinos in the fields.

Coordinated Opposition

The organization that played the primary role in mobilizing opposition to farm labor unions was the Associated Farmers. It was formed by a prominent American Legion official in February 1934, three months after the San Joaquin cotton strike. The shape of the organization had been established earlier through informal meetings attended by representatives of major railroad companies, utilities, banks, and packing companies, including Pacific Gas and Electric, the Bank of America, the Southern Pacific Railroad, and California Packing

Corporation (CALPAK) (La Follette Committee Hearings 1940, pt. 55, 20242). A number of other preparatory meetings in agricultural areas usually took place and included large growers in the region along with the sheriff, district attorney, the chief of police, and the chair of the county's board of supervisors (La Follette Committee Hearings 1940, pt. 55, 20248).

According to a report of its first convention in May 1934, the president of the Associated Farmers stated that while growers would staff the organization, both the majority of funds and ultimate control would come from banks and utility companies. Evidence gathered late in the decade by a U.S. Senate committee headed by Senator Robert M. La Follette, Jr., of Wisconsin confirmed that at least a large portion of the funding of the Associated Farmers had come from large corporations and corporate associations. The committee documented that from its founding until 1939, the 10 largest contributors to the Associated Farmers were, in order of amount donated, the Industrial Association of San Francisco; the Dried Fruit Association of California; the Canners' League; the Southern Pacific Railroad; the Southern Californians (a Los Angeles employers association); the Atcheson, Topeka, and Santa Fe Railroad; the Pacific Gas and Electric Company; the San Joaquin Cotton Oil Company; the Holly Sugar Corporation; and the Spreckles Investment Company. These represented less than 1 percent of all contributors, but they supplied 44.3 percent of the organization's operating funds. High-level officials in a number of prominent companies, including the Southern Pacific Railroad, Standard Oil of California, and the Bank of America, were appointed to solicit funds from their respective business networks (La Follette Committee Report 1942, pt. 8, 1152–53; La Follette Committee Hearings 1940, pt. 49, 17917). In a 1936 article John Steinbeck charged that the Associated Farmers were backed by speculative landowners, such as Alfred J. Chandler, publisher of the *Los Angeles Times*; Herbert Hoover; and William Randolph Hearst, as well as the Bank of America, which had significant agricultural landholdings (Steinbeck 1936). Many of the industrial supporters of the Associated Farmers were either invested in agriculture or were engaged in related fields, such as packing, shipping, and transportation.

The Associated Farmers played a major role in mobilizing vigilante groups that would physically assault strikers and union members. Sometimes these vigilantes would even be deputized by the local sheriff in the event of a farm labor strike. For example, during an August

1935 strike of 4,000 apple pickers and packing-shed workers in Sonoma County, the largest agricultural strike of that year, a mob of 250 disrupted a strike meeting. Two leaders were subsequently tarred and feathered, and the home of one of the strike organizers was shot up and tear-gassed.

As strike activity increased in 1936, so did vigilante responses. An armed force of 1,500, including "citizens" and private guards along with the police and sheriff department, violently disrupted strike-related activities by Mexican and Filipino celery workers south of Los Angeles. Parades and meetings by strikers and their supporters were broken up, and an estimated one-third of the strikers were arrested. Similar actions greeted an Orange County citrus pickers strike and a Salinas area lettuce packers strike. In the lettuce strike, the Associated Farmers, with the cooperation of the local sheriff's department, drew up plans for the successful intimidation of strikers and the elimination of their union, the AFL-affiliated Vegetable Packers Union. A National Labor Relations Board report on the strike stated that "the impression of these events . . . is one of inexcusable police brutality, in many instances bordering on sadism" (Jamieson 1945, 140).

Other aspects of the Associated Farmers anti-union campaign included seeking the passage of anti-picketing ordinances in agricultural counties and the denial of federal relief to strikers, hiring private investigators and spies to infiltrate agricultural labor organizations, mounting an intense anti-radical and anti-Communist propaganda campaign, and pressuring for prosecution of union leaders under the state's criminal syndicalism law. This last goal was epitomized by the previously discussed arrests and persecution of CAWIU leaders in 1934.

The Dust Bowl Migration and the Federal Response

The sources of the massive outmigration from the Great Plains states of Oklahoma, Arkansas, Texas, Kansas, and Missouri during the Great Depression are generally understood as a result of the mid-1930s droughts and dust storms and the impact of the Agricultural Adjustment Act. But the underlying causes were deeper. The depression hit when small farmers, tenant farmers, and sharecroppers were already burdened by a long economic decline during the 1920s. The decade-long deterioration in value of agricultural goods increased early in the 1930s. Markets dried up, exports of agricultural commodities plummeted, and large surpluses were created in wheat, cotton, and rice. By 1932 gross agricultural income was less than half of what it was in 1929. Thousands of banks that normally extended credit to farmers closed their doors, and an estimated failure of more than two million mortgaged farm businesses and tenant-farming operations occurred during the 1930s (Majka and Majka 1982, 97–98).

Compounding this situation were the effects of the Agricultural Adjustment Act (AAA). As described in Chapter 3, the AAA intended to improve the market price for agricultural commodities by offering payments for limiting the acreage planted and harvested. Since the program was administered at the county level where wealthier agricultural landowners could best exert their influence, these landowners were in positions to reap the financial benefits of AAA payments by keeping land uncultivated that normally would have provided a livelihood for many. As a result, the program had the effect of displacing thousands of tenants and sharecroppers at a time when urban areas did not have the employment opportunities to absorb them. The long-term effect was toward a greater concentration of agricultural land ownership (Tolan Committee 1941, 446–55). At the same time, wages for agricultural work in 1933 were only 46 percent of their 1927 level (La Follette Committee Hearings 1940, pt. 47, 17218).

The worst drought of the century, stretching from South Dakota to Texas, compounded the harshness of the situation for Great Plains agriculture. Wheat and cotton farmers were the worst hit. The much-publicized dust storms from 1933 to 1935 and their accompanying soil erosion affected relatively few farms, but those that were hit were likely to be devastated. Residents had few options other than to pack up and leave. Still, migrants from the areas where the dust storms were concentrated only composed around 6 percent of the total number of those from the south-central states who moved to California during the 1930s (Gregory 1989, 11).

More than half a million people left the south-central states during the 1930s, and between 315,000 and 400,000 ended up in California. The volume of migrants to California during this decade was actually smaller than in the preceding and subsequent decades. What made the dust bowl migrants significant was that they tended to settle in agricultural counties, as the urban areas were unable to absorb a population growth (Stein 1971, 3–16, 46; Gregory 1989, 6–10). This migration increased the pace of a transition in the agricultural labor supply that had started during the early 1930s, as unemployed whites from urban areas began replacing Mexicans in the fields, many of whom had been repatriated to Mexico (Majka and Majka 1982, 69–72; Hoffman 1974, 39–106; Reisler 1976). After the peak years of migration from south central states to California of 1935–37, the majority group supplying the farm labor force was white. While Mexican and Asian labor remained in the Imperial Valley and in many of the coastal areas, Anglo workers came to dominate the farm labor force of the interior agricultural valleys, especially the San Joaquin and Sacramento valleys. By 1940 Anglo Americans composed 76 percent of the farm workers in the San Joaquin Valley (Gregory 1989, 61–62).

This transition to a mostly white migratory labor force stimulated concern among agribusiness supporters and hope among farm labor advocates. Even though growers preferred to hire the desperate, new residents in preference to increasingly militant Mexicans and Filipinos, the long-term impact was unclear. Dr. George Clements of the Los Angeles Chamber of Commerce expressed the fears of agribusiness in 1936:

Can we expect these new white transient citizens to fill their [Mexicans] place? The white transients are not tractable labor. Being so-called American citizens, they are going to demand the so-called American standard of living. In our own estimation, they are going to be the finest pabulum for unionization for either group-the AFL or the subversive elements. (La Follette Committee Hearings 1940, pt. 53, 19467–68)

John Steinbeck, writing from a perspective supportive of agricultural labor, put it this way in 1938:

One has only to go into the squatter's camps where the families live on the ground and have no homes, no beds, and no equipment; and one has only to look at the strong purposeful faces often filled with pain and more often, when they see corporation-held idle lands, filled with anger, to know that this new race is here to stay and that heed must be taken of it.

It should be understood that with this race the old methods of repression, of starvation wages, of jailing, beating, and intimidation are not going to work; these are American people. (Steinbeck 1938, 3)

Both these assessments contain an implicit assumption that immigrant minorities would be more passive and content with low wages and living standards than would white American citizens. Even the increasing militancy and support for unionization among Mexican and Filipino farm workers did not deter this judgment. At least initially, however, the influx of migrants from the south central states only resulted in massive destitution, not a shot in the arm to agricultural unionism. The federal government was the first to respond to their situation.

An early federal program was the Federal Transient Service, established in May 1933 to assist interstate migrants. Although it was of no use to the intrastate migrants who composed the majority of agricultural workers in California, some migrants from south-central states did receive aid before the program was terminated in September 1935. Of more importance was the Federal Emergency Relief Administration that provided aid for the unemployed. Its director, Henry Hopkins, established a policy that relief funds were to be given solely on the basis of need. This made possible the granting of federal relief to workers on strike, and this assistance helped prolong the 1933 cotton strike and contributed to the concessions won by the cotton harvesters. Bitterly opposed by growers and by the administration of California's Republican governor Frank Merriam, it was finally abolished by December 1935, and responsibility for relief was taken over by individual states. Governor Merriam's program was considerably less generous with employment relief for farm workers. In fact, the director of California's State Emergency Relief Administration, Harold Pomeroy, became the executive director of the Associated Farmers when a new administration took office in January 1939.

The most significant federal program for the south-central migrants was the construction of migrant labor camps, initiated in 1935 by the Resettlement Administration (RA) and later transferred to the Farm Security Administration (FSA). During initial planning stages, options included resettling migrants in federally funded cooperative farms. For pragmatic reasons, including the advantage of achieving immediate results and reducing ideological opposition to the RA-FSA programs, the labor camps were given highest priority (Majka and Majka 1982, 109–10).

By 1940, 56 FSA camps were in operation. The 18 in California provided shelters, washrooms, and sanitation and cooking facilities for 20,000 to 30,000 migrants. The camps were strategically located in order to be useful to agricultural workers. Carey McWilliams, who was to become the head of California's Division of Immigration and Housing in 1939, believed that the federal camps were a key to the organization and residential stabilization of the farm labor force. He wrote,

The solution of the farm-labor problem can only be achieved through the organization of farm workers. The chief significance of the migratory camps is that they provide an agency through which organization can be achieved. Quite apart from this consideration, however, they are social agencies of great practical importance and they demonstrate that the stabilization of migratory labor can be accomplished. (McWilliams 1971, 303–304)

Since the federal migrant camps were outside of direct agribusiness control, union leaders and organizers could talk with residents without fear of reprisal. As such, the camps provided a considerable resource to union campaigns, which previously had been plagued by an inability to easily reach workers living in grower-owned camps. The managers of the camp were generally sympathetic to union appeals. In fact, many of the FSA camps were the sites of union meetings and sometimes even strike headquarters.

As might be expected, growers opposed the camp program. Even though FSA camps saved them money by relieving them of some of the burden of supplying temporary housing for their workers, the growers did not want to relinquish their ability to curtail access to labor camps by union organizers and control other aspects of the lives of the labor force. Grower organizations unsuccessfully fought the establishment of the program and later sought the removal of the camps. Some growers even refused to hire anyone living in several of the camps. The FSA camps continued, however, to provide shelter for tens of thousands of migrants until U.S. entry into World War II made them obsolete.

In the meantime, the next coordinated attempt to unionize California's farm labor force during the later 1930s enjoyed more supportive federal and, after January 1939, state policies than was the case with earlier union efforts.

Resurgence of Unionism and Government Policies

The establishment of the next national farm labor union was an outgrowth of the founding of the CIO, which initially was called the Committee for Industrial Organizations. When supporters for a national cannery and field worker union failed to win the support of the American Federation of Labor (AFL) for the idea, they decided to establish such a union on their own and affiliate with the CIO. The United Cannery, Agricultural, Packing, and Allied Workers of America

(UCAPAWA) was founded in Denver in July 1937. The Southern Tenant Farmers Union (STFU) became affiliated with the new union. UCAPAWA was supported by officials of many Mexican and Filipino farm worker unions in California, most of which were only local in scope. Also supportive were a number of agricultural unions outside of California. Farm worker unions from Alabama, Florida, New Jersey, Arizona, Colorado, Michigan, Ohio, Tennessee, and Texas were represented at UCAPAWA's founding convention. Among the matters discussed was a strategy to combat a campaign by anti-union conservatives to drive a wedge between organized labor and small farm owners, especially those in the Midwest. Also considered was a plan to unite small farmers, tenant farmers, members of farm cooperatives, and agricultural workers under a central organization.

During the last half of the 1930s a political climate supportive of unionization in general added to the hope that unions might be able to gain a permanent hold in agriculture. In response to depression-era strikes and protests, the federal government had finally acknowledged labor's right to organize. In July 1935 the passage of the National Labor Relations Act (NLRA) guaranteed the right for employees to join labor organizations and unions and made illegal most forms of interference and reprisals by employers. The NLRA also set up the National Labor Relations Board that conducted elections among employees to determine union preference, if any, and to investigate violations of the law on the part of both employers and employees. Agricultural workers were specifically excluded from coverage under the NLRA, however, mainly as a concession to representatives from southern and western agricultural states in order to ensure the legislation's passage. While there was optimism during the late 1930s that agricultural labor would soon be included, this exclusion continues to the present.

In the industrial sector, labor militancy was at its peak. Nearly half a million workers were involved in sit-down strikes during 1936 and the first few months of 1937 alone. Breakthroughs in early 1937 resulted in first-time contracts at General Motors and U.S. Steel. Other contracts in mass production industries and in mining and meat packing soon followed. The founders of UCAPAWA hoped that their union could take advantage of these circumstances. Packing and cannery workers covered by the NLRA could provide a stable membership base and resources to assist in the effort to unionize farm workers. At its height, UCAPAWA claimed 40,000 dues-paying members, most from Colorado, Wyoming, Arizona, and Florida and among the fish cannery and seafood workers in the Pacific Northwest and South Atlantic states. Also, the union was part of a growing industrial union organization, the CIO, and the formation of several national farm labor support groups could provide additional resources. In short, it seemed that the time was most promising for agricultural labor unionization.

UCAPAWA began serious organizing campaigns in California's agricultural operations during the summer of 1938. Among its leaders were several who had been active in CAWIU, including one of its vice presidents, Dorothy Ray Healey. The union conducted its most serious recruiting efforts in eight of the FSA camps and achieved moderate success in five of them.

The union initiated few strikes itself, putting a priority on building a stable organization. It did feel compelled, however, to direct numerous spontaneous strikes when workers appealed to the union for support (Jamieson 1981, 165). The demands it developed were similar to those of CAWIU earlier in the decade. Other than wage raises, these included the designation of a job steward in each field, closed shop agreements, hiring of union members and rehiring of striking workers without discrimination, drinking water in the fields, and the impartial testing of growers' weighing machines.

UCAPAWA led a number of relatively small strikes during 1938. Several of the larger strikes resulted in union victories. The largest, however, involving 3,000 cotton pickers in Kern County near Bakersfield, was unsuccessful. Tactics were reminiscent of the 1933 cotton strike. Car caravans of strikers took their message from field to field in order to publicize the strike and solicit support. In retaliation, the Kern County sheriff made numerous arrests under an anti-picketing county ordinance. Also, the Associated Farmers initiated a blacklist of workers involved in the strike, refused to talk to worker representatives, and declined mediation offers from the U.S. Justice Department. With growers unified in opposition and assisted by local law enforcement, the strike collapsed (Jamieson 1981, 171–72). The continued anti-union actions by agribusiness and local law enforcement not only continued what was a long-standing pattern in California but also mirrored similar violence against the STFU in the South during the same period.

By the 1939 harvest season a new administration had taken office in California. The outlooks and policies of its personnel appeared to represent a significant change from the usual accommodation by the state government to agricultural interests. In November 1938 Democratic candidates Culbert Olson and Ellis Patterson were elected governor and lieutenant governor, respectively. The contrast of their administration to that of the previous governor, Republican Frank Merriam, was immediately apparent. In his policy reports and later testimony to the La Follette and Tolan committees, Olson condemned agribusiness for disregarding the welfare of their workers. His administration adopted a reform-minded approach to agricultural conflict and endorsed the inclusion of farm workers under the NLRA. He also supported making farm workers eligible for existing social welfare benefits previously denied them.

Olson's appointment of Carey McWilliams as head of the Division of Immigration and Housing displeased agribusiness enormously. In their publicity the Associated Farmers referred to McWilliams as "Agricultural Pest No. One, outranking pear blight and boll weevil" (McWilliams 1979, 13). McWilliams attempted to revitalize a nearly moribund agency and announced that division inspectors would check grower-owned migrant camps for violations of the state's housing codes. Although the division was badly underfunded and considerably understaffed with only four inspectors for almost 5,000 labor camps, it was successful in publicizing some of the worst violations. McWilliams even organized public tours of some camps and went on radio to urge people to report the locations of hidden labor camps and serious violations of housing codes. McWilliams later estimated that growers spent over $1 million in 1939 to improve migrant housing in response to the division's efforts (McWilliams 1979, 77).

Perhaps the most significant aspect of the Olson administration was its elimination of several of the barriers to agricultural unionization created by his predecessor. As an example, Olson's director of the State Relief Administration (SRA), Dewey Anderson, announced a significant change in relief eligibility policy. Rather than automatically deny people relief when there were agricultural jobs offered, no matter how low the wage, the SRA would determine in advance what a "fair wage" would be, and no one would be removed from relief for refusing to accept a job whose wages were lower than that amount. In addition, Olson proposed formation of a fair wage standard board for agricultural labor in order to institutionalize this practice.

Twice during 1939 in response to labor strikes the Olson administration attempted to set a "fair wage" governing state relief eligibility. In May, McWilliams announced that a "fair wage" for cotton choppers (weeders and thinners) would be 27.5 cents an hour in contrast to the growers offer of 20 cents. In the fall the "fair wage" for cotton picking was also set at 27.5 cents an hour or $1.25 per hundredweight. The cotton growers rejected these recommendations and instead offered 20 cents an hour or 80 cents per hundredweight. The "fair wage" policy was quickly modified because of vehement opposition by growers and agricultural organizations. A compromise was reached with representatives of grower organizations and past and present government officials where a family would only be released from relief rolls when potential earnings from agricultural employment by all employable members of the family would exceed the family's relief budget. While not a complete reversal, the compromise illustrated the difficulties of the Olson administration in getting cooperation with its policies from economic elites and Republican and conservative Democratic members of the legislature.

Another potential resource for agricultural unionization was a Senate investigation, headed by Senator La Follette of Wisconsin. Popularly known as the La Follette Committee, it was formed in 1936 in order to investigate employer violations of the NLRA. Since agricultural labor was not covered under the NLRA, the committee had not intended to hold hearings on labor policies and patterns of conflict in the California fields. Then national attention increased when John Steinbeck's *Grapes of Wrath* was published in March 1939, Carey McWilliams's *Factories in the Field* was published two months later, and Olson was elected in California. At the height of the controversy over Steinbeck's book, Eleanor Roosevelt toured California for five days talking with migrants and visiting migrant settlements located in ditchbanks throughout the agricultural areas. Subsequently, she reported to Congress that Steinbeck had not exaggerated the living conditions of the migrants. These events persuaded a reluctant Senator La Follette to expand the scope of his committee's investigations.

The committee held 28 days of hearings in December 1939 and January 1940 and called about 400 witnesses. Governor Olson was the first to testify. Carey McWilliams issued a lengthy report on farm labor conditions in addition to his own testimony. The testimony the committee heard was issued in 27 volumes in October 1942. The volumes documented the blacklists, the anti-picketing ordinances passed specifically in response to strikes, the vigilante activities, the cooperation of local law enforcement in breaking strikes, and the cooperation between agricultural and industrial interests to maintain unorganized and inexpensive field labor. The committee paid special attention to the activities of the Associated Farmers, subpoenaed their files, and documented their central place in the prevailing pattern of vehement opposition to farm worker unions and collective bargaining.

In retrospect, the publicity given to Associated Farmers tactics by the La Follette Committee hearings appeared to have ended the effectiveness of the organization and blunted its aggressive approach. McWilliams later wrote that the hearings "put the Associated Farmers out of business" (McWilliams 1979, 78). The organization failed in its attempts to spread to other states and remained a California phenomenon. The initiative shifted to agricultural unions to reform farm labor circumstances under considerably more favorable circumstances. As it turned out, this was only an extremely brief window of opportunity before external events foreclosed the possibility of unionization for another two decades.

The Failure to Organize

UCAPAWA failed to achieve a solid organizational base among cannery and packing-shed workers. Instead, most of the unionization of cannery and packing-shed workers was taking place under AFL unions. UCAPAWA also did not have an adequate commitment of resources from its national office to carry out its campaigns in the fields. Lacking organizational strength, UCAPAWA continued to discourage farm worker strikes unless widespread support could first be demonstrated to their satisfaction. In fact, the union tried to prevent what proved to be the largest strike in many years, the fall 1939 cotton strike in the San Joaquin Valley.

The context for the cotton strike was the lowest wage offered by cotton growers since 1934. The fact that the SRA designated a considerably higher "fair wage" gave legitimacy to worker dissatisfaction. Also, under the restrictive program of the AAA, cotton cultivation had been cut nearly in half during the preceding two years, meaning fewer jobs were available as cotton pickers.

The strike spread quickly from the Madera area to involve several thousand workers over a wide region. In Madera County, observers estimated that the strike was 75 percent effective during its first week. Even members of the Associated Farmers admitted that the strike pulled large numbers of workers out of fields. Strike caravans roamed from field to field in order to gain additional support. UCAPAWA again assumed leadership of the strike and used several FSA camps as strike headquarters. In response, local law-enforcement agencies arrested hundreds of strikers for violating local anti-picketing ordinances. Growers evicted striking workers from private labor camps and openly displayed guns when confronting protesters. In the most violent incident, a group of 300 growers and vigilantes attacked people attending a late October strike rally in Madera with clubs, tire chains, fan belts, and pick handles while the local sheriff stood by. Finally, the state highway patrol was called in by the governor and ended the confrontation with tear gas. Other physical assaults on strikers followed, and local law-enforcement agencies cooperated with efforts to break the strike. Most of UCAPAWA's leadership were either put in jail or fled the area because of threats of assault or arrest.

Even with the considerable efforts to repress the strike, many growers broke away from the wage standard set by San Joaquin Valley Agricultural Labor Bureau and accepted a union compromise of $1 per hundredweight. In those cases the strike only lasted several weeks. In other areas strike activity continued for several months, but few desired results were achieved.

The piecemeal nature of whatever gains were made by the strike and the continued failure to reach union contracts meant that UCAPAWA made little progress during 1939 in establishing itself on a permanent basis. By assuming leadership of spontaneous strikes, the union contributed to achieving temporary gains for desperate people, but this did not provide a base for future organizing efforts. Estimates at the time suggest that the union's membership remained fairly constant at about 3,000 for the three years it was seriously involved in agriculture (Daniel 1981, 281). In fact, the continued resistance to farm labor unions by an organized agribusiness and the increasingly defensive posture of California officials when confronted with powerful opposition made the task of organizing farm workers seem impossibly difficult. UCAPAWA's president, Don Henderson, suggested at the union's 1939 convention that the disadvantaged position of farm workers was more than "just a trade union organizational problem." Instead, their situation was symptomatic of "a fundamental, deep-lying, widespread social problem that goes right to the roots of our whole social system here" (quoted in Daniel 1981, 281). The convention adopted a resolution that called on the federal government and "public conscience" to assume responsibility for the farm worker plight.

In 1940 UCAPAWA decided to concentrate its efforts on cannery and processing workers who were covered by the NLRA and thus protected from the kinds of intimidation and harassment tactics used by growers and vigilantes against farm workers. The STFU had already voted to secede from UCAPAWA. UCAPAWA's chances for a presence in the fields were dealt another serious blow by the decision of the Filipino Agricultural Labor Association (FALA) to affiliate with the AFL. This union represented a temporary revival of independent, ethnic agricultural unions that tended to become more prominent when larger, more inclusive agricultural unions were not present or lost their effectiveness. In fact, FALA led the only agricultural strike of any consequence in the United States in 1940, involving several thousand Filipino celery workers in California's Delta region. Almost anticlimactically, UCAPAWA quietly gave up its efforts in the fields early in 1941.

The final chapter of Carey McWilliams's *Factories in the Field* is titled "The End of a Cycle." Instead, unionization efforts during the late depression years turned out merely to be another chapter. The failure of UCAPAWA was more than just another attempt to organize farm workers that fell short. After all, the history of the western states contains numerous examples of such unsuccessful efforts. Instead, UCAPAWA appeared to be in the strongest position of any previous attempts. It was part, however tangential, of a national labor movement that was winning union contracts for the first time in many urban mass-production industries. UCAPAWA was also affiliated with the CIO and could make some claims on the labor organization's resources. Nationally, a liberal political climate helped make unions respectable, and in January 1939 a progressive administration took office in California. In addition, a good deal of national publicity concerning the plight of farm workers in California resulted from the publication of John Steinbeck's *Grapes of Wrath*. Finally, the exposure given the violent and often unlawful tactics used by vigilantes, local law-enforcement agencies, the Associated Farmers, and individual growers began to undermine their effectiveness. Still, these developments were not enough, and those who looked to UCAPAWA to end the prevailing pattern of labor exploitation in the fields were very disappointed.

Three factors have been given most frequently to explain the failure of agricultural unionization during the period when unions in industry were succeeding. These are the lack of appeal of unionization to many of the white migrants, organizational deficiencies of UCAPAWA, and

the continued power of the agricultural industry to defeat union campaigns and block changes in state policy. Finally, it should be noted
that the window of opportunity for agricultural unionization was brief.
Different circumstances and priorities that accompanied the United
States' entry into World War II eliminated any further possibility for
change during this period.

The political history of the south-central states seemed to suggest
that its citizens would be receptive to an appeal for unionization. The
white migrants originated from an area that had a strong Populist legacy, including the appeals of a strategy to form producer cooperatives.
In the decade before World War I the Socialist party was as strong in
parts of the western South as anywhere else outside certain urban
areas in the industrial North. None of this suggests the "rugged individualism" that some historians have cited as preventing migrants
from participating in cooperative efforts necessary for successful organizing (Stein 1971, 264–68). Instead, some of the migrants were strong
supporters of UCAPAWA. Gregory (1989) estimates that perhaps as
high as one-third of the white migrants sympathized with the union.
He also notes that union supporters among the migrants were more
likely to have prior experience with unions or radical causes, most frequently in their home states (Gregory 1989, 158–59).

The normal difficulties a union would have in reaching a new group
of workers in an unfamiliar environment was exacerbated, however,
by certain other aspects of the migrants' prior experiences. The two
decades since World War I had transformed the political consciousness of much of the western South. Nationally, beginning with the
"Red Scare" during the early 1920s, radicalism had become equated
with being "anti-American." More specific to the western South, the
growing strength of both nativism and fundamentalist religions during
the 1920s led to a deeply felt suspicion of organizations and leaders
identified as radical. Finally, the Ku Klux Klan made considerable
inroads during the 1920s in many of these states, particularly Texas,
Arkansas, and Oklahoma (Gregory 1989, 159–60). This increased the
tendency toward racial and ethnic prejudice and the scapegoating of a
minority group as the cause of economic hardships.

These political themes resurfaced once the migrants were in
California. A substantial proportion accepted right-wing propaganda
that equated the CIO with communism and agreed with those growers
who saw UCAPAWA as a Communist organization. Also, many
white migrants objected to the presence of Mexicans and Filipinos in

UCAPAWA and were especially offended that some of these "foreigners" were in leadership positions. The union maintained a strict policy of inclusion, regardless of racial, ethnic, and national background. Some Mexican farm workers—many veterans of the 1933 cotton strike—had prominent roles in later strikes and organizing efforts, which kept some white migrants from participating. Citing the work of researchers who interviewed farm workers during the 1930s, Gregory points out that a number of the white migrants expressed anti-Mexican sentiments once they were in California (Gregory 1989, 162–69).

It should be noted that many white migrants subsequently did become involved in union campaigns in the oil fields, canneries, shipyards, and factories they entered during and after World War II. Also, a substantial proportion of those participating in the largest farm labor strike between 1939 and 1965—a 1947 strike at DiGiorgio Farms in southern San Joaquin Valley—were remnants of the dust bowl migration. In fact, five of the six members of the executive board of the National Farm Labor Union local that initiated the strike were from the western South. But these events took place at a later time and under different circumstances.

Another factor in the failure of unionization lay within UCAPAWA. For example, there was a considerable cultural gap between much of UCAPAWA's staff and the white migrants. Many of UCAPAWA's organizers were college-educated people from urban areas. They were considerably more "class-conscious" than the migrants and tried to reach UCAPAWA's potential constituency by using a class analysis that did not fit well with the migrants' background as small farmers. UCAPAWA simply was not in the fields long enough to cultivate a substantial leadership with roots in the south-central states who might have been more successful in reaching the white migrants.

Also, as part of a national labor union, UCAPAWA's efforts in agriculture were subject to policies originating at the national level. UCAPAWA's strategy was to bring as many people into the union as quickly as possible. Since the California fields did not prove to be a fertile ground for the union's growth, efforts to organize agricultural workers there were given increasingly less attention and fewer resources.

The third and perhaps most significant factor was the continued ability of agribusiness to resist unionization. Even though the vigilante and related activities to defeat farm labor unionization were gradually becoming discredited during the late 1930s, they were still effective for the duration of UCAPAWA's presence in the fields. For its part, the union and its supporters blamed its failure primarily on continued repression by large agricultural landowners and their organizations, the local police, and vigilante groups.[9] Meanwhile, the political power of the agricultural industry remained strong at the state level. In practice, this meant defeat for nearly all of the agricultural reform proposals of the Olson administration. Defeated by a conservative coalition of Republicans and rural Democrats were proposals to build 30 migrant labor camps to supplement the FSA camps, create a permanent fair-wage standard board for agricultural labor, require the registration of private labor camps, and tighten the regulations concerning these camps. Only a proposal to regulate labor contractors passed. The conservative coalition was supported by the California Farm Bureau, the Associated Farmers, and most of California's major corporations. What this meant in practice was that agricultural unions gained only very limited assistance from the California government under Olson, and that assistance came in the rather piecemeal fashion described previously.

In retrospect, it should be noted that prevailing conditions were not very conducive to the success of unionization efforts. An enormous number of people were looking for work, and only a minority could be absorbed by the agricultural labor market. Typically, there were three or four workers for every job in agriculture, according to some estimates. Many people were desperate and would take any job offered, no matter how low the pay. Also, a new migrant or immigrant group usually needs to find a niche before feeling confident enough to embark on collective efforts to improve its situation. The migrants from the south-central states were not in California long enough to establish themselves before UCAPAWA's organizing campaigns tried to reach them. Given a longer time span, some of the resistance to farm labor unions by the white migrants might have been overcome.

But the "window of opportunity" for change was brief. By the middle of 1940 preparations for war were already creating jobs in urban industries. Like sharecroppers and tenant farmers in the South, large numbers of migrants left the fields for better prospects in the improving urban economies. By 1942 there was already an actual labor shortage in the fields of California and several other western states. While this tight labor market was far more conducive to organizing, there were no unions ready to take advantage of the situation. Without this pressure, the priority of government turned to ensuring an adequate supply of farm labor. This set the stage for a "guest worker" agreement with Mexico that lasted 22 years. Known as the bracero system, its impact was to essentially eliminate the possibility of a farm worker movement effectively pressuring for reforms until after the program ended in December 1964.

Chapter 6

The United Farm Workers Era

The latest large-scale farm worker movement and its accompanying attempt to unionize much of the agricultural labor force has again been concentrated in California, spinning off smaller-scale efforts in a number of other states, including Arizona, Texas, Florida, Washington, Ohio, and Michigan. The dominant force behind these attempts has been the United Farm Workers Union (UFW), headed since its inception in 1962 by Cesar Chavez until his death in April 1993. Although its activities have been at a low ebb since the early 1980s, as of the early 1990s, the UFW continues to be the largest agricultural labor union in California.

A comparison of the similarities and differences between the backgrounds of the insurgencies of the 1930s and from 1965 to the late 1970s is instructive. One major difference is the general national economic climate. The depression era was of course a time of economic hardship and marginality for many throughout the nation. In agriculture, both those who participated in insurgency and those who did not generally shared similarly desperate financial circumstances. By comparison, the 1960s and early 1970s were a period of national economic expansion and increased expectations by citizens. This was reflected in the better circumstances prevailing generally for domestic farm workers. While many were considerably below the poverty line, few in California were on the edge of destitution, and options outside of agricultural work were available for many.

The gap between the circumstances of farm workers and those of urban workers, however, loomed particularly large. Relatively speaking, most segments of the agricultural labor force had lost ground during the preceding 25 years when compared with urban, blue-collar workers. Much of this can be explained by the outcomes of unionization movements during the 1930s: their successes in most industries and their failure in agriculture. In addition, it is difficult to overestimate the deleterious effects of the bracero programs on conditions of agricultural employment for U.S. citizens and permanent residents. The dissatisfactions experienced by agricultural workers that resulted in their widespread support for unionization efforts were in part due to their poverty-level wages, lack of any meaningful job security and stability, and generally poor working conditions. But they were also in part due to feelings of relative deprivation when comparing their circumstances to the improved standards of living experienced by many urban workers, especially those in unionized industries.

The most important similarity between the 1930s and 1960s was that nationally both were reform-minded, liberal periods. In addition, national social movements provided much of the early stimulus for the farm labor movement. During the 1930s agricultural insurgency was promoted as a part of the larger labor movement that had finally come to maturity. During the 1960s initial farm labor protests were tied ideologically to the civil rights movement, and protesters cultivated close ties with many industrial labor unions.

In both cases the farm labor movement could utilize resources freed up by both the national political climate and the movement's ties to existing, successful social movements. Some of this came in tangible forms, such as donations and contacts with politically influential individuals and organizations. Much of it, however, was in the less tangible forms of widespread publicity of grievances and the recognition of the legitimacy of farm worker protests.

The impact of these kinds of external supports was tempered in California during both periods since conservatives, and ones not particularly favorable to farm labor, were in control of state government for much of the time. The possibilities of consolidating gains had to wait for the election of governors who supported reforms.

The Bracero Programs as an Interlude

The "guest worker" arrangement with Mexico, known as the bracero agreement, began in 1942 as a response to potential and actual shortages of harvest workers during World War II. Mexican nationals were recruited for agricultural work for the duration of a season and returned to Mexico on the completion of a harvest. Bracero work contracts stipulated wages and length of service in advance. Mobility was strictly limited by law and leaving the job made bracero workers subject to deportation. Their situation led Lee G. Williams, a U.S. Department of Labor official supervising bracero employment from 1959 to 1964, to refer to the programs as "legalized slavery." In fact, a well-known study of the bracero era was succinctly titled *The Slaves We Rent* (Moore 1965).

The initial bracero agreement was meant only to last the duration of World War II. Bracero workers were highly desirable to growers, however, and agribusiness successfully sought a number of extensions of the agreement beyond its December 1945 expiration date. In 1951 the bracero system was placed on a more permanent basis with the passage of Public Law 78 by Congress. This law established an administrative framework supervised by the U.S. Department of Labor for recruiting, contracting, and transporting bracero labor to participating growers. With the legal basis for the programs more firmly established, use of braceros skyrocketed, from 67,500 in 1950 to a record 445,000 in 1956. Texas and California accounted for 50 to 80 percent of all braceros contracted during any single year (Majka and Majka 1982, 151–53).

The widespread employment of braceros had an adverse effect on domestic farm workers who experienced increasing difficulty in obtaining agricultural work. One impact was downward pressure on agricultural wages, particularly in regions and in crops where braceros were most extensively utilized. In 1948 when the number of braceros utilized was still relatively small, farm labor wages in California were 65 percent of national manufacturing wages; by 1959, at the height of bracero importation, this figure had declined to 47 percent (Jenkins 1978, 529). During the bracero period the pay offered for field work frequently was so low that domestic workers had to look for elsewhere for better-paying jobs. In addition, braceros frequently were hired in preference to domestic workers, despite the fact that braceros were not supposed to compete with domestic workers for jobs. The overall consequence for many domestics was dislocation. Farm workers who had settled out of the migrant stream into small agricultural communities were once again faced with migrancy in order to survive (Galarza 1977, 226–30).

The emergence of widespread farm labor protests had to wait until the last bracero program was terminated. Hiring bracero workers proved to be an effective weapon in the arsenal of growers to prevent or undercut attempts to improve conditions of agricultural employment. Also, in several instances braceros were used as strike-breaking crews, most notably in a well-documented 1948 strike at DiGiorgio Farms in the southern San Joaquin Valley (Galarza 1964; Galarza 1970; London and Anderson 1970). Both the hiring of braceros in preference to domestic workers and the use of braceros as strike breakers were illegal according to the terms of the bracero agreement, but the law was inconsistently enforced. Instead, the bracero option doomed farm labor organizing efforts in advance. Still, farm labor unionism maintained a presence in the fields, first with the National Farm Labor Union and later with the Agricultural Workers Organizing Committee.

The termination of the bracero system was a result of profound changes in American politics stimulated by the civil rights movement. The widespread abuses of bracero labor and the detrimental impact of this system on domestic farm workers attracted the attention of a number of organizations concerned with civil rights, particularly for minorities. The spread of the civil rights movement to the Mexican-American population first manifested itself in demands for the termination of the agreement. In this they had the support of the AFL-CIO and many liberal political leaders.

The anti-bracero coalition that successfully pressured for termination of the programs consisted of representatives of labor, religious, civil rights, civil liberties, and social action organizations. Spearheading the assault were two citizens organizations explicitly dedicated to reforming farm labor conditions: the National Advisory Committee on Farm Labor and Citizens for Farm Labor. Their goals were given additional support by the CBS television documentary "Harvest of Shame" aired on Thanksgiving Day in 1960. One of those leading protests against the abuses of the bracero system and its impact on domestic workers was Cesar Chavez, who during the 1950s and early 1960s was working for the Saul Alinsky–affiliated Community Service Organization.[10]

These organizations and support groups pressured a reluctant Kennedy administration into a more strenuous enforcement of the terms of the bracero contracts, particularly the prohibition against using bracero labor to replace striking domestic employees. Most notably, they were able to forge an anti-bracero coalition in Congress who opposed renewal of Public Law 78. In March 1963 the House voted 174 to 158 against a two-year extension of Public Law 78 and only approved a one-year extension after an appeal by California governor Pat Brown. The bracero programs, initially intended as a temporary wartime emergency measure, finally ended on 31 December 1964. Their 22-year existence conveyed enormous benefits to agribusiness, both in terms of keeping labor costs at a minimum and eliminating the possibility of reforms (Majka and Majka 1982, 158–66). It is no coincidence that the first in a series of strikes and product boycotts that marked the resurgence of the farm worker movement and led to the establishment of the United Farm Workers began during 1965, the year after the termination of Public Law 78.

Strikes, Boycotts, and the First Table-Grape Contracts

The gains made from 1965 to 1970 illustrate the importance of citizens' support for farm worker movements. External resources were made available as a result of the three related factors suggested earlier. First, a liberal, reform-minded national political climate focused on ways to ameliorate social injustices. Second, the civil rights movement had successfully legitimized grievances of ethnic minorities. Third, an expanding economy and some degree of financial security for many Americans, especially the middle class, coincided with an increased generosity toward the less fortunate. These three factors "freed up" resources that were used to assist the farm worker movement. The support offered farm workers took both tangible and symbolic forms.

While public support was crucial, early successes depended on the mobilization of farm workers themselves. Demonstrations of solidarity among farm workers were necessary to guarantee a continual flow of donations and support for the strategy of product boycotts, especially the table-grape boycott. Initial mobilization of farm workers was facilitated by the existence of agricultural labor organizations with considerable farm worker membership that had formed prior to the strikes. Studies of social movements indicate that insurgency is most effective in gaining widespread support from constituents if it is sponsored and coordinated by already-established organizations. In the case of farm workers in California in 1965, these organizations were the National Farm Workers Association (NFWA), founded by Cesar Chavez in 1962, and the Agricultural Workers Organizing Committee (AWOC), established in 1959 and affiliated with the AFL-CIO. Although AWOC was poorly supported by the national AFL-CIO, AWOC locals initiated several important strikes, including the Delano-area (California) table-grape strike of 1965.

Early in 1965 California growers sought the continued importation of braceros under Public Law 414 of the McCarran Act, which stipulated that foreign workers could be recruited in the event of a shortage of domestic workers. Pressured by California governor Pat Brown, U.S. Secretary of Labor Willard Wirtz set $1.40 an hour for any braceros used that year. In the spring of 1965 table-grape growers in Coachella Valley in southern California offered only $1.25 to domestic Filipino workers affiliated with AWOC. Instead, AWOC demanded the hourly rate set for braceros that might be recruited that year and called the workers out on strike. Without easy access to braceros, the Coachella growers quickly settled. When the grape harvest moved north, grape growers in the Delano area in the southern San Joaquin Valley offered many of these same Filipino migrants $1.20 an hour. In response, the Filipinos refused to leave the grower-owned labor camps to go to work.

The NFWA under Chavez was based in Delano, and many of its members worked in the same grape fields as the striking Filipinos. The Delano area contained a large number of settled (nonmigrating) agricultural workers, and Chavez had built the NFWA largely on their support. Even though the organization had virtually no financial resources to support striking members, on 16 September, Mexican Independence Day, NFWA's membership voted overwhelmingly to join AWOC in its strike.

Once AWOC and the NFWA formed an alliance, the strike spread quickly. By early October dozens of table-grape operations in the southern San Joaquin Valley were being struck by about 3,000 farm workers. Grower responses were reminiscent of the 1930s. Individual growers attempted to intimidate strikers. This included spraying strikers on picket lines besides struck ranches with sulfur meant for killing roadside vines, displaying shotguns and taunting pickets, beating individual strikers who came too close to property boundaries, and driving pickup trucks at excessive speeds past picket lines. Striking workers were evicted from grower-owned camps, and strike breakers were recruited, many from other states. Local courts issued injunctions limiting the number of pickets, and local police made mass arrests and virtually ignored grower acts of intimidation.

Unlike the few strikes during the bracero era, many sympathizers came to Delano to offer their support. Clerics, representatives from a variety of church groups, members from urban labor union locals, civil rights activists, and college students stood on the picket lines beside the strikers. Chavez initially sought financial assistance for the strikers from California's universities, making early appearances at the University of California at Berkeley, Stanford, San Francisco State, and Mills College in Oakland, collecting $6,700 (mostly in dollar bills) from students attending the support rallies (Levy 1975, 192–93).

Despite these impressive demonstrations of support, the NFWA was aware that the table grape growers had considerable resources of their own. It was extremely unlikely that negotiations would take place before the growers were pressured by either the threat or experience of financial losses. The chronically oversupplied agricultural labor market meant that strike-breaking crews eventually could be recruited. The support for growers by the local courts and law-enforcement agencies made it unlikely that a successful strike could be sustained over a long period. In short, it was not realistic to expect stable, long-term union contracts resulting from pressure by field workers alone.

Reacting to these conditions, the NFWA called for a boycott of table grapes in October. The response was initially encouraging. The International Longshoremen's and Warehousemen's Union in San Francisco briefly halted loading table grapes onto ships. The United Auto Workers president, Walter Reuther, participated in a December march in Delano in support of striking workers, pledged $5,000 a month from the UAW to support the strike, and helped bring national attention to the grape boycott. The U.S. Senate Subcommittee on Migratory Labor, headed by Senator Harrison Williams, Jr., conducted hearings in Delano in March 1966, focusing attention on the mass arrests of pickets as an anti-union tactic. In a well-publicized exchange concerning the arrests of lawful pickets, Senator Robert Kennedy suggested to the Kern County sheriff that he "read the Constitution of the United States" (R. Taylor 1975, 158).

After several months the NFWA decided to concentrate its boycott efforts on two companies that had easily identifiable products: Shenley Industries brand of liquor and DiGiorgio Corporation subsidiaries of S & W Fine Foods and TreeSweet Products. Both Shenley and DiGiorgio were ideal representatives of agribusiness corporations. Most of Shenley's nonfarm enterprises were unionized, and its table grapes comprised a small segment of its entire operations. DiGiorgio at the time was one of the largest fresh fruit growers and distributors.

It owned packing houses, cold-storage facilities, processing plants, warehouses, and a cannery, many of which were unionized. Its 30,000 acres of agricultural land included several large table-grape ranches. Its extensive corporate interlocks included the Bank of America, as Robert DiGiorgio was one of its directors, and one of the Bank's vice presidents was a DiGiorgio director.

In March and April of 1966 the NFWA mounted a 300-mile, 25-day march from Delano to the capitol building in Sacramento, arriving on Easter Sunday. The march served multiple purposes. Initially, it was intended as a protest against the spraying of pickets with insecticide and fertilizer by a Shenley crew. But it also served several larger goals: to gain publicity for the strikes and boycotts and to explain the purposes of the protests to farm workers outside southern San Joaquin Valley. Nightly programs and rallies were held in farm worker communities along the path of the march, and the theatrical group El Teatro Campesino performed skits illustrating various abuses endured by farm workers. The march was inspired by the civil rights movement's Freedom March from Selma, Alabama, to the state capitol of Montgomery two years before. But it also combined themes of pilgrimage and penitence, building on the cultures and religious heritage of both Mexican and Filipino farm workers.

On 6 April, four days before the march ended, Shenley Industries agreed to recognize the NFWA. The initial contract included a $1.75 base wage and a union-run hiring hall to replace hiring through labor contractors. A day after Shenley's announcement the DiGiorgio Corporation called for secret-ballot union elections on its ranches, and representatives of the corporation and the NFWA began to work out the details.

While negotiations with Shenley were relatively smooth, those with DiGiorgio were not. Since farm workers are not covered under national labor laws, there were few, if any, precedents or norms for union recognition elections for farm workers. Negotiations were difficult, as DiGiorgio tried legal maneuvers to inhibit NFWA organizers' access to DiGiorgio employees. Also, the Teamsters Union entered the controversy, and the NFWA claimed that the Teamsters had DiGiorgio's full cooperation in getting workers to sign Teamster recognition cards, a procedure that sometimes has been used by unions as an alternative to union recognition elections.[11] This marked the first of many times in subsequent years that the two unions would be competitors in seeking to represent field workers.

Finally, a 30 August election was agreed to under the supervision of the American Arbitration Association. In order to improve its chances of winning the election, the NFWA decided to accept an offer to merge with FLOC as an AFL-CIO–affiliated union. The decision to merge was not an easy one for NFWA leaders. The main reservation was over the extent of autonomy that the NFWA would retain. Since the situations and legal status of agricultural and industrial workers were so different, the NFWA leadership reasoned that they would need to have the freedom to make strategic decisions that might set them at odds with the advice of the national labor federation. The terms of the merger satisfied Chavez that the NFWA would have enough autonomy to operate without undue AFL-CIO restrictions. For example, the consumer boycott would be continued, with or without AFL-CIO endorsement, and volunteers would remain as NFWA staff members. Farm workers themselves overwhelmingly voted for the merger, and on 22 August the United Farm Workers Organizing Committee (UFWOC) was created. In 1972 the union's status was further changed from that of an organizing committee to an independent union affiliated with the AFL-CIO. (For simplicity's sake, we will begin here referring to the union by its current name, the United Farm Workers of America, AFL-CIO [UFW].)

The merger was timed to influence the DiGiorgio election. The NFWA had staked its future on its outcome but was unsure of the extent of its support among DiGiorgio field workers. Many NFWA supporters had left DiGiorgio when the strike began the previous year. Even though most of the strikers were eligible to vote in the election, many had left the area in search of employment. Finding and transporting as many as possible back for the election was a difficult task. Also, the NFWA had experienced difficulty in reaching current DiGiorgio field workers, and the union was aware of cooperation between DiGiorgio managers and Teamster organizers. To offset Teamster claims that the NFWA was too small and weak to adequately represent farm worker interests, the UFW now could claim access to resources of the AFL-CIO. Still, on the eve of the election two national television networks predicted defeat for the UFW, and a *Los Angeles Times* reporter told Chavez that betting in Las Vegas was three to one against his union.

The 30 August election involved workers at two DiGiorgio ranches—one near Delano and the other in northeastern San Diego County. On 1 September the American Arbitration Association announced that field workers had voted for the UFW over the Teamsters, 530 votes to 331. Only 12 votes went to a "no union" option. An election at another DiGiorgio vineyard near Arvin took place on 4 November after a UFW-sponsored sit-in at DiGiorgio headquarters in San Francisco. The Teamsters decided not to pursue this contest, and the UFW won 285 of the 377 votes cast.

Despite the favorable outcomes of these elections, subsequent events illustrate many of the difficulties that farm worker unions have had in translating worker and public support into lasting concessions. DiGiorgio continued to resist unionization. Basic differences between the corporation and the union were over the establishment of a union hiring hall and a strict regulation of pesticide use. Negotiations over contract terms finally went into arbitration after three months. Although the UFW did get a contract with a hiring hall and pesticide protection, it was not given a "successor clause" that would have carried the contract over to new ownership in the event the ranches were sold. At this time DiGiorgio was planning to sell its agricultural land, since the U.S. government had ruled DiGiorgio was ineligible to benefit from federally subsidized water prices as DiGiorgio's holdings exceeded the maximum limit of 160 acres. When the sale was completed at the end of 1968, the UFW was left without a contract. Also, during the time the contract was in force, the UFW claimed DiGiorgio managers consistently attempted to evade the terms of the contract through obstruction and refusal to cooperate. For example, the corporation did not establish an employee seniority list for use by the union hiring hall (Levy 1975, 253–56).

A boycott of Perelli-Minetti brand liquors resulted in a contract for the workers in the company's vineyards near Delano. Also, in 1967 and 1968 the UFW signed contracts without as much contention with a number of wineries with vineyards, including Almaden, Paul Masson, Gallo, Christian Brothers, Franzia, and Novitiate. Several of these contracts resulted from card-check elections where the UFW received authorization cards signed by the majority of field workers. Still, the UFW's dozen contracts only covered 5,000 workers, and its goal of organizing table grape workers was scarcely begun. In the summer of 1967 the union decided to devote exclusive attention to obtaining table-grape contracts in what turned out to be a three-year struggle, centered on the success of the consumer boycott.

During June and July of 1967 the UFW conducted an organizing campaign at Giumarra Vineyards, owned by the Giumarra Brothers

Fruit Company, California's largest table-grape grower, having 6,000 of its 11,000 acres in grapes and employing nearly 2,500 workers during harvest. When Giumarra refused to recognize worker-signed UFW authorization cards and declined to meet with union representatives, a strike began on 3 August. Around two-thirds of the 1,200 workers at the Delano vineyard walked out. Giumarra recruited a replacement work force, however, largely composed of undocumented workers. After the Department of Immigration removed 500 undocumented workers from Giumarra's vineyards, they were replaced by green-card Mexican workers (immigrants with temporary work visas) in violation of government regulations forbidding the use of green-carders as strike breakers. Still, the UFW did not have the financial resources to provide strike benefits and so turned to a consumer boycott of table grapes marketed under the six Giumarra-owned labels. After several months of the boycott, however, Giumarra began to ship its table grapes under other growers' labels. The UFW responded by calling a boycott of all California table grapes, beginning in January 1968 (Majka and Majka 1982, 186–87; Jenkins 1985, 162–63).

As in the 1965 Delano strike, the UFW sought support from among labor leaders and union rank-and-file, civil rights and antiwar activists, college students, Chicano communities, and environmental groups. Volunteers were recruited from these constituencies to spread the message of the boycott to mainstream America, and soon boycott organizations were active in 40 or 50 cities, with boycott committees operating in hundreds of other communities. Two hundred strikers and their families joined the boycott effort full time.

The boycott was promoted by three different constituencies. Full-time UFW volunteers worked long hours, were paid $5 a week and provided subsistence, and lived in boycott houses. Students and other young people made up the vast majority of the full-time volunteers, especially during the summer months, while clerics, Chicanos, and farm worker families comprised much of the rest. The full-time volunteers did most of the daily work of organizing picketing and leafleting, holding meetings to promote the table-grape boycott, and arranging financial contributions. They also recruited part-time volunteers. This second constituency included sympathetic supporters who would lend several hours a week to boycott activities, such as picketing stores, attending rallies, and helping distribute leaflets. Their participation was crucial to successful demonstrations of support—for example, at

Saturday picketing and leafleting outside supermarkets. In addition, a third constituency of institutional supporters, such as church executives, political leaders, and union officials, contributed by endorsing the boycott, soliciting donations, arranging meetings with influential individuals, and offering free office space, phone use, and practical advice. The coordination of the efforts of these constituents was crucial to building a multidimensional farm worker network that both supported the grape boycott and lent legitimacy to the movement and its goals. This same strategy of mobilizing external support continued during the UFW-sponsored boycotts during the 1970s as well.

In the liberalized political climate of the late 1960s, the UFW's strategies proved to be effective. The mayors or city councils of more than three dozen cities, including Cleveland, New York, Detroit, and San Francisco, endorsed the boycott, and some ordered municipal agencies to suspend their purchases of grapes. Protestant, Catholic, and Jewish leaders pressured influential figures to lend their support. The AFL-CIO executive council urged its locals to support the grape boycott, and several unions gave wholehearted support. Locals of the Seafarers, Butchers, Retail Clerks, and Teamsters unions all mounted job actions in support of the boycott. Several major supermarket chains stopped carrying California table grapes owing to pressure of a "secondary boycott" of their stores. Labor unions in Britain and Sweden were especially strong in their support, and in some cases dock workers refused to unload California grapes from cargo ships.

But support for a consumer boycott often takes years to fully mobilize. Perhaps out of frustration from the lack of immediate results, some farm workers began to debate using violent tactics. This prompted Chavez to initiate the first of several fasts he undertook over the years to dramatize farm worker issues. This initial fast had the purpose of reaffirming a philosophical as well as strategic commitment to a Gandhian nonviolence. Beginning in February 1968 it continued for 25 days before culminating in a Mass attended by Senator Robert Kennedy who was then considering running for the Democratic presidential nomination. Six days later Kennedy announced his candidacy and chose Chavez to be one of his delegates to the Democratic Convention. For two weeks prior to the California Democratic Primary, UFW volunteers devoted most of their effort to campaigning for Kennedy, concentrating on heavily Chicano precincts. Several observers pointed to the UFW's efforts as decisive in Kennedy's narrow victory. Dolores Huerta, one of the UFW's vice presidents, was walking with Ethel Kennedy behind the senator when he was assassinated the night of the primary.

The table-grape boycott stimulated a reevaluation of the UFW's position toward inclusion of farm workers under national labor legislation. Even though both Chavez and Larry Itliong, another UFW vice president, testified before a House subcommittee as late as spring 1967 in favor of incorporating agricultural labor into the NLRA, strategic considerations caused the union to change its position by the following year. Specifically, the 1947 Taft-Hartley amendment to the NLRA had prohibited secondary boycotts and mass picketing, both successful strategies for the UFW. Taft-Hartley also prohibited organizational strikes. In addition, the normal operations for NLRB-supervised elections was cumbersome, and UFW leaders feared growers would use legal maneuvers to delay elections until after the end of the harvest season. The change in the UFW's legislative position set the context for the union's later strategy of seeking a California law that did not have the drawbacks of the NLRA, and this eventually resulted in the passage of the California Agricultural Labor Relations Act (ALRA) in 1975.

The boycott received an unexpected boost early in 1969 after an increasing number of workers became violently ill after contact with pesticide residues on grape vines. After checking with the state's Department of Public Health, the union claimed that California regulations were too weak to prevent pesticide poisoning by the phosphate-based chemicals that were replacing the still-legal DDT-type chlorinated hydrocarbons. What began as a worker health issue, however, turned into one of consumer safety when tests on table grapes sold at several Safeway supermarkets revealed concentrations far in excess of government limits of Aldrin, a pesticide later banned by the Food and Drug Administration as a carcinogen.

Anti-boycott initiatives took several forms. A coalition of California agribusiness organizations hired a public relations firm that organized a campaign around the phrase "consumer rights," promoted grape sales using a bumper sticker "Eat California Grapes, the Forbidden Fruit!," and ran newspaper ads claiming the health benefits of grapes. Delano growers created the Agricultural Workers Freedom to Work Association and sponsored a national tour for its "leader" to denounce Chavez. Then California governor Ronald Reagan promoted grapes on trips throughout the nation and often denounced the UFW's boycott as illegal and immoral. Reagan also directed the state's Board of Agriculture to engage in an anti-boycott publicity campaign. He even ordered state agencies to provide struck growers with welfare recipients and prison inmates until this effort was blocked by a state Supreme Court ruling. While accompanying Republican presidential nominee Richard Nixon on a September 1968 campaign tour, Reagan referred to picketing grape strikers as "barbarians." Nixon called the boycott "illegal" and said it should be put down "with the same firmness we condemn illegal strikes, illegal lockouts, or any other form of lawbreaking." After Nixon became president, his administration directed the Defense Department to increase its grape purchases, and the quantity of grapes shipped to U.S. forces in Vietnam increased from 555,000 to 2,167,000 pounds from 1968 to 1969 (London and Anderson 1970, 161; Matthiessen 1969, 312; Levy 1975, 302).

These efforts were ultimately unsuccessful, however. U.S. Department of Agriculture statistics testified to the strength of the boycott, even though its figures were conservative estimates. Between 1966 and 1969, two years when the grape harvest was roughly equivalent, shipments to the top 41 grape-consuming cities, accounting for 75 percent of the table-grape market, were down 22 percent overall. The decline was most apparent in the largest urban markets: shipments to New York were down 34 percent, Chicago down 41 percent, Detroit down 32 percent, Boston down 42 percent, and Baltimore down 53 percent. Coachella Valley grape grower Lionel Steinberg estimated that 20 percent of the market was lost and that Coachella Valley growers lost $3 million during the 1969 harvest (Meister and Loftis 1977, 161–62).

By the 1970 harvest, the table-grape industry was ready to negotiate. Early in 1970 a committee initiated by the U.S. Conference of Catholic Bishops began attempts to facilitate an agreement. On 2 April two Coachella ranches partially owned and managed by Steinberg were the first to sign UFW contracts. Over the next three months the UFW signed contracts with nearly all the table-grape growers in the Coachella and southern San Joaquin valleys. Then on 29 July all 26 of Delano grape growers followed suit, including Giumarra. The UFW now had three-year contracts with California grape growers representing 85 percent of the table grapes produced in the state. Besides providing wage raises (to $1.75 or $1.80 an hour plus 25 cents a box piece rate), the contracts included a union hiring hall with guarantees of worker seniority, formal grievance procedures, protective pesticide regulations, a joint worker-grower committee to oversee pesticide use, a union-sponsored health plan supporting a series of medical clinics, and grower contributions to an economic development fund to aid elderly or disabled workers or those displaced by mechanization. Also included were a variety of seemingly mundane but nevertheless significant measures, such as providing workers with cool drinking water, rest periods, and field toilets and prohibiting profiteering on meal arrangements. By September the UFW had contracts covering 150 agricultural operations and representing 20,000 jobs and more than 10,000 members.

By the time the table grape contracts were reached, several characteristics of the UFW as a labor union and as a social movement organization were well established. While these features were generally beneficial during the movement's insurgency phase, the failure to transform these into more stable forms of organization would result in internal disagreements that contributed to the departure of a significant number of UFW officials and staff. This left the union particularly vulnerable in later years to sustained counterattacks by agribusiness and hostile government officials.

First, Chavez's leadership style developed to approximate that of a charismatic authority as he quickly emerged as the dominant farm worker leader. Certainly for much of the public, the farm worker movement became personally identified with Chavez. This quite naturally concentrated much of the movement's power into his leadership. Despite the fact that the union's major decisions were made by an executive board, Chavez had a dominant influence. In the meantime, there were few viable alternative sources of leadership among farm workers. For example, Filipino farm worker leaders faded from prominence, although many, such as Larry Itliong and Philip Vera Cruz, continued to play important roles in the union. And the Teamsters continued to be too closely tied to agribusiness to be seen by many as a viable representative of farm worker interests.

Second, the UFW institutionalized a reliance on volunteers to form its staff. While this initially was a financial necessity, the failure over time to provide for paid positions in the union made it difficult to build an organization that maintained a permanent core of experienced officials who could efficiently administer labor contracts and conduct routine business. While many of the union's staff had an admirable distrust of large-scale bureaucracies and did not want the UFW to become similar to most labor unions in this regard, the union's inclination toward the other extreme created different sorts of problems. The UFW's flexibility had the considerable advantage in allowing volunteers and staff members to be moved around virtually on a moment's notice in order to respond to the constantly changing challenges. For example, during the next three years the union would frequently need to redirect its energies to defeat a number of restrictive legislative proposals and to respond to encroachments by the Teamsters Union. The constant shifts in the use of volunteers did, however, disrupt both personal and organizational routines. Combined with the absence of regular salaries, one result was that the union had some difficulty developing a sizable core of officials who could maintain commitment over the long run. Many of the union's officials devoted over a decade to the movement, but it was difficult to reconcile their service with any needs they had for a stable personal life.

Assault on UFW Successes

Despite the success in signing table-grape contracts, the UFW's celebration was short-lived. On 28 July, the day before the Delano-area contracts were signed, the 29 Salinas Valley lettuce growers comprising the Grower-Shipper Vegetable Association signed five-year contracts with the Teamsters Union covering field workers. Several days later, a number of Santa Maria and Imperial Valley growers also signed Teamster contracts. Interestingly, the contracts were signed before their actual terms had been worked out.

The Teamsters were being used by Salinas growers to undermine an organizing campaign among farm workers in lettuce begun during the preceding spring. In fact, lettuce workers in Salinas and Santa Maria had been asking the UFW to intervene on their behalf for two years, and Chavez announced that lettuce would be the union's next target as soon as the grape contracts were concluded. In fact, the initiative for the Teamster field contracts appeared to have come from the Grower-Shipper Vegetable Association. While renegotiating contracts with the Teamsters covering non–field workers, association representatives initiated discussions with the Teamsters for contracts covering field workers. But the opportunity was also used by William Grami, the director of organizing for the Western Conference of Teamsters, to build a power base, in part to increase his chances of being selected as the next director of the Western Conference.

The signing of the Teamster contracts illustrated the vulnerability of farm labor since it was not covered by the NLRA or similar legislation. Such "sweetheart" contracts between employers and labor unions would be illegal under the NLRA. There were no unionization elections or even attempts to ascertain the preferences of field workers covered by the contracts. Nor were workers given an opportunity to ratify the contracts, although they were required to join the Teamsters and have weekly union dues deducted from their paychecks. In fact, the contract announcement came as a surprise to the lettuce workers. When the terms of the contracts were announced later, they were similar to the UFW's grape contracts in wages but differed in terms of employment practices and working conditions. Hourly wages were set at $1.85 during harvest and $1.75 at other times. Hiring halls were forbidden, however, and hiring was left up to labor contractors and individual growers. Also, the contracts contained no provisions concerning pesticide use or protection against replacement by mechanization.

After attempts to renew an earlier jurisdictional agreement between the UFW and the Teamsters was unsuccessful, a UFW-sponsored strike was initiated on 24 August. Estimates of the number of workers participating ranged from 7,000 to 10,000, mostly in the Salinas, Watsonville, and Santa Maria areas. Lettuce shipments quickly declined from the prestrike 200 to 75 railway carloads a day. Strawberry growers admitted that after the strike began, strawberry shipments were only 14 percent of prestrike figures. Neither of these declines was due to the conclusion of the harvest season.

Anti-UFW assaults during the strike were reminiscent of the 1930s. Teamster officials brought in "strong-arm men" carrying chains and shotguns to intimidate pickets. Local "patriotic" organizations were quickly formed that branded the strikers as "Communist." A total of three UFW pickets were shot. UFW attorney Jerry Cohen was beaten unconscious by a Teamster "guard" and hospitalized for four days. The UFW's Watsonville headquarters was bombed, and bomb threats against the UFW were almost a daily occurrence.

Despite overwhelming initial support by the regular farm labor force, the long-term effectiveness of the strike was hampered by court injunctions limiting UFW picket activity intended to reach strikebreaking crews. In fact, legal restrictions turned out to be more effective than physical intimidation. On 16 September a local judge prohibited all UFW picketing in the Salinas area, contending that the strike was in reality a jurisdictional dispute between two unions and that neutral employers were legally protected from harm in such cases. Even though this ruling was overturned by the California Supreme Court on 29 December 1972, the two years that the injunction was in force made effective strike activity very difficult. In overturning the decision, the Supreme Court noted that the growers displayed the "ultimate form of favoritism" in selecting the Teamsters and made no attempts to ascertain the preferences of field workers. Instead, it appeared to the court that "probably the majority of the workers desired to be represented by the UFWOC rather than the Teamsters" (Majka and Majka 1982, 206).

The UFW did gain several contracts in the Salinas area while the strike was in progress. The largest was with Inter Harvest, a subsidiary of United Fruit. Fearing a boycott of its Chiquita brand, the company had requested and obtained a rescission of its Teamster contract. A card check tabulated by Monsignor George Higgins had already revealed that the vast majority of Inter Harvest field workers wanted UFW representation. The UFW contract was notable for its inclusion of crew bosses and its ban on the pesticide DDT, which would be outlawed by the federal government several years later. Other contracts obtained by the UFW included Purex subsidiary Freshpict and several strawberry, tomato, and artichoke growers. By the end of 1970 the UFW represented 15 percent of the head lettuce grown in California and Arizona.

Once again, the inability to win contracts through strikes revealed the structural weakness of farm labor. The lack of inclusion under labor laws gave growers options that would be illegal if undertaken by most employers. Also, the UFW still did not have adequate monetary resources to support a long strike. As a result, strikers began to return to work after several weeks out of financial necessity, and within a month crop shipments were two-thirds of normal volume. Once again the UFW turned to the sympathetic public it had developed, and in late September the union announced a boycott of head or iceberg lettuce not harvested under UFW contracts.

This time, opposition to the UFW took more coordinated forms. The main threats came from proposed legislation that would severely restrict tactical options for any farm labor union. A number of key agricultural states introduced similar bills, and the Nixon administration introduced its own proposal in Congress. All of the proposals included provisions for secret ballot elections, but all outlawed secondary boycotts. Other provisions made it difficult for seasonal farm workers to participate in elections. For example, a number of proposals stipulated "cooling off" periods of 30 days or more in the event of farm worker strikes before an election could be held, in practice eliminating the possibility of elections during harvest season in most cases. Other proposals required a 10-day notice before strikes were initiated, outlawed harvest-time strikes or product boycotts, made illegal union hiring halls, and stipulated that collective bargaining could not involve issues of pesticide controls and mechanization.

The UFW diverted much of its energies from the lettuce boycott in order to counter such legislation in California, Oregon, Washington, Arizona, New York, and Florida. One of the most anti-union bills was signed in Arizona in May 1972 by Republican governor Jack Williams less than an hour after its passage. The UFW chose Arizona to make a stand against this kind of legislation and launched a recall campaign against the governor. Even though the 108,000 certified signatures gathered were in excess of the number needed, the certification procedure was delayed long enough so that the 1974 gubernatorial election was too near to schedule the recall election. Nevertheless, the campaign registered nearly 100,000 new voters and was credited with providing the victory margin for a number of Chicano and Navajo candidates for local and state offices during the next several years.

In California, after a similar bill failed to get out of committee, the Farm Bureau sponsored a proposal as a ballot initiative in 1972, known as Proposition 22. The bill was one of the most restrictive, outlawing secondary boycott and placing severe restrictions on product boycotts. Also, it required a 10-day strike notice and stipulated a 60-day "cooling off" period. Unionization elections could only be held when the number of "temporary" employees did not exceed "permanent" ones, making elections during harvest season virtually impossible. Unions were forbidden from negotiating about working conditions, and growers could hire nonunion workers even when under a union contract.

Once again the UFW had to ignore the lettuce boycott to direct its efforts to defeat this proposition. Despite the expenditure of nearly $500,000 in support of Proposition 22, it was defeated by 58 to 42 percent. In summary, the union was able to prevent passage of restrictive legislation in all but three states—Idaho, Kansas, and, most importantly, Arizona—while the Nixon administration's proposal made little progress in Congress. While the UFW was mostly successful in containing these threats, the union diverted much of its attention from the lettuce boycott. These struggles also placed the union on the defensive, and it took a sophisticated explanation to convey why the UFW was opposing legislation that on the surface appeared to give farm workers the right to free union elections.

In the meantime, the table-grape contracts were due to expire in 1973. The UFW realized that many of the growers would resist renewal, or at least bargain for concessions from the union. Some grower dissatisfaction stemmed from the implementation of a union hiring hall. The rationale for replacing labor contractors and direct grower hiring was that a hiring hall would help prevent abuses of employees, such as absconding wages, charging excessively for room and board, and firing workers arbitrarily.[12] More importantly, a hiring hall was intended to keep employment records for the purpose of creating seniority. The goal was to guarantee employment security for longtime workers. The hope was that this would reduce the proportion of migrants, since some could "settle out" of the migrant stream if guaranteed jobs with the same companies from one season to the next (L. Majka 1981). Many growers complained, however, that the hiring hall was inefficient, such as its failure to dispatch a sufficient number of workers on time—a charge with some merit, given the union's lack of administrative experience. For their part, union representatives charged that many growers had deliberately failed to cooperate with the hiring hall in order to generate confusion and dissatisfaction.

Still, some workers had genuine grievances against the hiring hall as well. The hiring hall was based on union, not ranch, seniority. This meant that longtime union members would be given preference for jobs with a particular ranch over workers who might have been employed there longer. This method of determining seniority sometimes worked at odds with the goal of providing employment security so that more migrants could become stable residents, particularly since migrants were less likely to have built up union seniority. Also, families and crew used to working together were sometimes broken up and dispatched to different ranches, creating additional confusion and resentments. In general, UFW contract benefits, such as year-round health care, were more beneficial for nonmigrants (locals) than for migrants. In later years the UFW would modify hiring-hall practices to base seniority at least in part on employment at specific ranches. At the time, however, growers could claim, with justification, that some workers were dissatisfied with UFW contracts.

In December 1972 Teamsters International Union president Frank Fitzsimmons made an unprecedented appearance at the American Farm Bureau Convention. In his speech Fitzsimmons proposed an "alliance" between his union and the grower organization. He also chastised Chavez and called the union "a revolutionary movement." Later it was revealed that the initiative for Fitzsimmons's appearance had come from officials in the Nixon administration, most likely originating with White House counsel Charles Colson. In fact, Colson had written several memos to the NLRB and the Justice and Labor departments suggesting that these agencies should only intervene in any conflict between the Teamsters and the UFW if it would help the Teamsters. One memo, written prior to Fitzsimmons's Farm Bureau appearance, stated, "The Teamsters Union is now organizing in the area and will probably sign up most of the grape growers this coming spring, and they will need our support against the UFW." In January 1973, 25 growers or their representatives began unpublicized negotiations with Teamster representatives (Levy 1975, 473; Majka and Majka 1982, 212–15).

When negotiations with the UFW stalled over the union's refusal to give up the hiring hall and pesticide controls, representatives of Coachella Valley growers suspended talks. On 15 April, as UFW contracts expired, all but two Coachella Valley grape growers announced that they had signed four-year contracts with the Teamsters covering field workers. The next day 2,000 workers involved in thinning grape vines for these growers responded by going on strike. Strike-breaking crews were immediately recruited, many from the Mexican border area. Court injunctions were quickly issued limiting picketing activity, and more than 300 UFW supporters were arrested during the first week. The AFL-CIO pledged $1.6 million for the UFW strike fund, making this the first well-financed farm work strike in California's history. AFL-CIO president George Meany, who had previously been unenthusiastic about the UFW, called the actions of the Teamsters "the most despicable strikebreaking, union-busting activity I have ever seen in my lifetime in the trade union movement" (R. Taylor 1975, 202–203).

In response, Teamster "guards" were again brought in to intimidate pickets. The Riverside County Sheriff Department deployed lines of police to keep apart the Teamster guards and the chanting pickets. In fact, the police received as much verbal abuse from the some of the guards as did the UFW pickets. Not all violence was averted, however. In one incident 56 people were hurt when Teamster guards charged unprotected UFW pickets; in another a Catholic priest sustained three

broken facial bones when assaulted by a guard in a restaurant. Dozens
of people were injured in other attacks.

As the strikes moved north with the UFW contracts being replaced
by ones with the Teamsters, so did the violence. On 28 June an estimated 40 armed guards charged 200 UFW supporters picketing a
southern San Joaquin Valley grape grower. Also, the police in San
Joaquin Valley counties were considerably more aggressive than they
had been in Coachella Valley. In a number of attempts to enforce
injunctions limiting picketing and demonstrations, police charged
picketers with clubs, often beating them and using mace, whether
they met with resistance or not. The UFW counted 44 people beaten
by the police that summer, including several AFL-CIO officials who
had come to witness the strike. Nearly 3,600 UFW members and supporters were arrested over the summer, including 70 clerics. Despite
spending $3 million on the strikes, the UFW had lost nearly all of its
grape contracts, as well as its contract with Gallo wine. By year's end,
UFW contracts had declined from approximately 180 covering 40,000
jobs for 67,000 workers to 14 covering 6,500 workers (Martin et al.
1988, 35; Meister and Loftis 1977, 160).

The strikes had ended tragically. Within two days, two UFW members were killed. On 14 August Nagi Daifullah, a UFW picket captain
from Yemen, died as a result of an altercation with a Kern County
deputy outside a bar in Arvin. Two days later 60-year-old Juan de la
Cruz was fatally shot while on a silent picket line mourning Daifullah's
death by someone driving past in a pickup truck. Chavez immediately
decided to halt picketing and other strike activity. Within days of the
two funerals, hundreds of strikers and UFW volunteers were dispatched to various cities to begin a second boycott of table grapes, this
time combined with the ongoing head lettuce boycott and a new boycott of Gallo-owned wines.

Passage of the ALRA and Initial Implementation

The renewed boycott operations resembled the original table-grape
boycott in most respects. The UFW quickly recruited additional volunteers to bolster their staff in a number of cities. House meetings, infor-
mational leafleting, store picketing, and fund-raising campaigns were
emphasized. Sympathetic supporters who could contribute several
hours a week on boycott activities were mobilized. As before, full-time
volunteers were paid $5 a week and provided housing and food.

Attention shifted dramatically from the fields to urban areas, from coordinating strikes to promoting the boycott.

The purpose of this boycott was different in one significant way, however. Without legislation regulating unionization of agricultural labor, there was no guarantee that growers would not continue to sign "sweetheart" contracts, either with established unions like the Teamsters or with company unions. The UFW was now more aware of the importance of labor legislation that would supervise union certification elections but leave reasonable tactical options available to farm labor unions to pressure recalcitrant growers. Chavez later said he had decided to pursue a legislative strategy several weeks after the table-grape boycott was reintroduced. Accordingly, part of the purpose of the boycott was to put economic pressure on agribusiness to agree to agricultural labor legislation. Also, the boycott became the focal point for securing endorsements from political leaders and influential organizations that would constitute a political alliance to pressure both agribusiness and government officials for what was hoped would be a legislative resolution to the conflict. The UFW successfully pursued this strategy during the next two years.

The boycott began with considerable momentum. The national media exposure given to the violence initiated by the police and Teamster "guards" produced considerable public sympathy for the UFW. Numerous church organizations, including the National Conference of Catholic Bishops and the World Council of Churches, endorsed the boycott, as did a number of labor unions, including the United Auto Workers, the Longshoremen's, and several AFL-CIO–affiliated unions. British, Norwegian, and Swedish unions promised to coordinate the boycott in Europe. The AFL-CIO withheld its endorsement, however. This was partially due to George Meany's lack of enthusiasm about UFW's grass-roots, militant nature and its boycotts. The UFW's independence of spirit led the union to take stands on political issues, such as the Vietnam War, and to endorse a number of candidates for public office who were not supported by the AFL-CIO. Another reason was that the UFW's secondary boycotts of grocery chains were often opposed by a few AFL-CIO member unions, such as the Retail Clerks and Butchers, in part because of fear of job loss with declining sales (Majka and Majka 1982, 227–31). As the boycott campaign progressed, the UFW became increasing aware that without AFL-CIO endorsement, the boycott was deprived of an important resource.

A compromise was worked out in April 1974 in which the AFL-CIO agreed to endorse the head-lettuce and table-grape boycotts in return for the UFW giving up its secondary boycotts of retail outlets where other AFL-CIO unions had members working. This condition effectively ended the boycott of supermarket chains. The AFL-CIO did not endorse the Gallo-owned wines boycott, in large part because of contracts other unions had with Gallo. After the AFL-CIO endorsement, the national federation and individual unions publicized the grape and lettuce boycotts, many unions took up donations for the UFW, and a number of union locals provided office space and phones for boycott organizers.

Throughout 1974 the UFW received reports of declining grape sales. Also, some figures showed that Gallo wine sales were down as much as 20 percent nationwide. While accurate figures are difficult to obtain, it seemed as if the boycotts were having a significant impact. A Louis Harris poll released in October 1975 found that nationwide 12 percent of all Americans were boycotting table grapes, 11 percent head lettuce, and 8 percent Gallo wines. Some analysts claimed that these figures indicate that the UFW had sponsored the most effective union boycotts in U.S. history.

In 1974 the UFW put together a legislative proposal written largely by UFW attorney Jerry Cohen with help of the head of the California AFL-CIO, Jack Henning. The bill was co-sponsored by two Democratic members of the state Assembly who were strong supporters of the union, Richard Alatorre and Richard Burton. The proposal provided for supervised union certification elections if at least 50 percent of employees signed authorization cards for a specific union. Specifics of the proposal were adapted for the circumstances of agriculture work. For example, hearings on most procedural challenges to an election were postponed until after the election had been held. This was intended to prevent using challenges to delay elections until most or all harvest workers were no longer employed. The bill was approved by the California Assembly too late during the legislative session to be considered by the state Senate. In any case, given the likelihood of a veto by Governor Reagan, this attempt was a trial run to see what kind of support such a proposal would receive.

With the election of Jerry Brown as governor in November 1974, the threat of a gubernatorial veto was diminished. Throughout his campaign, Brown emphasized that one of his first priorities would be to seek the passage of legislation guaranteeing secret-ballot union

elections for farm workers. Most observers believed that this meant
he would support the Burton-Alatorre Bill, especially since Brown had
endorsed this proposal during his campaign. A proposal was not forthcoming for several months after Brown was inaugurated, however.
Finally, on 10 April, Brown's proposal was made public. Much of it was
similar to the Burton-Alatorre Bill, but Brown's proposal contained
several restrictions on secondary boycotts and recognition strikes that
displeased the UFW. Negotiations followed among representatives of
the Brown administration, the UFW, and California growers. While
negotiations were in progress, Brown lobbied other interested parties,
including supermarket executives and church officials, to seek their
support for an eventual compromise.

The amended proposal, the Agricultural Labor Relations Act
(ALRA), was announced on 5 May, and the UFW officially endorsed it
on 8 May. A five-member Agricultural Labor Relations Board (ALRB)
appointed by the governor was designated to supervise secret-ballot
union elections. Also, the board would make determinations on challenges and set precedents on procedures and issues that would surface during elections and negotiations. To secure an election, a union
would need to collect signatures from at least 50 percent of employees
certifying that union as their bargaining agent. Other unions could get
on the ballot with signatures from another 10 percent of employees. A
"no union" option would be on all ballots. As in the Burton-Alatorre
Bill, elections would be held quickly during harvest time, and determination of challenges would be postponed until after the election. This
meant that challenges by unions or employers to election-related
issues—such as election procedures, eligibility of individuals voting,
and methods of persuasion—could hold up certification of election
results but were not intended to postpone the elections themselves.
No restrictions were placed on primary boycotts, harvest-season
strikes, or issues that could be covered by contract negotiations. The
restrictions on secondary boycotts contained in Brown's original proposal, however, remained. An agricultural labor union could only use a
secondary boycott to pressure a reluctant grower into negotiating a
contract after that union had won an ALRB-supervised election and
was certified by the board as the bargaining agent. Secondary boycotts could not be used to gain union recognition.

The bill passed the state Senate 31–7 and the Assembly 64-10. It
was signed into law by Brown early in June and took effect 28 August,
in time for the fall 1975 grape harvest. As the law proceeded through

the legislature, this reflection by an anonymous grower appeared in the *Los Angeles Times*: "We might never have had any union if we hadn't cooperated with the Teamsters to keep Chavez out."

In preparation for the expected elections, both the UFW and the Teamsters worked to strengthen their support bases. The Teamsters had the most farm workers under contract, claiming over 400 contracts covering 50,000 workers. In addition, they were the "incumbents" at many ranches where elections were likely. In contrast, the UFW had fewer than 20 current contracts, covering around 10,000 of California's 220,000 agricultural workers during peak harvest time.

Campaigning for the UFW involved reaching workers who had not yet been involved in movement activities. Since the recent focus of the UFW had been on boycott activities, less attention was paid in the union to recruiting new farm workers. Many of the current workers were relatively new in the fields. Federal officials estimated that as much as one-third of those comprising the 1975 harvest crews were undocumented workers, the most difficult constituency for the UFW to reach. Also, support for the UFW was strongest among farm workers with relatively stable residences (locals) in contrast to migrants who benefited less from hiring halls because they tended to have briefer as well as irregular employment with the same grower.

Several patterns worked against the Teamsters, however. Unlike the UFW, the Teamsters Union had no ethnic identity that could facilitate bonds with Mexican-American and Filipino-American farm workers. In fact, Teamster efforts to undermine the UFW—a union largely rooted in the Mexican-American experience and culture—was resented by many. Also, Teamster contracts were the result of grower cooperation, not worker support. There was not the kind of loyalty to the Teamsters as there was among UFW supporters. The Teamsters additionally had not been enforcing many of their contracts for several years, which deprived the union the full benefits of their incumbency. To offset these disadvantages, Teamster officials began to adopt a more militant tone, and contract renegotiations with 135 growers gave those workers significant wage gains.

The ability of the UFW to reach newer workers, especially migrants, was made much easier by an important ALRB procedural ruling. Throughout the summer of 1975, UFW officials who attempted to meet with workers living on grower property were frequently denied entry. Some UFW organizers were arrested, and a few were assaulted. Teamster officials, on the other hand, were often given the freedom to meet with workers whenever they wanted. Despite UFW protests, there was nothing illegal in differential access to grower-owned property, at least until the ALRA took effect. Reasoning that unions needed to have fair access to workers, the ALRB ruled that union organizers would be granted the right to meet with workers for one hour before and one hour after work as well as a maximum of one hour during lunch and rest periods. For the legal right to gain access, a union first had to file a notice with a specific employer. This "access rule" was later upheld by the California Supreme Court.

During the first month after the ALRA went into effect, the UFW won 86 elections with 52 percent (13,410) of the total number of votes cast. The Teamsters won 73 elections with 31 percent (8,037) of the vote, and the "no union" option won 19 elections with 17 percent (4,175) of the vote. After the second month the UFW increased its total to 114 victories, and the Teamsters increased theirs to 86. The Teamsters did best at operations where they already had contracts, but the UFW did win elections at a number of sites covered by Teamster contracts. By the end of the year the UFW had won 76 percent of the 191 certified elections, with another 191 elections remaining to be certified by the ALRB.

The first weeks of the elections were less than amiable. Numerous claims of grower and Teamster threats and intimidation of workers were reported, and the UFW filed more than 100 complaints of irregularities accompanied by worker affidavits. Two members of the ALRB estimated that intimidation lowered the UFW share of the vote by 15 to 20 percent.

In response, the board issued several unfair labor practice charges against growers. One of those was against the Joseph Gallo Company, headed by the younger brother of Ernest and Julio Gallo of Gallo Wines. Included in the charges against the company was the removal of UFW supporters from company-owned housing and the hiring of workers on the basis of union preference. Also, the ALRB tightened its enforcement of the terms of the law and increased its supervision of the elections.

The UFW victories contributed to a growing opposition to the law by many growers. While some UFW supporters may have been disappointed that the UFW did not win nearly all the elections, it appeared that many growers were genuinely surprised by the extent of farm worker support for the UFW. Also, with the enforcement of the ALRA, agribusiness could no longer exercise the kinds of control over its work force that it had been accustomed to for most of this century. When funds provided for the ALRB ran out late in 1975, both agribusiness and the Teamsters demanded alterations in the law before additional funds would be allocated to continue operations until the next fiscal year. Their demands included eliminating the access rule, defining labor contractors as "employers," extending the length of time between filing an election petition and holding an election, and reducing financial liabilities for parties found guilty of violating of the law. Although legislative proposals to amend the ALRA failed badly, a coalition of Republican and rural Democrats managed to block appropriation of emergency funds. Accordingly, the ALRB shut down its offices in early February 1976, and it had to wait until 1 July, the beginning of the next fiscal year, to resume operations.

The temporary suspension of operations had several long-term consequences. First, ALRB's staff was laid off, and a number of staff members permanently left the agency, including many of the hardest-working and most dedicated. If staff members chose to remain with the agency, there was nothing for them to do in the interim, and they did not get paid. When the ALRB resumed operations, considerable time had to be devoted to recruiting and training new staff members. Also, the disruption in ALRB activity contributed to the departure of its general counsel and three of its five board members.

Second, according to several ALRB officials and UFW organizers, many farm workers themselves became restless and disillusioned. They had voted for a union of their choice assuming a union victory would result in a union contract, but nothing happened. Expectations had been raised but not met, and their enthusiasm was dampened. Also, union organizers curtailed their activities. Without the board in operation, there was no reason to continue filing certification petitions for elections.

Third, the ALRB could not continue with a variety of duties necessary for the intended operations of the law. Scheduled elections were postponed. Also, if elections held before the ALRB ceased operations were not yet certified by the board, then no official results were declared, and no union had the legal right under the ALRA to attempt to negotiate a contract. The ALRB could not continue its investigations and rulings on numerous unfair labor charges, most of them filed by the UFW or by pro-UFW farm workers. Many of these needed to be determined before an election could be certified or declared invalid. Also, while the board ceased operations, growers could defy the terms of the law with relative impunity—for example, by refusing to negotiate "in good faith" with a union certified as the sole bargaining agent for employees. All of this slowed down the considerable momentum stimulated by the ALRA: organizing workers, petitioning for elections, holding elections, certifying the results, and beginning contract negotiations.

The suspension of ALRB's operations demonstrated the drawbacks of a legislative solution. The struggle was taken out of terrain familiar to the UFW and transferred into the legislative arena where agribusiness in California traditionally has had enormous influence. Individual growers and agribusiness organizations began to shift their focus to explore a variety of legal and political means to slow down or render ineffective the operations of the law. The initial manifestation of this change was to lobby for amendments to the law favorable to agribusiness and to pressure legislators to vote against temporary funds for the agency. These were harbingers of strategies that agribusiness and its political supporters would use with increasing effectiveness.

Because of the uncertain status of the ALRA, the UFW decided to seek voter approval of the law as a ballot initiative. If passed, the ALRA could only be changed through another ballot referendum, making the law more difficult to amend. This strategy was intended to offset the considerable legislative influence of agribusiness and prevent the passage of restrictive provisions once the legislative coalition that originally passed the law had eroded. The proposal also wrote the access rule into the initiative, changing its status from a procedural regulation. When enough signatures were gathered, the initiative was placed on the November 1976 ballot as Proposition 14. It was endorsed by Governor Brown, Democratic presidential candidate Jimmy Carter, most elected Democratic officials in California, and many former ALRB officials. Agribusiness mounted a well-financed advertising campaign, however, built around the theme that the access rule was a violation of the rights of private property and portrayed this as one more example of increasing government involvement in the private lives of citizens. This message had considerable appeal, especially coming in the first post-Watergate presidential election. Despite initial polls that showed considerable public support for Proposition 14, it was defeated by a 20 percent margin. Chavez reportedly took this defeat very hard, and some ex-UFW officials later reflected that the union's internal crisis began shortly thereafter.

While the Proposition 14 campaign was in progress, secret deliberations between the UFW, the Teamsters, and grower representatives were successful in reaching another jurisdictional agreement between the two unions that was signed in March 1977. The five-year agreement gave the UFW jurisdiction over workers covered by the ALRA, while the Teamsters would limit themselves in agricultural operations to workers covered by the NLRA. The Teamsters also indicated that they would cease organizing efforts among farm workers and would not renew their current agricultural labor contracts, with the exception of one with Bud Antle that they had since the early 1960s. Also, Teamster Local 63 in Los Angeles would continue to seek contracts covering dairy workers in southern California.

This agreement presented the UFW with the kind of advantageous position it had sought. The union now had little competition in certification elections, and growers could not use the presence of the Teamsters to their advantage. There were a number of small unions that were involved in organizing activities in specific localities. But besides Teamster Local 63, the only other union to be involved in a number of certification elections was the Christian Labor Association (CLA). Like the Teamster local, the CLA secured contracts at a number of dairies in southern California and the San Joaquin Valley, covering on the average three workers at each dairy.

The UFW won 33 of the 48 nondairy elections supervised by the ALRB during a seven-month period ending 30 June 1977. Of the 9,163 farm workers voting in these elections, 61 percent were for the UFW, 5 percent for other unions, and 21 percent for no union representation, while the remaining 13 percent were challenged votes. Still, election victories were not easily translated into union contracts. By the time the table-grape boycott was officially suspended in January 1978, the UFW had won more than 250 elections, and the ALRB had certified more than 180 of these. But the union had signed only 80 contracts covering about 25,000 workers, compared with 250 in 1973, before the union's initial table-grape contracts expired. By the end of 1978 the UFW had increased its number of contracts to 108: 42 in vegetables and lettuce, 20 in grapes, 24 in tree fruits, and 13 in nursery. The average hourly wage under these contracts was $3.38. Fringe benefits raised the average hourly compensation to $4.01. These figures varied little from one crop to another (Martin et al. 1988).

Nevertheless, the ALRB was a crucial factor in reaching contracts. In 1977 and 1978 the agency found a number of violations of the law, mostly by individual growers. This put pressure on growers to keep from illegally interfering with certification elections and to bargain in good faith after union certification was given. One breakthrough was the contract agreement between the UFW and seven Delano-area table-grape growers in May 1978, two and a half years after elections at these ranches. They represented the first contracts in the Delano region since 1970. Although the contracts raised hourly wages, they did not include a union hiring hall. Instead, growers would hire through their own central hiring system. Several observers have claimed that the UFW agreed to contracts without a hiring hall because there were problems with the hiring hall in the past, the UFW had a relatively weak position in the grape industry, and the union simply desired to sign a contract covering grape harvesters.

In 1979 the UFW's primary focus was on renewal of the contracts signed in 1976 covering vegetable and lettuce operations in the Imperial and Salinas valleys. Contract demands centered mainly on wages, with the UFW pushing for hourly wage increased from $3.70 to $5.25. While this was considerable, the union argued that the discrepancy between industrial and agricultural workers continued to be very large, and this 42 percent increase would help close the gap. Growers offered a 7 percent wage increase, arguing that this was in keeping with President Carter's Wage and Price Stability Council guidelines, although these guidelines were not intended for agricultural workers. When contracts with a number of Imperial Valley growers expired in January 1979, workers went on strike. By early February, 10 companies were being struck, affecting 4,300 workers. Violence broke out as gunshots were directed at labor camps and farm worker buses. Ku Klux Klan posters appeared, and crosses were burned in several fields. On 10 February Rufino Contreras, a seasonal harvester from Mexicali who had struck grower Mario Saikhon, was killed by gunfire. He was part of a group of strikers who had entered a Saikhon field attempting to talk to a group of 70 strike breakers. Two Saikhon ranch foremen and another employee were subsequently booked on murder charges.

In February 1979 strike activity moved north to the Salinas Valley. As UFW contracts expired, workers joined the strike and were replaced by strikebreaking crews. Growers hired armed guards to prevent strikers access to replacement harvesters. Chavez charged the Immigration and Naturalization Service (INS) with failure to enforce against the importation of undocumented workers. When such pressure resulted in increased INS surveillance, raids on Salinas fields resulted in the arrest of three times the number of illegal aliens normally apprehended during the season. Most of those arrested were working as strike breakers.

This strike was in some ways different from previous ones. On the surface, it did not concern union recognition. Rather, its intention was to pressure for a better contract. In this sense it was similar to many strikes in other industries. Most growers were still not resigned to unionization of field workers, however, especially under UFW contracts, making UFW survivability a continuing issue.

One consequence of these two challenges was a difference of opinions within the union concerning strategies. Chavez reportedly leaned toward a suspension of the strike before a resolution had been reached. Instead, he favored a renewal of the consumer boycott of head lettuce and threatened this action several times during the strike. He did announce a secondary boycott of Chiquita-brand bananas in order to pressure the largest lettuce grower, Sun Harvest, a subsidiary of United Brands, for contract renewal. But well-organized and sometimes militant tactics by striking workers also brought considerable pressure on reluctant growers. Roving caravans of 150 to 200 strikers each visited struck ranches attempting to reach strike breakers and sometimes disrupt production. This precipitated a certain amount of violence by both sides. Confrontations between strikers and strike breakers or private security guards resulted in injuries to scores of people. As a reaction to the growing violence and to the frustration that seven months of strike activity had not brought a resolution, Chavez undertook a 12-day march from San Francisco to Salinas in early August 1979 accompanied by hundreds of striking workers and UFW supporters. The march ended with an estimated 5,000 marchers joining 7,000 others for a rally in Salinas that was addressed by Governor Brown.

While the march was in progress, the Teamsters reached a contract agreement with Bud Antle raising the hourly wage to $5. This did not make the UFW demand of $5.25 seem exorbitant. Gradually, the UFW began to reach contract agreements with struck growers raising wages to $5 an hour and including various clauses covering future mechanization. These mechanization clauses were intended to facilitate union-grower negotiations regarding the introduction of labor-saving machinery in order to minimize job loss or plan for a gradual displacement, with retraining of workers when feasible.

The major breakthrough came on 31 August, when the UFW signed a renewed three-year contract with Sun Harvest covering 1,200 lettuce and vegetable workers. Besides a $5 hourly wage, raises in piece rates, cost-of-living adjustments, and a union-run hiring hall, the contract provided for binding arbitration to handle disputes over mechanization. Another contract provision allowed for two full-time union representatives to serve as liaisons between the company and the union, with their salaries paid by the company. While the mechanization clause was viewed at the time as being more significant, the union representative issue later became the more controversial, particularly with respect to internal union politics.

During the first several weeks in September the UFW signed with 11 other growers, with the Sun Harvest contract providing a model. Most of the growers who began negotiating with the UFW the previous year in lettuce and vegetables had now signed. These contracts appeared to represent advancements in the UFW's attempts to institutionalize worker representation in decision-making and emphasize "control issues" in changes the union was promoting in agribusiness operations. But other growers continued to resist, including the large lettuce grower Bruce Church. Also, violence continued as strike activity resumed once again in the Imperial Valley early in 1980. Some observers traced a significant hardening of grower intransigence to the period immediately following the 1979 strike. After the union signed three-year contracts in July 1980 with the Vinter Employers Association representing 1,500 grape harvesters for four wineries, the position of the UFW began a steady erosion for the rest of the decade.

In retrospect, the last half of the 1970s marked the peak of the United Farm Workers. The union had successfully mobilized not only a substantial proportion of farm workers but also built an admirable support network, both among ordinary citizens and political allies. The UFW also helped change the political opportunities structure in California to its advantage, as it had become a moral voice for change in agricultural class relations. The UFW had a strong enough impact to pressure for passage of one of the most progressive pieces of labor legislation in the nation. After a rocky start, the implementation of the ALRA began to be more steady, and many activists and observers believed that gradually increasing numbers of growers were becoming resigned to unionization and willing to work within the law. The situation was undoubtedly the most promising ever for permanent improvements in the status of farm labor in California. This "window of opportunity" was brief, however, undermined by unresolved internal disputes within the union, a closing of political opportunities, and a hardening of grower opposition to unionization once again.

Chapter 7

Unionism during the 1980s and Early 1990s

The Decline of the United Farm Workers Union

The situation in 1980 appeared to be a window of opportunity for the UFW finally to become firmly established in California's agribusiness and use its position to spearhead or assist unionization drives by farm workers in other states. Instead, since the early 1980s farm worker unionization in California reversed its direction. Much of this was reflected in the decline of the number of contracts held by the UFW and the number of workers under contract. For example, in 1987 the union held just 31 contracts, down from 162 contracts in early 1982 and 115 in 1984. These 31 contracts represented between 12,000 and 15,000 workers, a decline from 60,000 workers under contract during the early 1980s.[13] By 1987 the UFW had contracts with only one-sixth of the agricultural operations where they had won elections supervised by the Agricultural Labor Relations Board (Martin et al. 1988, 48). At the time of Chavez's sudden death on 23 April 1993, the UFW held only a handful of contracts covering about 5,000 workers out of the 769 operations where they were certified. In the Salinas Valley, which was their strongest base a decade earlier, the union had but one remaining contract. In fact, most of the remaining contracts were with nurseries, mushroom farms, and similar specialty crop operations, not with the large farm companies.

Throughout the 1980s the patterns were that fewer union representation elections were held; those that resulted in union victories were much less likely to culminate in labor contracts; UFW contracts up for renewal faced stiffer opposition by employers and were less likely to be renewed; some companies that had UFW contracts went out of business, most notably Sun Harvest; union decertification elections comprised an increasing proportion of Agricultural Labor Relations Act (ALRA) elections; and later contracts contained significantly weaker provisions than earlier agreements.

In addition, the number of certification elections declined. After the initial flurry of elections during the first four years of the ALRA, from 1975 to 1979, the demand for certification elections might have been expected to reach a stable situation. According to ALRB annual reports, however, the number of union certification elections showed a steady decline throughout the 1980s. During the three-year period from 1 July 1979 to 30 June 1982, the number of certification elections averaged 37 annually. During the next three-year period, fiscal years 1983–85, this declined to 29 elections per year. And from 1 July 1985 to 30 June 1988, the annual average was just 17 elections. During this time the number of elections to decertify a union that had previously won a representation election increased slightly, from an average of six per year during fiscal years 1979–82, to eight per year during fiscal years 1986–88. During this first three-year period, however, decertification elections represented 13 percent of the total number of elections, whereas during the later three-year period they represented 31 percent of the total (ALRB 1977–88).

There were three sources for the decline in farm labor unionization, particularly with respect to the UFW, and each reinforced the others. First, the UFW experienced a serious internal crisis during the late 1970s and early 1980s that resulted in the departure of a substantial proportion of the union's organizers, administrators, and staff. Even more than a decade later, during the early 1990s, it appeared that the union still had not rebuilt its organizational structure to a level comparable to what it was previously. In fact, a number of staff members either quit or were fired during the late 1980s, further decimating the union's pool of talent. Second, with the change in governors from liberal Democrat Jerry Brown to conservative Republican George Deukmejian in January 1983, state administrators and appointees to the ALRB were far less sympathetic to farm labor unionization, and some were publicly hostile to the UFW.

The administration of the law gradually shifted to impede rather than facilitate settling unfair labor practice charges, holding certification elections, and encouraging good-faith bargaining. Finally, in this climate strategies growers had been using to prevent or delay unionization became more effective, in part because there was less active enforcement of the law. Most of these were legal maneuvers, challenging actions by the ALRB that they did not like. Also, several growers filed expensive lawsuits against the UFW, which shifted the union's declining resources to fight defensive court battles. In addition, some observers have claimed that there was an increase in the use of undocumented workers mainly from Mexico but also from Central America in some crops and localities, including those where the UFW formerly had substantial worker support and labor contracts.

Since the election of Deukmejian, the UFW repeatedly claimed that his policies and appointments led to changes in the operations of the ALRB that resulted in a decline in UFW membership and contracts. The internal crisis the union experienced, however, preceded by several years the election of Deukmejian. After the departure of much of the union's leadership, there was little momentum left for continued organizing. The UFW was then in a position that made it extremely vulnerable to attacks by agribusiness and, later, by the new administration.

The UFW's Internal Crisis and Its Consequences. After the jurisdictional agreement with the Teamsters in 1977, the UFW went through a difficult period of personnel changes. What seemed to be an ideal period for consolidating gains and launching a new round of organizing efforts and election campaigns instead was one in which much energy was turned inward in what proved to be a spectacularly unsuccessful attempt to resolve internal differences. Energies that could have focused on winning elections and contracts were instead directed to a bitter internal struggle over power and loyalty.

The result was the departure of a substantial proportion of UFW organizers, administrators, and staff from several levels of leadership below Chavez. Among those who resigned from the union between 1978 and 1981 were Jerry Cohen, chief legal counsel and director of the legal office for 17 years; Marshall Ganz, the union's chief organizer for nearly 15 years; Gilbert Padilla, one of the union's founders and its secretary-treasurer; Jessica Govea, director of the union's health service program; and Marc Grossman, spokesman for Chavez and longtime UFW volunteer. Also resigning was Eliseo Medina, who, with Ganz, Padilla, and Govea, was at the time a member of the UFW's executive board. Some of these were amiable departures; others were not. In addition, nearly all the UFW legal staff under Cohen subsequently left. Finally, many of the full-time union representatives in charge of administering Salinas-area contracts were fired. Many of these union representatives had been strike leaders during the 1979 lettuce and vegetable workers strike.

Some top-level officials resigned in part because of the unwillingness of Chavez and his supporters on the union's executive board to establish regularly paid positions and to delegate more authority. Most of the legal staff left rather than relocate from Salinas to UFW headquarters at La Paz, located in a very small town 30 miles east of Bakersfield. The union representatives from the Salinas area were fired after they were accused of disloyalty for their support of an opposition slate for election to the UFW's executive board. Because these departures were spread out over several years, it is perhaps clearer that they represented a failure to resolve several long-standing issues. They also represented a decimation of various levels of leadership within the union. There is no doubt that this slowed the momentum of the union substantially.

In a small organization where there were only as many lines of initiative as there were leaders able to take charge and direct them, the decimation of organizing talent on the executive board, among other volunteers, and within the ranks of paid representatives left the union unable to sustain the kinds of mobilization necessary to win collective bargaining agreements.

In addition, without a smoothly operating legal staff, the UFW proved unable to negotiate contracts for ranches where elections had been certified. The union's goal of having farm workers themselves conduct all aspects of union business did not prove capable of delivering contracts. Always ready to find profound fault with the union, growers used this as evidence that the UFW was poorly organized and in disarray from internal disputes and certainly could not be counted on to uphold their obligations in a contract. Growers acted as if they believed they had little to fear if they failed to renegotiate their contracts with the union. Several former ALRB officials during the Brown administration agreed that the demise of the well-coordinated legal staff in the union was a decisive factor in slowing down the momentum of farm labor unionization under the aegis of the ALRB.

The broader issues behind the departures point to weaknesses associated with charismatic forms of authority and reliance on volunteers. These features suggest that the internal difficulties the UFW experienced were due to the tensions between two different modes of organization. The UFW was unable to translate personal forms of authority and a loose, volunteer organization into more formal, stable patterns. While charismatic authority—often valuable in inspiring people to take up difficult challenges—is often crucial to develop and sustain protests and social movements, it is also inherently unstable. Because it emerges when traditional norms of authority have become untenable and usual patterns of dominance and subordination intolerable, it can concentrate an enormous amount of unrestrained power into the hands of a leader. This power may be exercised in what appears to be arbitrary, unpredictable, and volatile ways.

To sustain changes made under charismatic leadership and to preserve gains achieved by constituents, this authority needs to be transformed into a more stable form. This has usually meant a transition to more formal organizations with written rules and managerial hierarchies. Authority then becomes associated with offices rather than with personal qualities and extraordinary abilities. Transition between these two forms is often difficult, and some of the enthusiasm and commitment that marks the protest phase is dissipated by the more routine operations that follow.

Chavez provided charismatic leadership to the movement since the 1965 Delano grape strike. Not only has he been the ultimate decision-maker in most important matters but even has involved himself periodically in such things as the details of day-to-day operations of UFW field offices. Although the union has claimed that its decisions were reached in accord with a model of community consensus, it was not easy to take positions contrary to Chavez's. The UFW's rhetoric of self-determination and the democratic values held by many of its staff sometimes clashed with Chavez's leadership style.

With the union's success, other needs came to the fore. Contract negotiations and renegotiations required different skills. Also, a stable structure would be best suited to administering contracts, especially those that attempted to institute substantial changes in worker-management relations. The UFW had a number of offices with specialized functions, such as medical clinics, retirement plans, and other services. The union additionally had a number of field offices around the state. The enormous number of union certification elections held throughout the state during the first four years of the law, however, and the potential to negotiate large numbers of contracts in different crops after the elections put the requirements far beyond what reasonably could be closely supervised by any one person. A more widespread delegation of authority to groups within the organization—such as the legal staff, field offices, ranch committees, and union representatives—seemed a necessary step. But this also meant a certain loss of control by Chavez, a transition from power concentrated in the hands of a charismatic leader to a more decentralized, and perhaps more formal, system of authority. The departures from the UFW, however, eliminated the possibility of this kind of transition of authority. In addition, the election of Chavez's son-on-law, Arturo Rodriguez, as the new president of the UFW after Chavez's death is consistent with a tendency of charismatic authority to create a "family line" of leadership and may indicate that the union will resist changes in its organization and strategies.

Further impeding this transition were the explicit values of Chavez and some others in the union's leadership that emphasized sacrifice and total commitment. The union's administrators, organizers, and staff had been largely volunteer since the union's founding. Officials, Chavez included, were "earning" $10 a week by the late 1970s and were provided living quarters and food. Such subsistence helped ensure that union staffers and officials were dedicated, but this poverty was less conducive to building a larger staff engaged in specialized operations.

Chavez seemed to have a deep ambivalence regarding successful institutionalization of the union and certainly had a distaste for some changes that success may bring. It was clear to most observers that Chavez did not want the UFW to become like a normal AFL-CIO labor union. One former union official remarked, "He saw them [union officials] at the conventions in their gray pinstripe suits and red ties. They looked like the employers of their workers. Cesar wanted to do it with an army of true believers" (*Press Enterprise*, 6/5/89). Several observers speculated that the "breakthrough" of a minimum earning of $5 an hour in the Salinas contracts may have epitomized for Chavez a fear that the union was becoming too similar to conventional labor unions. When the struggles were about union recognition, they were also implicitly about recognition of the human dignity of Chicano, Mexican, and Filipino farm workers. Renegotiating contracts where wages were a major issue did not directly possess the same quality.

In addition, the Salinas workers displayed considerable independence from the union hierarchy, resisting giving up strike activities. These workers tended to comprise tightly-knit crews who had a stable pattern of migrating between the Imperial and Salinas valleys. They generally were better paid than farm workers in the San Joaquin Valley (Friedland et al. 1981; Thomas 1985). These crews and their leaders comprised a potential power base within the union that might successfully challenge Chavez and his supporters. Some observers interpreted this possibility as the larger context behind the firing of Salinas union representatives.

The most significant result of the internal crisis was that the UFW could not institutionalize its position in agriculture while the ALRA was still functioning to remove barriers to unionization. For all the difficulties experienced under the ALRA, there were signs that the law had begun to provide a means of resolving at least some capital-labor conflicts. Under the expectation that the UFW was going to be the likely bargaining agent, some growers began to make improvements in their operations—for example, installing toilets in the fields and showers in the labor camps. While these and other improvements were often made out of some growers' hope to avoid unionization, they still represented actual changes in the quality of life for both union and nonunion farm workers.

What made it possible for the ALRA to be passed in 1975 was in part the willingness of a segment of agribusiness to accept collective bargaining and unionization. Some growers no doubt saw that if they could obtain a cheap enough labor contract, they could afford the enlightened paternalism of entering labor agreements. Some agribusiness firms were used to dealing with unions and lacked the historical animosity toward labor organizations typical of many growers. Furthermore, some were vulnerable to UFW campaigns that involved boycotts of well-known products and pressure from churches that endorsed UFW efforts.

The UFW did not, however, become institutionalized enough to prevent erosion of its position during the 1980s. The union had worked for 15 years to create the favorable opportunities that presented themselves in the late 1970s. Governor Jerry Brown was highly supportive of the UFW. A legislature favorable to farm labor unionization was in office. The ALRB and the California Supreme Court were staffed by individuals with strong backgrounds in U.S. labor law. Divisions had appeared in the agribusiness community yielding at least one segment ready to participate in collective bargaining. A vast public had been created by international product boycotts that pressured for resolution of capital-labor conflicts in California. Nevertheless, the UFW did not build a secure dues base among better paid farm workers, did not obtain contracts on many ranches where the union had been certified as the bargaining agent, and did not stabilize its leadership ranks. Thus when an unsupportive governor took office what might have been a difficult but sustainable period of retrenchment became a life-and-death struggle for the survival. A "normal" cycle of reaction by vested interests against a successful farm labor campaign developed into devastating conditions that all but undermined farm labor organizing.[14]

Changes in the ALRA Administration. George Deukmejian, the Republican candidate for governor, campaigned in 1982 with heavy donations from agricultural corporations. During the campaign he made the operations of the ALRA a major issue, claiming that the law was "biased" in favor of the UFW. During the 1982 race he criticized his Democratic opponent, Los Angeles mayor Tom Bradley, for having nominated Chavez for the Nobel Prize in 1974. Also, during both his 1982 race and his successful reelection campaign in 1986, Deukmejian denounced the UFW and attacked Chavez personally. Once in office, Deukmejian took a public stance in opposition to the renewed UFW table-grape boycott. When the union attempted to link alleged health hazards for field workers—including cancer and respiratory ailments from pesticides used by the growers—with the boycott, the governor responded in a radio address that these "charges made by the boycott sponsors are false and irresponsible" (*Los Angeles Times,* 8/28/88). One of the priorities of his administration was to reverse the pattern of implementation of the ALRA.

During the eight years of the Deukmejian administration, from January 1983 to January 1991, the ALRA was transformed from a law that facilitated agricultural labor unionization to one that placed increasing obstacles in its way. This was accomplished primarily in four ways. First, a number of appointments to the ALRB and its staff were persons who either had backgrounds in agribusiness or were known to be grower supporters in labor disputes. Second, several basic provisions of the ALRA were not enforced systematically or at all, making it easier for individual growers to circumvent the law with little fear of penalties. Third, the budget of the ALRB was severely cut, reducing its ability to enforce the law. Fourth, decisions by the state Supreme Court began to overturn legal precedents that had been established during the first five years that the law was in effect.

The position of general counsel to the ALRB is of considerable importance in carrying out the enforcement of the law. Unfair labor practice charges can be filed with the ALRB by interested parties against an employer, a union, or an agent of either. Usually, these involve illegal interference by either side with certification elections, employer discrimination against individual workers because of their union activities, and failure by either side to negotiate in "good faith" once a union has been certified. Charges are often resolved informally soon after they are filed. If they are not settled, however, the general counsel is in a crucial position to assess their merits and decide whether to issue a complaint or dismiss the charges. These decisions are intended to be based on investigations by ALRB staff. If a complaint is issued and is not then settled by the disputing parties, it is heard by an administrative law judge who takes testimony, makes a decision, and, if warranted, issues a remedy for redress. This decision can be appealed to the five-member board and can further be appealed to the California Court of Appeals. Finally, the California Supreme Court may be petitioned by one of the parties for review of the Court of Appeals decision.

The importance of the office of general counsel makes the impartial disposition of its duties central to the administration of the ALRA in ways that influence the willingness of all sides to resolve differences and abide by ALRB decisions. Deukmejian's appointment of David Stirling, a former Republican assemblyman from Whittier, as the ALRB's general counsel was confirmed after a polarizing debate in the state legislature. Once in office, Stirling demonstrated a barely concealed contempt for the UFW. On several occasions he essentially served as a spokesman for agribusiness. In one instance he undertook a speaking tour in a number of eastern states to attack the grape boycott and the UFW's attempts to portray heavy use of certain pesticides as a public health issue. While on this trip Stirling lobbied the United Methodist Church at its national convention to withdraw its support for the UFW (*Bakersfield Californian*, 10/13/85). On other occasions he called Chavez's focus on the pesticide question a "vicious" and "utterly contemptible" tactic (*Los Angeles Times*, 9/18/85) and claimed the UFW suffers from a "victim's complex" (*Wall Street Journal*, 9/9/86). Concerning his attitude toward the ALRA, Stirling claimed that, before his appointment to the ALRB, "the purposes of the law were confused and abused." The evidence he cited in support of his assertion was that "the grower community felt oppressed. Actions of the agency were unacceptable to the grower community." He asserted that the agency favored the UFW, "assisted in the demise of the Teamsters," and acted in a way that resulted in unjustified and "onerous" financial burdens on growers. Concerning the actions of the agency under Deukmejian, he took satisfaction in declaring that "the board is no longer responsive to the needs of farm workers."[15]

While not all Deukmejian appointments to the five-member ALRB were as openly partisan, observers described the relationship between board members and the UFW as "open warfare" once the governor's choices dominated the board. According to one former member of the ALRB during the Brown administration, "It's no secret that Deukmejian appointed people unsympathetic to the UFW and labor law" (Waldie personal communication 1989).

A second way that the ALRA shifted from facilitating to inhibiting unionization during the Deukmejian administration was the lack of implementation of crucial aspects of the law. Two patterns in the actions of the general counsel were especially important: the failure to act on grievances brought by farm workers and by the UFW, and the unwillingness to administer the "make-whole remedy."

With respect to the first, during much of the 1980s an increasing percentage of unfair labor practice charges were dismissed by the general counsel rather than turned into complaints and passed on to the board for hearings. During 1975–80, the first five years of the ALRA, an average of 27 percent of all unfair labor practice charges filed with the ALRB were dismissed, representing 33 percent of all the charges that were not withdrawn. By contrast, during the four-year period of 1983–87, 71 percent of unfair labor practice charges were dismissed, representing 77 percent of those not withdrawn (ALRB 1975–87). According to ALRB officials, this increasing rate of dismissals was the result of requiring more evidence before the board investigated charges. This was intended to reduce time spent on relatively minor or frivolous charges.

Many of the charges dismissed during the last half of the 1980s were, however, anything but minor in their consequence. Included among those dismissed were a number stemming from certification elections conducted by the ALRB that had not been acted on after several years. Some dated back to the late 1970s, but most were from the early and mid 1980s. Even though the UFW won many of these elections, no hearings were conducted on the charges prior to their dismissal, and no union contracts were signed. The UFW claimed with some justification that without resolution of charges, growers did not fear reprisals from the ALRB for failure to undertake serious contract negotiations. Dismissal of charges brought by farm workers and by the UFW seemed to become the norm, while charges brought by growers were treated more seriously by the general counsel. By the late 1980s observers estimated that 80 percent of all charges filed with the ALRB by farm workers or unions were dismissed by the general counsel. In fact, the UFW simply stopped filing grievances with the board and encouraged farm workers to do the same.

The other way in which the implementation of the law was changed to the advantage of agribusiness was in pursuing charges of "bad-faith bargaining" and the use of the "make-whole remedy." While not intended to apply where tough but sincere negotiations occur (hard bargaining) and when unresolvable differences among the parties prevent a contract resolution, the make-whole remedy in theory eliminates monetary incentives for grower to delay negotiating a contract. A grower found guilty of bad-faith bargaining may be obligated to "make whole"—that is, to pay workers the difference between what they actually earned and what they would have earned had bad-faith bargaining not occurred. Determination of a precise amount has been somewhat difficult, however, and different methods have been controversial.

As in the case of other kinds of charges, the ALRB insisted on more evidence before initiating an investigation of charges of bad-faith bargaining. Also, the general counsel restricted the use of the make-whole remedy, intending to apply it only in an exceptional case. Finally, the basis for calculating the sums of money growers owed to workers under a damage award for bad-faith bargaining was changed to reduce grower costs.

General Counsel Stirling delayed ordering payment of the make-whole remedy in many cases where it was awarded before he took office. Hundreds of these remedies had been ordered, but little of the money awarded was actually disbursed (*Los Angeles Times*, 12/8/87). In fact, in order to expedite several long-standing cases where make-whole remedies were instituted but had not been paid out, Stirling ordered payments to workers of 10 cents on the dollar of the amount awarded.

Greater discretion was granted the general counsel in enforcing the law. For example, the general counsel was given the full power to determine whether a grower was in full compliance with ALRB's orders when the grower had been found guilty of violation of the law. Previously, the general counsel needed to offer the board documented proof of compliance. This concentrated power of the ALRB into this office and made it considerably easier for decisions by general counsel to escape scrutiny. In addition, the ALRB's files on specific complaints brought by workers were open to the very growers who were charged (*Los Angeles Times*, 7/31/85). This gave individual growers access to what was believed to be confidential testimony by farm workers and created the possibility of retaliation against specific employees. It also allowed a grower to read ALRB staff memos detailing strategies for prosecuting the grower for noncompliance and plan a legal strategy based on that information.

The third major shift in the implementation of the ALRA was accomplished by reducing the agency's operating expenses. The budget of the ALRB declined steadily during the Deukmejian administration, reduced by over 60 percent. The cutbacks were concentrated during the mid-1980s, as the 1988–89 ALRB budget was only 48 percent of what it was three years previous. The result was a 60 percent reduction in staff as investigative positions were eliminated. By the late 1980s there simply were not the personnel necessary to administer the law even if officials wanted to enforce it.

Finally, decisions by the California Supreme Court began to undercut the effective operations of the ALRA. Changes in appointments to the court corresponded to changes in appointments to the ALRB, and this proved to have important consequences for the implementation of the law. Previously, the ALRB had begun to build a solid judicial record established through matters going before the state Supreme Court. Following NLRB principles, the state Supreme Court generally affirmed ALRB decisions. This was particularly important since about 40 percent of ALRB rulings were appealed to the courts. Neither side was willing to simply abide by board rulings, but the number of grower appeals was far greater than the number of UFW appeals. When the political climate shifted, the Supreme Court judges who had tended to uphold ALRB rulings gradually were replaced by judges who lacked backgrounds in labor law. The ALRB proved vulnerable because, unlike the NLRB, it effectively operated in one industry, in one state, with one union, and it faced all the political hazards this exposure entailed. One result was that the courts became more likely to over-turn ALRB rulings and established operating procedures. This in turn undercut the integrity of the law.

One example in particular illustrates the consequences of changes in court decisions for the implementation of the ALRA. In 1988 the California Supreme Court invalidated a 1981 ALRB order that granted UFW organizers access to employees of a Kern County grower, including visits to labor camps. Consequently, individual growers became able to impose rules limiting union access to workers that then might be subject to review by the board. This in effect overturned the "access rule," which had given farm labor unions the right to reach migrant workers who were housed on company property (*Los Angeles Times*, 11/18/88).

The result of all these changes in the enforcement of the ALRA was that the resolution of agricultural conflicts with the assistance and pro-tection of governmental machinery had largely dissipated. While the federal NLRA went through a similar process of contention during the late 1930s, it gradually became an institution capable of persisting over time. The ALRA was not allowed to go through the same evolution. The transformation of the ALRA had become so profound that by 1988 the UFW, the union that was the chief beneficiary during the early years of the law, called for the complete elimination of the budget of the ALRB, reasoning that its continued operation was detrimental to farm workers.

The Impact of Agribusiness Strategies. The impact of the ALRA has proved to be unlike that of the NLRA during the late 1930s and 1940s. Although almost all industrialists initially opposed the NLRA, they gradually resigned themselves to unionization of their labor force. Later, management recognized that some aspects of unions and labor contracts functioned to their advantage, such as preventing wildcat strikes and providing a method for disciplining the rank and file. Management, once it accepted labor unions, encouraged the development of union structures and policies that were most compati-ble with corporate goals. And the political influence of labor unions gradually diminished, making them less of a challenge to corporate-supported economic and social policies (Montgomery 1979).

After the passage of the ALRA agribusiness tactics have in many respects not been much different from those traditionally used by industrial management. Agribusiness responded in predictable ways when the struggle shifted from the fields and boycott efforts to the ALRB and the courts. After the ALRA went into effect, "the number of grower attorneys tripled," according to former UFW attorney Jerry Cohen. Several law firms retained by growers relocated to California. Growers hired management experts and consultants to counter union strengths. But instead of accepting the mandate of the law and seeking an optimal negotiated settlement, agribusiness increasingly used these various legal strategies to oppose unionization in general and the UFW in particular. Its goal was to maintain a union-free situation in the California fields.

In many instances legal maneuvers on the part of growers followed UFW-won elections. This typically involved filing objections to the elections. Delays built into procedures associated with due process generally worked to the advantage of agribusiness. The array of legal impediments available as tactics for growers to delay unionization illustrates the drawback of the legal approach to secure contracts.

Still, many growers did sign contracts with the UFW, but their resistance to unionization gradually stiffened. When the implementation of the ALRA shifted under the Deukmejian administration, growers interpreted this as an opportunity to get out of contracts with the UFW and retaliate against its supporters. Penalties for such practices exist within the law, but during the Deukmejian administration labor laws were infrequently applied. One tactic used by several agribusiness operations was to declare bankruptcy. This allowed agribusiness enterprises to extract wage concessions from workers under union contract. For example, after Egg City declared bankruptcy, wages of workers under a UFW contract were reduced $2 an hour. Another strategy was to undergo a "paper" reorganization, a bogus plan by which the company is "sold" and "reorganized" in ways that were used to eliminate the UFW as a bargaining agent. In both these situations the ALRB has the jurisdiction to investigate whether the law has been violated by such actions, but it generally failed to do so. Other growers brought lawsuits against the UFW. At the time of his death, Chavez was in Arizona to testify in a retrial of a lawsuit against the union by the large Salinas lettuce grower Bruce Church, Inc., which had won $5.4 million award from the union in 1988.

Finally, many growers with UFW contracts discovered there were few risks in simply not renegotiating a contract with the union. In fact, in several cases the UFW gave in to grower demands for changes in the new contracts, and the growers still refused to sign. With little to fear from investigation by the ALRB, growers ceased cooperation with the UFW. The result was that most of the contracts won by the union as a consequence of ALRA elections were never renewed after the initial contracts expired.

UFW's Decline in Perspective. The impact of the internal crisis of the UFW, the changes in the administration of the ALRA, and the success of agribusiness in reversing the momentum toward unionization must be looked at as part of a larger pattern. What gave farm workers the ability to make gains was the strength of their insurgency that created a crisis in agricultural production. The resulting government mediation facilitated for around five years the implementation of gains that shifted power relations to the advantage of farm worker unions. The crisis that produced the ALRA passed, however, and the alliance that the UFW had built with progressive groups dissipated. Additionally, the UFW's structure weakened considerably through unresolved disputes, key resignations, and staff firings. Agribusiness then took advantage of a new, conservative administration to undercut the effectiveness of the law. Significantly, the law itself has not been modified and as of the early 1990s remains one of the most liberal pieces of labor legislation in the nation. Thus it is possible that under more favorable circumstances the ALRA could again be used to facilitate farm labor unionization. More than simply a change in administrations would be required, however.

The ALRA has shown limitations in its ability to facilitate unionization that parallel the weaknesses of the NLRA in several respects. Neither labor law has been able to prevent employer retaliation against workers who engage in union activity, although for different reasons under each law. The NLRA lacks penalties capable of functioning as a real deterrent, while the ALRA currently suffers from nonenforcement of existing penalties. Long delays are involved in settling unfair labor practice charges under both laws, especially as employers appeal their defeats through the courts. Employer resistance to union contracts after unions have won representation elections undermines collective bargaining.

On a more general level these events illustrate a cycle of protest, creation of a crisis, government mediation that contains significant concessions, disappearance of the crisis, and a subsequent erosion of concessions. It also illustrates that government agencies created to mediate disputes become themselves objects of struggle between dominant and subordinate groups. Without substantial pressure from below, reform structures can be then turned to the advantage of powerful groups. These patterns are not determined in advance, however; some concessions may persist. Reforms then become the basis on which future episodes of protest begin.

This suggests that disputes over the implementation of the ALRA will most likely continue. Despite the mixed blessing that any legislative strategy involves, the history of farm labor movements in California has given ample evidence that any long-term satisfactory resolution of this hundred-year conflict will most likely involve some form of government intervention. Next we cover another farm labor unionization campaign in the upper Midwest that has so far proven successful without legislative involvement. But the situation there has been quite different from that in California, where agribusiness has been truly dominant and the variety of tactical options available to it have been simply too formidable for farm labor unions to become institutionalized. Also needed is farm worker leadership that, while recognizing the double-edged nature of government intervention, is capable of using the next window of opportunity to become as established in agribusiness operations as circumstances permit.

The Success of the Farm Labor Organizing Committee of Ohio

The organizing campaigns and boycotts of the United Farm Workers Union helped stimulate related activities in a number of states during the past 20 years. Several efforts were either sponsored by or coordinated with the UFW, such as those in Texas, Florida, Arizona, and Washington. Others were separate from the UFW, while a few were seen as rival efforts by the union. Most of these have been of short duration, however. Achieved gains tended to be temporary, and few farm worker organizations survived for more than a year or two. By contrast, farm worker advocacy groups in a number of states have tended to persist, in large part because many have had some minimal government funding and paid personnel. These have not been strictly social-movement organizations, however, nor have their efforts been oriented toward organizing farm workers, either for negotiating with employers or union campaigns. Instead, their concerns typically have been the improvement of housing conditions, job safety, health care, and educational opportunities for migrants and their children.[16]

One exception has been a successful unionization effort by the Farm Labor Organizing Committee (FLOC) headquartered in Toledo, Ohio. What makes FLOC particularly interesting is that its campaigns brought results during the 1980s and early 1990s while the UFW's efforts were losing momentum. By contrast, FLOC's efforts culminated in June 1986 when FLOC and Campbell Soup Company announced a labor agreement covering a number of tomato and cucumber farms in Ohio and Michigan that were contracted to Campbell. This ended a lengthy boycott of Campbell products undertaken by FLOC. The contracts were subsequently renewed with little of the antagonism that has characterized management-labor relations in California's agricultural industry.

The similarities between the UFW and FLOC are considerable. Both concentrated on consumer boycotts of products connected to their targets, which required both unions to devote considerable effort in soliciting public support. Also, FLOC explicitly adopted much of the UFW's general organizational style as well as that union's strategy of developing a network of support groups. The national political climate shifted dramatically, however, between the UFW's most successful boycotts during the late 1960s and early 1970s and the time of the Campbell boycott during the 1980s. Under more difficult circumstances, FLOC was unable to elicit the kind of widespread support for the Campbell boycott that the UFW had achieved for its boycotts. Instead, FLOC increasingly relied on endorsements of the boycott by social-action organizations (many affiliated with mainstream religious denominations) and by denominational governing bodies. It was the negative publicity Campbell received rather than financial losses owing to the boycott that prompted the company to negotiate a contract with FLOC.

Approximately 65,000 migrants make up the harvest labor force for Ohio, Indiana, and Michigan. Most are Mexican-Americans or legal Mexican immigrants. Many have home bases in the lower Rio Grande Valley in Texas, but an increasing number spend the winter months in Florida working on the citrus crops. They comprise part of a mid-continent migrant stream working in a variety of crops: tomatoes, cucumbers, cherries, sugar beets, apples, peaches, strawberries, and asparagus

Conditions of Midwest farm workers typically have been worse than in California. While it has been difficult to get accurate average income for migrant families, all sources agree that it has been quite low. For example, in a report to the Ohio State Senate in 1981, the average family income of farm workers was estimated at $3,381 per year. In 1989 the Michigan State Social Services Department estimated that a Mexican-American migrant family of four earned between $7,000 and $9,000 in a *good* year. A 1983 survey of Midwestern tomato workers put the average family income before taxes at $6,450, about half of which was earned in the Midwest. In addition, employers have the choice of whether to provide for medical insurance and worker's compensation (Barger and Reza 1994).

Low income has made it difficult for farm workers to put down roots and instead has encouraged continued migrancy. Working as frequently and as many hours as possible, migrant farm workers still have to endure periods of unemployment, since their jobs depend on favorable weather and the health of the crops. Housing in labor camps often has provided only one room per family, no indoor plumbing, and water contaminated by pesticide runoff. In Ohio much of the migrant housing has been in violation of state laws, as inspections by state health officials periodically confirm. In addition, child labor has been widespread; a 1984 BBC documentary on Ohio farm workers concluded it would be difficult *not* to see child labor in the fields.

Many of the midwestern farm workers are employed through a labor contracting system similar to that in California. Individual farmers arrange with crew leaders to supply the required number of workers when necessary. Generally the farmers pay the crew leaders, who in turn pay the workers—an arrangement open to abuse. On some cucumber farms a form of sharecropping has been exercised in which the harvest workers are considered independent contractors instead of employees and typically receive 50 percent of the value of the crops they harvest. This arrangement, however, means that workers are not legally employees and as a result are not covered by worker's compensation and unemployment insurance. It also exempts farmers from meeting minimum-wage requirements and taking responsibility for child labor. In addition, since social security and other taxes are not withheld or filed, individual sharecroppers had to file these themselves. Because the self-employed business income taxes are higher than those for wages, many farm worker families found themselves strained financially, and some owed thousands of dollars in taxes as they were unaware for years of their responsibility to pay (Lopez 1990, 16–20; Barger and Reza 1994, 73–74).

The Farm Labor Organizing Committee was founded in 1967 by a group of farm workers, including 20-year-old Baldemar Velasquez, who remains as FLOC's president. Velasquez came from a migrant farm worker family who settled out of the Texas-to-Ohio migrant stream early enough to enable Baldemar to complete high school and attend college. FLOC initially called for talks with a group of tomato farmers in northern Ohio to discuss housing and wages for migrants. When few growers responded, FLOC called a strike and quickly won labor agreements with 33 growers for the years 1968–70. These contracts proved to be temporary, however. During the following years, under pressure from large processors, many farmers had to change crops. In some cases processors refused to renew contracts with individual growers unless the harvest was mechanized. The processors claimed that by entering contracts with farm workers the farmers were no longer a reliable source for produce (Valdez 1984, 46–48).

The relationship between processors and farmers in midwestern tomato and cucumber agriculture gives the processors rather than the farmers decisive, if indirect, power over farm worker employment. Each year many farmers enter into contracts with corporate food processors, such as Campbell and Heinz U.S.A. (a division of the H. J. Heinz Company), to supply their entire crop to the processor. Price and use of pesticides are usually set by the processor and stipulated in the contracts. In fact, the company often sells seedlings to contracted farmers to ensure product consistency. As a result individual farmers have had little flexibility to negotiate significant changes in wages and working conditions with farm labor organizations. For example, they cannot pass on increased labor costs by increasing the price of their commodity.

Recognizing these structural limitations, FLOC allowed its contracts with tomato growers to expire and shifted the focus of its efforts to community organizing and countering discrimination against farm workers. The organization also prepared itself for taking on the food-processing corporations that had to be brought into negotiations if any permanent changes were to result. During these years FLOC built up a membership base of about 700 persons, most of whom were seasonal workers who had settled out of the migrant stream.

In 1978 FLOC asked for union recognition not only from individual growers but also from Libby's and Campbell Soup Company, two of the major food processors with contracts in northwest Ohio. Both companies refused to discuss employment issues with FLOC, and fewer than 5 percent of growers contacted agreed to meet with the union. In response, 2,000 farm workers went on strike. The reaction of many growers was similar to the situations in California. Some faced strikers on picket lines with guns, one sprayed pesticides on a picket line, and another ran a pickup truck into a line of strikers. Some FLOC sympathizers working at farms not being struck were fired and black-listed. Subsequently, crops were harvested by replacement workers and, eventually, mechanical harvesters. Because of the strike, however, an estimated 25 percent of the local tomato crop was not harvested that year.

In 1979 Campbell mandated that all contracted tomato farms harvest their crops mechanically, dramatically reducing the number of harvest workers necessary. Other growers and processors followed Campbell's initiative, and by 1982 85 percent of tomatoes in northwestern Ohio were machine harvested (Valdez 1984). Responding to Campbell's actions and the corporation's lack of willingness to meet with worker representatives, FLOC called for a boycott of all Campbell Soup Company products in the summer of 1979. It asked consumers not to buy from Campbell or its numerous subsidiaries until labor agreements could be signed covering wages as well as health and safety conditions. Products bearing the Libby's label were initially included but dropped when Libby's sold its agricultural operations in northwest Ohio.

Campbell countered the boycott by arguing that because it did not hire any farm workers it could not be accountable for their wages, working conditions, and housing. Those issues were between individual farmers and their employees, and it would be inappropriate for Campbell to interfere in these matters.

Initially FLOC conducted the boycott according to a consumer strategy reminiscent of UFW boycotts. A network of past supporters of farm labor issues were activated to persuade consumers not to buy Campbell products. FLOC used mass-mailing strategies to disseminate information about its goals and generate publicity for the boycott, as the media was providing little coverage. By 1980 FLOC support groups were being organized in a number of major cities in the Midwest and the East. FLOC supporters attended rallies, leafleted and picketed at supermarkets, and solicited support from labor unions and church groups. Another similarity with UFW campaigns was a 560-

mile march in 1983 by about 100 FLOC members from Toledo to Campbell's corporate headquarters in Camden, New Jersey—one of the few FLOC-sponsored events that generated any significant national media coverage.

It soon became apparent to FLOC that even if it was successful, the consumer strategy would take many years to have the desired impact on Campbell. Consequently, FLOC shifted its emphasis from an exclusive focus on the consumer boycott of Campbell-owned products to what can be called an organizations strategy. This had two components. First, it attempted to persuade clients of firms and organizations having financial and administrative ties with Campbell to use their influence to persuade these firms to pressure Campbell to support farm worker elections, union recognition, and contract negotiations. Second, the organizations strategy sought the endorsement of national organizations of the consumer boycott of Campbell products. This included but was not limited to those traditionally sympathetic to farm labor goals. Both of these components would not only give needed publicity to the consumer boycott but also generate negative publicity about a well-known food corporation that was particularly dependent on public trust.[17]

Although the consumer boycott continued, the organizations strategy dictated a different emphasis. FLOC aimed to enlist the support of organizations, such as unions and churches, that had sizable assets in corporations with Campbell ties. The principal goal was for these organizations to make their future association with firms with financial and administrative ties to Campbell conditional on that firm pressuring Campbell about its labor practices. The ultimate threat to Campbell's corporate associates was the loss of accounts of client organizations sympathetic to FLOC as well as the possibility of a consumer boycott of their own services.

In addition, FLOC hoped to persuade members of these organizations to participate in demonstrations at the corporate headquarters and stockholder meetings of the firms with Campbell ties. While FLOC continued to disseminate information about the consumer boycott, its primary focus became mobilizing the clients of targeted organizations rather than the mass of consumers.

The second component of this strategy was FLOC's solicitation of endorsements for the Campbell boycott from sympathetic organizations like labor unions, church councils, and national social-action committees of churches. FLOC's major purpose in securing boycott endorsements was to use the prestige and legitimacy of these groups to apply moral pressure on Campbell and gain a hearing in still other organizations that might further influence the corporation and consumers.

Beginning in September 1984 FLOC's organizations strategy became focused on a corporate campaign against several companies with Campbell links, most importantly Philadelphia National Bank. The bank had particularly close links with Campbell, as the president of Campbell, R. Gordon McGovern, was a director of CoreStates Financial Corporation, the bank's parent company. Also, the chair of CoreStates, G. M. Dorrance, was a cousin of retired Campbell chair John T. Dorrance. In fact, the Dorrance family was the major Campbell stockholder. In addition, Philadelphia National Bank held a substantial number of Campbell shares in trust for its clients.

FLOC sought to apply pressure to Philadelphia National Bank by publicizing its links with Campbell, a corporation FLOC argued was profiting from poor working conditions and child labor in fields under contract in the Midwest. It was hoped that adverse publicity would persuade the bank to influence Campbell to resolve the farm labor dispute. At the bank's 1984 stockholders meeting, FLOC supporters threatened to boycott the bank if it failed to pressure Campbell to permit farm workers to vote in union elections. In addition, FLOC supporters leafleted branches of the bank. Volunteers conducted door-to-door canvassing to petition Philadelphia National Bank to remove or accept the resignation of McGovern as a director of the bank. In April 1985 more than 100 FLOC supporters demonstrated at a Philadelphia National Bank stockholders meeting, publicizing the conditions of farm labor under contract with Campbell. No policy changes were made, however, either at the meeting or subsequently by the bank.

Prudential Life Insurance Company was also targeted in FLOC's corporate campaign. The chair of Prudential's board, Robert Beck, was a member of the Campbell board of directors as well as the overseer of a $40 million pension fund for Campbell. The campaign culminated in July 1985 when FLOC supporters presented a statement signed by 100 union officials, community leaders, and clergy at Prudential headquarters in Newark, New Jersey, urging Beck to use his influence as a member of the Campbell board of directors to bring about a resolution of the farm labor dispute and to resign as a Campbell director if an agreement was not reached.

Although neither the Philadelphia National Bank nor the Prudential Life campaigns resulted in any policy changes, FLOC officials and supporters could point to the additional publicity for the boycott. Also, there were indications that Campbell was experiencing some pressure and was increasingly concerned about its corporate image. By the end of 1984 Campbell protested in its defense that it had been willing to negotiate all along—somewhat of a shift from past statements. In fact, secret negotiations between FLOC and Campbell began early in 1985 during the middle of FLOC's corporate campaign.

The second component of the organizations campaign, obtaining endorsements for the Campbell boycott, was more successful. Endorsements by church-related organizations included those by the Ohio and Indiana Council of Churches, several Catholic archdioceses in Ohio and Michigan, the Illinois Catholic Bishops, the Episcopal Diocese of Ohio, the National Conference of Catholic Charities, and several commissions and councils of the United Church of Christ, the Disciples of Christ, the United Methodist Church, and the American Friends Service Committee. A number of state and local political and civic organizations also endorsed the boycott. The AFL-CIO, however, declined to recommend that its member unions boycott Campbell products as it had done for the UFW table-grape and head-lettuce boycotts during the mid-1970s. Still, a number of unions and state federations did endorse the Campbell boycott, including the state AFL-CIO affiliates in Ohio and Indiana. More than 200 religious, labor, and other organizations formally endorsed FLOC's goals or the boycott of Campbell products. In addition, FLOC estimated that 1,200 public and private schools dropped participation in Campbell's "collect the labels" program in support of the boycott.

A critical endorsement came in June 1985 when the Ohio Catholic Bishops issued a press release supporting the Campbell boycott and urging all Catholic schools and hospitals in Ohio not to buy products from Campbell Soup Company. In their statement the bishops pointed out the necessity of including the processor in any negotiations, as processors like Campbell set the economic realities of both growers and farm workers and acted as an "indirect employer" of farm workers.

Campbell's response to the bishops' press release was swift but misleading. The following day Campbell leaked information to the press and church groups that it had reached an agreement with FLOC. This was limited, however, to the formation of a commission chaired by John Dunlop, former U.S. secretary of labor and a professor at Harvard. Some observers felt that Campbell was attempting to offset negative publicity from the Ohio bishops' recommendations as well as making it appear as if the boycott was over. Nevertheless, the formation of the commission was a significant step forward, and the commission proved instrumental in facilitating subsequent agreements. Its eight members were given the tasks of overseeing secret ballot elections for union recognition, assisting in contract negotiations if workers voted for union recognition, and serving as an arbitration board in the event of unresolved negotiating issues. In effect, the commission had many of the same functions as the ALRB in California, but without legislative authority. While some viewed the formation of the Dunlop Commission as the resolution of the dispute, the agreement did not require Campbell to enter negotiations with FLOC and the growers or be bound by an agreement between the growers and harvesters. Even growers were not strictly obliged to negotiate with FLOC.

FLOC quickly petitioned for elections on 28 farms in Ohio and Michigan. The Dunlop Commission conducted elections during the last week of August 1985 on seven cucumber and 13 tomato farms in northwest Ohio. These farms were all contracted to Campbell or Vlasic Foods, a Campbell subsidiary that produces and markets pickles. Results released by the Dunlop Commission showed that more than 60 percent of the cucumber workers voted for FLOC. No announcement was made on the tomato elections because the results were challenged before the commission by FLOC, which submitted more than 40 charges of unfair labor practices. These included claims of harassing FLOC staff and intimidating FLOC supporters, hiring local residents the day before the election to provide anti-FLOC votes, and denying voting rights to regular harvest workers. After the elections there was little progress toward contract negotiations. FLOC continued to pursue its boycott of Campbell products and sought additional boycott endorsements while hoping for a settlement with Campbell under the aegis of the Dunlop Commission.

The breakthrough came early in 1986. The executive committee of the National Council of Churches was scheduled to vote on an endorsement of the Campbell boycott in February 1986, and observers expected the endorsement to be passed. The National Council of Churches represented the largest national interdenominational Protestant organization, and its endorsement of the boycott would have had far more significance than any of the previous endorsements. Two days before the vote was to be taken Campbell, FLOC, and the Campbell Tomato Growers' Association signed a three-year contract. Almost certainly the timing of the agreement reflected Campbell's interest in avoiding the negative publicity that would have resulted from a boycott endorsement by the Protestant organization.

With the Dunlop Commission as mediator, Campbell entered agreements with FLOC covering 400 farm workers on 20 tomato farms around Toledo. Campbell also entered into agreements with approximately 400 cucumber workers on 12 Michigan farms on behalf of its subsidiary, Vlasic Foods. The contracts provided a precedent for three-party agreements among processors, growers, and farm workers. They included a wage increase up to $4.50 per hour and provided major medical and hospitalization insurance, a grievance procedure, one paid holiday, two paid union representatives, and establishment of study committees to discuss pesticide use, housing, health care, safety, and day care programs. Union dues of 2.5 percent of earnings were to be paid to FLOC. Also, farm workers who were tomato strikers from 1978 could receive compensation from Campbell of up to $2,000 per family. The contracts ended seven years of FLOC-sponsored strikes and boycotts.

The day after the Campbell contracts were signed, representatives of Heinz U.S.A., another major purchaser of tomatoes and cucumbers in Northwest Ohio, announced that the company was willing to begin contract negotiations with FLOC, thus avoiding a probable FLOC-sponsored boycott of Heinz products. Contracts similar to those with Campbell were reached in June 1987.

FLOC did experience considerable difficulty in obtaining contracts covering cucumber farms contracted to Vlasic. Animosity toward the union was considerable among a number of Vlasic growers. Some refused to recognize the election results from 1985, and others simply would not allow supervised elections on their farms. The union claimed that particular growers intimidated its organizers, threatened workers if they talked to organizers, and took reprisals against some who publicly supported FLOC. After FLOC signed three-year contracts covering harvesters on cucumber farms contracted to Heinz in April 1987, however, many of the Vlasic growers followed by signing similar contracts that August. Contracts with several other growers brought the number of workers under FLOC contracts to 3,300 by the 1989 harvest season.

After the Heinz and Vlasic signings FLOC began negotiations with Dean Foods Company, another major purchaser of cucumbers for its subsidiary Aunt Jane's Pickles. In a Dunlop Commission–supervised election, 72 percent of Dean Foods' field workers voted for FLOC representation. The subsequent contracts covered 1,200 workers.

The sharecropping arrangement for cucumber harvesters was a major negotiating issue in FLOC's renewal of its contract with cucumber growers who sold their produce to Heinz in 1990. The subsequent three-party agreement effectively signaled the end to the sharecropping arrangements between cucumber growers and harvesters in Ohio and Michigan—a major achievement for the union. From then on workers would have the legal status of employee and have their worker's compensation, unemployment insurance, and Social Security paid for by their employers, in this case Heinz U.S.A. Sharecropping arrangements were to be completely phased out by the end of 1993. The sharecropper status of migrant workers was also being challenged in the courts by reform groups acting on behalf of migrants. In 1990 the California Supreme Court ruled that migrant workers are indeed employees, and similar suits were being filed in other states. By the 1991 harvest season FLOC contracts covered more than 5,000 workers. As of the early 1990s, most observers believe that FLOC will eventually sign contracts with Hunt-Wesson (Hunt's) and Stokely U.S.A., the two remaining major processors in the tomato and cucumber industries.

The importance of FLOC's contracts is not limited to better wages—in fact, the potential for mechanization places limits on gains in income. Perhaps more significant are achievements that give workers greater job security, protection from dismissal without adequate cause, and channels for filing grievances. Also, recent interviews with workers under contracts and FLOC officials suggest that intangible benefits have accompanied the formal achievements. Farm workers are more likely to speak out and file complaints if they think their rights under the contracts have been violated. Some of this is facilitated by the presence of camp representatives selected jointly by their harvest crews and FLOC, whose responsibilities include monitoring the implementation of the contracts and initiating procedures for grievances brought to their attention. Also, field representatives from FLOC are involved in contract administration. As a result, growers and crew leaders are less likely to disregard the rights of workers. In general workers have become more self-confident and assertive, aware that they have the ability to influence the conditions of their work and lives (Barger and Reza 1994; Lopez 1990).

Such three-party agreements—virtually unique in American labor relations—may additionally set an important precedent. They might not only become models for other agricultural industries but also be applicable outside agriculture. Currently, many unionized corporations contract out for products and services with smaller nonunion companies, and this trend has been rapidly growing as corporations relentlessly strive to reduce production costs. Corporations can claim that they bear no responsibility for the wages, working conditions, or job security of employees of these firms. When major corporations sign three-party contracts they tacitly admit that the welfare of workers providing them goods—although technically employed by someone else—is dependent on the terms they themselves dictate.

FLOC's eventual goal is to organize farm workers along the migration paths that lead to fall harvests in the upper Midwest. The union periodically has sent organizers to Florida and Texas both to elicit support for FLOC when the workers are in Ohio and Michigan and to assess what might be done to improve situations in other states. Also, North Carolina has become a target for the union's campaign to end sharecropping arrangements for migrant harvest workers. Meanwhile, FLOC celebrated its twenty-fifth anniversary in December 1992, and the union has been recognized by *Washington Monthly* magazine as one of the "best" unions in the nation. In fact, FLOC president Baldemar Velasquez was awarded a MacArthur Foundation fellowship "genius grant" of $265,000 in 1989.

But for all its achievements, FLOC remains a small organization with limited resources. In the context of the diminishing strength of organized labor on the national level, FLOC will be fortunate to keep its existing contracts, sign agreements with the remaining large processors for Ohio and Michigan produce, and stimulate modest changes elsewhere. The difficulty for the union is that it is under pressure to organize an entire industry. There is always the possibility that one or several processors will contract growers in other states or in other countries such as Mexico in order to reduce their costs. In fact, FLOC claims that Campbell issued it an ultimatum to either attain similar contracts among tomato growers in other states or face the possibility of losing tomato contracts in the upper Midwest.

The trajectories of farm labor movements have differed dramatically during the 1980s and early 1990s. In California farm labor unions historically found it exceedingly difficult to get contract renewals, especially when the pressures generated by strikes, boycotts, and public attention that led to initial contracts dissipated. The UFW was no exception to this pattern, as the union lost contracts, members, and influence throughout the decade. By contrast, FLOC achieved precedent-setting three-party contracts that hold an "indirect employer" partially responsible for the wages, working conditions, and living circumstances of migrant harvesters. The difference between the situations of these two unions perhaps is best symbolized by the ease with which FLOC signed contract renewals with both Campbell and Heinz and their respective growers in 1988 and 1989 and again with Campbell in 1993 and Heinz in 1994. The newer contracts with Campbell included field sanitation facilities and pesticide protections. They also stipulated that only people 15 years and older could be employed, formally eliminating child labor in operations covered by FLOC contracts. Ninety-seven percent of 2,000 workers on 52 farms voted to accept the new contract. The 1994 contracts with Heinz will run until 1998 and include a 22 percent pay increase for preharvest work implemented incrementally, bringing the hourly wage up to $5.15 in 1998. These contract renewals and the gains they achieved may represent a major step toward institutionalization of farm labor unionization in the upper Midwest if the processors keep contracting small growers in the region. A further indication of FLOC's stability is that it was scheduled to receive its charter from the AFL-CIO at FLOC's convention in July 1994, marking its formal affiliation with labor organization.

Differences between the UFW and FLOC

There are several patterns that account for the differences between FLOC's successes and the UFW's failures during the 1980s and early 1990s. These differences are structural, historical, strategic, and organizational. First, the structure of agricultural production in the Midwest is fundamentally different from that in California. The situation in the Midwest is conducive to a successful bargaining among three parties. Smaller growers would like to command higher prices for their products from food processors as well as have a more regularized schedule of production. Migrant workers would benefit considerably from better guarantees of employment from one year to the next and from higher wages as a result of higher prices paid smaller growers for their produce. Finally, large food corporations and processors have considerable stake in preserving a positive corporate image and are used to dealing with unions.

During the Campbell boycott a number of growers understood potential benefits of a trilateral agreement. Taking a pragmatic approach, these growers cooperated with attempts to resolve the dispute between FLOC and Campbell. Once the trilateral agreements were signed, growers were assured of contracts with a processor for three years instead of the usual one. Although other growers continue to resist unionization, arguing that workers are contented and paid well, most who have agreements have been quite cooperative with the process, especially in comparison with California growers. Growers covered by FLOC contracts are guaranteed a more stable and experienced work force.

According to Heinz figures, cucumber productivity has increased over 40 percent under the FLOC contracts. Also, many growers have worked with FLOC to improve housing and field conditions. In fact, FLOC's campaign necessitated the organization of tomato and cucumber growers into associations in order to negotiate agreements with the large processors. Under the agreements growers did not have to fear that costs from worker or union demands—for improved housing, for example—would be borne solely by themselves. More rational recruiting methods and grievance-resolution procedures and steady increases in wages and benefits have resulted in a lower level of overt conflict between individual workers and growers, making for a smoother, more predictable harvest. Much of the hostility of the strike years has largely disappeared. In fact, the president of the Campbell Tomato Growers' Association, Wally Wagner, has publicly supported much of FLOC's agenda.

For their part, the major food corporations realize the importance of a positive corporate image in selling easily identifiable products. This concern over legitimacy seemed to be the major reason that Campbell decided to initiate negotiations with FLOC. Even FLOC officials admit that the boycott probably had not hurt Campbell economically.[18] But the negative publicity generated by FLOC's campaigns needed to be confronted. When Campbell's strategy of claiming not to be a party in the dispute failed to be convincing, the corporation took the reasonable step of bargaining a resolution that would best preserve its corporate image.

By contrast, many of the largest California growers are also processors. There is not the clear division between growers and processors as there is in much of the Midwest. Also, relatively few of the Californian grower-processors who have been the targets of UFW campaigns have readily identifiable products. Therefore, boycotts of a fruit or vegetable, such as head lettuce or table grapes, is the logical consequence. One result is that UFW boycotts needed to have a *signif icant* economic impact before growers would negotiate. Because a generic product and not a corporate name is being boycotted, corporate image usually is not relevant. The exceptions have been when major food corporations were involved. For example Sun Harvest, a subsidiary of United Brands, broke ranks with other growers and negotiated a contract with the UFW during the 1979 strike, largely because of its concern over a proposed boycott of its Chiquita line of fruits. By contrast, tainting an entire product with a negative image—for example, grapes with worker exploitation and pesticide poisoning—has proved more difficult, and during the latest boycott this strategy was not very effective.

A second pattern that accounts for FLOC's successes and the UFW's failures is that midwestern agriculture does not have the history of acrimonious labor relations that has polarized the different sides in California for most of this century. Although we have concentrated on the 1930s and the UFW period, large growers have also strenuously opposed organizing efforts by both Japanese and Anglo-American workers during the first two decades of this century and several attempts at unionization during the bracero era. The long history of prejudice and discriminatory legislation in California aimed at Asians and Mexicans has coincided with the interest of growers in keeping labor costs low and workers under their control. By the time the UFW became the latest of a number of agricultural labor unions in California, the lines of conflict had long since been drawn. By contrast, the lack of long-standing polarization in midwestern agriculture meant that FLOC could seek potential allies in some of the small growers. Also, FLOC has avoided much of the inflammatory rhetoric that the UFW sometimes used. In fact, FLOC has publicly praised Campbell and Heinz for their help in ending sharecropping arrangements and has appeared willing to discuss ways to preserve the economic health of the industry with the processors and growers.

A third difference is that legislative involvements have been avoided in the Midwest. In contrast, legislation in California that established a government agency to supervise and certify union elections has provided just another battleground. In fact, the struggle between agricultural labor and capital simply changed focus, from the fields and supermarkets to the legislative and legal arenas. The ALRA has not proved to be able to resolve the long-standing dispute as many of its supporters had hoped. While the Dunlop Commission provides some of the same functions as the ALRA, it is a private body, not as open to political pressure such as withholding operating funds. More importantly, the Dunlop Commission has been called on only infrequently to settle disputes.

Finally, there is an important difference in the trajectory of both organizations. FLOC has so far avoided the debilitating internal conflicts and abrupt departure of talented organizers and staff that have plagued the UFW. The fact that FLOC's staff is small in number and the union's achievements modest by comparison may account for the relative lack of debilitating internal conflict. But differences in leadership styles may also have contributed to FLOC's avoidance of the kind of internal crisis that decimated the UFW.

Discussion and Conclusions

The difference between the UFW's and FLOC's strategies revolves around the fact that the external resources needed to run a grass-roots consumer boycott were no longer available by the time FLOC began its boycott. A national grass-roots campaign requires a huge staff. In the case of the UFW, this staff was largely volunteer, comprising individuals with roots mostly outside farm labor, the largest category being college students. Because it consisted of volunteers, the staff primarily found its rewards through solidarity: identification with and participation in a cause in which members firmly believed. A similar number of such individuals was not available for mobilization by FLOC.

Also needed was some indication that grass-roots boycott efforts would be received in ways that translated into tangible results. In studies of social movements it is axiomatic that a liberal political climate fosters liberal movements and a conservative political climate fosters conservative ones. Perhaps the national political climate during the 1980s was not as explicitly conservative as many analysts suggest, but it was certainly politically apathetic. Appeals to even minimal forms of social commitment were not so much overtly opposed as they were ignored by a large proportion of the population. This situation made it difficult for FLOC to continue putting all its emphasis on a grass-roots boycott effort aimed at hurting Campbell enough financially to convince the corporation to change its policies.

A comparison of these two successful episodes of agricultural labor unionization support the general conclusions of Tilly (1978), among others. Social movement success is frequently related to the ability of protesting groups to build political alliances with groups who either can exercise decisive influence or can make moral claims on behalf of their members. Influence over the polity is crucial in the long run. For example, the UFW was successful when it was in a position to influence legislation and its implementation. But FLOC's successes during the 1980s also suggest that advances for progressive movements are possible in conservative political climates when the protesting group understands the limits of mass protests during such periods and is carefully reflective about opportunities and strategies. When insurgents are particularly selective about the targets of protests, they can apply the kinds of pressure that would convince elites that it is in their interest to alter prevailing practices.

Conclusion

Continuities in Farmer and Farm Worker Movements

The preceding chapters have covered a wide range of American history. As we have seen, agriculture in the late twentieth century entails a vastly different complex of social, economic, and political relationships than it did in its origins as a European colonial enterprise. Nevertheless, in this concluding chapter we would also like to explore some possible linkages across the history, regions, and classes that have been discussed in this book. Given the great transformation of agriculture during the period covered, we may expect that historical continuity, regional similarities, and the intersection of class interests will provide insight into some essential qualities of agrarian mobilization. We must also continue to recognize the discontinuities, dissimilarities, and distinct class interests that have tended to be our focus. This approach will provide a point of departure for additional speculation on the directions that agrarian social movements may take in the near future.

Both farmer and farm worker movements have primarily centered on economic issues. This is not surprising since the occupational categories of farmer and farm worker are, after all, economic in nature. In this limited sense farmer movements and farm worker movements can be seen as class-based. At the same time these two occupational categories represent different classes. Farmer movements represent a defense of simple commodity or petit bourgeois production—that is, independent ownership and control of one's means of production such as land and machinery. Farm workers represent other levels of the working class, usually part of the working poor. Neither group seems able to claim strong allies among the rest of their class. Farmers, in fact, often find themselves in conflicts of economic interest with other petit bourgeoisie, from whom they must purchase goods or services. Farm workers have recently found allies in organized labor, but this has come only in recent decades after many previous decades when neglect and sometimes exclusion had been the norm. The low wages and lack of labor law protection for agricultural workers reflects not only the opposition by large growers and agribusiness corporations but also the historically weak support that farm workers have had from the working class as a whole.

While we can recognize a class base for both farmer and farm worker movements, their common economic situation is not sufficient to generate mobilization. One reason might be a lack of consciousness of themselves as groups whose interests were being opposed by more powerful groups. For example, Marx, in his well-known analysis of the French peasantry, held that although the peasants constituted a common class situation at the level of economy, there was insufficient consciousness among them for unifying or mobilizing themselves to collective action in pursuit of their common interests. Instead, at least the conservative segment of the peasantry was dominated ideologically by clerics and persuaded to support the national chauvinism of the regimes of both Napoleon and Louis Bonaparte.

While neither farmers nor farm workers are particularly good examples of contemporary counterparts of Marx's analysis of the French peasantry, perhaps a similar lack of understanding of their collective situations by American farmers and farm workers may account for some periods of passivity or misdirected efforts. What is more prominent in their social histories are the ways that both farmers and farm workers have acted in pursuit of their class interests. In becoming insurgents, both groups have embraced ideologies that recognize that each of their shared interests is thwarted or threatened by existing institutional arrangements. McAdam (1982) calls this realization "cognitive liberation." Recent social movement theorists have suggested that a coherent ideology among an insurgent group is particularly important to preserve the unity of a social movement (e.g., McNall 1988; Snow and Benford 1988; Schwartz 1976).

Farmer Movement Ideologies

Carl C. Taylor's *The Farmers' Movement, 1620–1920* (1953) is based on the provocative hypothesis that there is a single, unitary farmer movement (analogous to the labor movement) throughout U.S. history. He focuses on ideology as the "glue" that holds this movement together. Taylor's thesis raises specific questions concerning the role of ideology with respect to both the class basis and historical continuity of agrarian mobilization. What ideologies permit the development of an analysis that suggests a common struggle against capital, or a class basis to the economic and political problems of farmers' everyday lives? What ideologies persist such that participants recognize and learn from common historical experiences in agrarian struggles against landlords, bankers, merchants, and so forth? We turn now to a brief examination of Taylor's thesis as a means of considering these questions.

Taylor's study is one of the few attempts to review the history of farmer movements in the United States. More significantly, Taylor hypothesized a continuity that links these various farmer movements to one another. Indeed, Taylor contends that "the various farmer revolts have only been the high tides of a Farmer Movement which is as persistent as the Labor Movement" (1953, 2). His thesis stands out against a literature that is primarily oriented toward analysis of each episode of agrarian mobilization as distinct. Taylor defends his position by arguing that it is a movement insofar as it has been "a continuous, and probably a progressive, adaptation to economic and cultural situations" (1953, 499). This progress and continuity is based in the development of "ideologies and philosophies which buttressed the farmers' opinions and sentiments about these conditions" (1953, 499).

Taylor's analysis of the farmer movement as grounded in ideologies that interpret the political economy is strikingly similar to Zald and McCarthy's more contemporary use of the concept social movement to broadly denote "a set of opinions and beliefs" in favor of social change (1987, 20). Indeed, Taylor concludes that the farmer movement "is not so much a social structure as it is a body of ideologies and sentiments about a continuing set of issues" (1953, 499). Taylor is less clear about the content of such ideology, other than to contend that the philosophical development of the Farmer Movement was a "progressive" adaptation to an increasingly commercialized agriculture.

Instead, his thesis requires greater specificity concerning the substance of the ideology in order to demonstrate a continuous farmer movement.

From our discussion of the history of farmer movements we can identify at least three particularly resilient ideologies or "master frames" (Snow and Benford 1988) that have guided collective action. One is "agrarian fundamentalism," the belief that the larger economy—and sometimes even the polity—are dependent on agricultural prosperity. This ideology has been remarkably persistent, in part because it has appeared to be validated by the experience of rural people, especially in times of economic crisis. As we have discussed, this ideology recently appeared with considerable potency in the collective actions associated with the farm crisis of the 1980s. Agrarian fundamentalism does not, however, by itself lend to the perception of class-based antagonism. The development of class consciousness is, rather, distorted and obscured by its focus on a status (farm/nonfarm) difference.

Similarly, a second common farmer ideology of "competitive capitalism" cannot directly enhance class consciousness. Indeed, the farmers' lack of concrete experience with truly competitive markets tends to invert this ideology into a sort of immanent critique, an "injustice frame" (Gamson et al. 1982) that is then fragmented into two critical frameworks—an anti-state intervention ideology and an anti-monopoly capital ideology (see Mooney and Hunt 1994). The complexities of this inversion, fragmentation, and subsequent realignment of competitive capitalist ideology make it difficult to argue for the continuity of this ideology as an effective analysis guiding a farmer movement.

Perhaps only a "producer" ideology that sees all economic rewards as the rightful due of direct producers has the consistent material basis to provide continuity between various movements. The producer ideology is capable of abstraction and generalization to diverse historical conditions. It repeatedly finds both fertile material conditions (e.g., tenancy, indebtedness, merchant or processor domination) and other complementary popular ideologies over a long historical period. The producer ideology, in what Rude (1980) calls its "derived" or theoretical form (i.e., the labor theory of value), has broad historical and regional applicability by claiming relevance to class society. A producer ideology that saw both farmers and workers as commodity producers and viewed capital as their common opponent has been the basis for maintenance of repeated attempted alliances between these classes. Furthermore, the interaction of the producer ideology with agrarian fundamentalism or the critical forms of competitive capitalist ideology can create potent frameworks inspiring mobilization around specific analyses.

We have argued that the farmer movement is historically divided by an alternation of political and economic strategies. This, too, is no different from the labor movement, where political resources are sometimes more useful than economic ones. Taylor seems to be partially correct in attributing the continuity in the movement to its ideologies rather than particular organizations and specific goals. Movement ideologies have often interacted to link diverse economic and political strategies over time. The emergence of a single farmer movement was impeded, however, by the relative absence of any potent ideology claiming that theirs was an inevitable future. In fact, their experience has been the opposite. As soon as feudalism was overthrown, the promise of simple commodity production was overtaken by other forms of capitalism. Simple commodity producers enjoyed a brief moment of hope in the New World, but even Jefferson's vision was probably more wishful thinking than reality. That vision remained out of reach as tenancy and indebtedness continued to dominate agriculture, while the ranks of hired workers swelled and competitive capitalism gave way to monopoly capitalism.

The movement is also divided by farmers' variable relationships with capitalist production. At any given moment, capitalist practices involving, for example, rent, credit, contract production, off-farm employment, or the use of hired labor generate different economic, political, and ideological strategies and tactics. The internal division among farmers along such lines as income, net worth, prestige, and political power also promotes diversity in political action. Similarly, the constant transformation of large-scale capitalist enterprises through expansion, technological innovation, stagnation, and reactions to crises requires continuous adaptation of class strategies, tactics, and analysis. Each mobilization takes on a distinct character that reflects interactions between a particular period's economic, political, and ideological constructions. The interaction between simple commodity and other capitalist production constantly changes. All of these conditions pose major barriers to our discovery of continuity in the class practices of simple commodity producers in their struggles against capital over any extended length of time.

Some threads of continuity are discernible, however. Within many of these movements there has been a cohesive core of participants who share in the vision of a cooperative economics and a democratic politics. The connection between farmer movements may derive from a producer ideology that is grounded in the material relations of agricultural production. Tenancy and indebtedness, for example, tend to reveal, rather than obscure, exploitation in production. Each mobilization varies in the extent to which it is receptive to a core movement subculture. The resilience of this subculture rests on its material grounding in continuous forms of exploitation, its internal coherence, its relative compatibility with labor movements, and its incompatibility with monopoly capital.

To the extent that there is, as Taylor argues, a farmer movement that is analogous to a labor movement, it is perhaps in the beginnings of successful formal cooperation that we find continuity, when an "organizational learning" is taking place. Here various participants in the movement learn from the mistakes of past efforts at cooperation, gradually adapting their actions to the ever-changing political economy farmers face. For example, cooperative services and marketing do provide a thread by which we can follow the development of a number of major farmer organizations. The Farmers' Alliance, the Farmers' Union, and the Farm Bureau, as well as numerous cooperatives that market agricultural commodities, are among the more significant organizations that have built on the cooperative experiments of the Grange. It was often the case, however, that the strategy of economic cooperation was harnessed by elites to reproduce existing inequalities. For example, patronage refunds were tied to the volume of business transacted, and management practices that were indistinct from those in private-sector, capitalist enterprises were adopted.

Thus what was sometimes presented as a revolutionary strategy for the development of agrarian (and petit bourgeois) socialism was coopted by elites into a reform movement that no longer threatened capitalist hegemony. The notion of a cooperative form of social organization has, however, been a vision that has inspired various experiments throughout agrarian history. Extending Taylor's argument, one might contend that formal cooperation among simple commodity producers is the functional equivalent of the working-class trade union. That some cooperative organizations have been more bureaucratic than democratic or manipulated toward politically conservative ends is perhaps not much different from corporate cooptations of some labor unions.

Farm Worker Movement Ideologies

While the class position of agricultural labor is more clear-cut than that of farmers, farm workers have been a diverse group, both by race/ethnicity and national origins/citizenship status. On the one hand, farm worker movements need to be understood as part of the larger labor movement. They are part of the larger working class, although occupying one of its lowest levels, at least as measured by income and job stability. A substantial part of their goals is simply better pay and working conditions, and there are few groups in American society who are more deserving. Most farm labor movements have attempted to form unions, either independent ones or affiliates of a national union or the AFL-CIO, and have attempted to bargain collectively with their employers.

But this understanding by itself is not sufficient. For farm labor movements have also tended to be movements of immigrants, usually recent ones. This has been particularly true on the West Coast, as one immigrant group after another—from Chinese, Japanese, and Asian Indians to Filipinos and Mexicans, among others—have attempted to improve their lives collectively. In addition, the experiences and circumstances of white migrants from the Dust Bowl during the 1930s in California were more similar to those of Mexican and Filipino farm workers than to other whites.

The minority status of most farm workers, whether or not they happen to be U.S. citizens, adds another dimension to their movements. As a consequence, farm worker movements have important similarities to the civil rights movement. Both these movements recognized the importance for their constituency of being treated with dignity and respect and recognized as fully capable and worthy human beings. These forms of "empowerment" would increase self-respect and instill the courage necessary to take a stand against degrading and humiliating situations. The rhetoric of various farm labor movements echoes these sentiments and suggests that the desire for inclusion into the mainstream of American social institutions was part of the participants' understanding of the meaning of their activism. In fact, the UFW grew out of the civil rights movement, and Chavez himself was previously an organizer for a community action agency focused on empowering Mexicans and Mexican Americans. Similar to the civil rights movement, farm labor leaders and organizations frequently have invoked religious symbols to emphasize the legitimacy of their cause, and church organizations and clergy members have often come to the support of the movements.

One of the ways in which the dual emphasis on economic gains on the one hand and full participation and self-determination on the other is manifested is in the central role of "control issues" for most farm labor movements. A major continuity from one period of insurgency to the next has been in terms of the presence of "control issues" (Majka and Majka 1982; L. Majka 1981). These issues are those that go beyond wage demands and instead seek qualitative changes in work relationships. Some changes may involve economic costs for growers, such as providing fresh drinking water and field toilets, without yielding direct economic advantages to workers. But at their most basic, "control issues" have attempted to give workers and their organizations more autonomous power to influence employment and working conditions, more dignity and self-determination for employees and their representatives.

The specifics of control issues vary from one period and movement to another. Without being exhaustive or detailed, control issues for farm workers have included the abolition of the labor contractor system that places workers in extraordinary dependency on individual contractors; improvements in job safety, particularly with respect to use of pesticides; changes in timing of work and the rate of production that has often been used by employers to victimize older workers; changes in the types of tools and equipment used, such as the banning of the short-handled hoe; changes in hiring practices and guaranteed seniority; and improvements in meals and sanitary conditions in the labor camps.

These and similar goals have been taken up by diverse farm labor organizations and movements. Various ethnic associations acted as labor agents for Asian farm workers, most notably Japanese immigrants during the early decades of this century. These organizations often tried to obtain "closed shop" conditions in negotiations with growers and thereby gain some degree of job security and seniority for their members. The Industrial Workers of the World (IWW) active during the 1910s in California and midwestern agriculture agitated for better sanitary conditions in labor camps and improved food for workers. During the early 1930s CAWIU sought election of rank-and-file worker committees to negotiate with growers, preferential hiring of union members, rehiring of union members and strikers without discrimination, and hiring free of racial and ethnic discrimination. Around the same time, the Confederacion de Uniones Obreras Mexicanas struggled for job preference for its members and arbitration of disputes. Later in the decade two other unions took up control issues. UCAPAWA sought job stewards in each field, drinking water at the job site, rehiring strikers without discrimination, the end of lockouts and discrimination against union members, and a closed-shop agreement. Finally, the Filipino Agricultural Labor Association (FALA) pushed for closed-shop agreements, reinstatement of strikers without discrimination, seniority rights for its members, and job preference for the next year's harvest.

The UFW developed control issues to their broadest point for agricultural workers. In fact, most of the changes the union sought revolved around nonwage issues. The most significant of these were the replacement of the labor contractor system with a union or joint union-grower "hiring hall" that would help give job security and seniority to longtime farm workers; restriction of pesticide use by ensuring that state and federal laws were enforced and even instituting stricter controls in some cases; establishment of arbitration when labor-displacing mechanization was to be introduced; and election of union representatives to handle implementation of union contracts and disputes at individual agricultural operations. That the union had difficulty implementing some of these reforms does not take away from the overall direction of the changes sought. Finally, FLOC has achieved the elimination of sharecropping where it has contracts and even indirectly "empowered" small growers through the three-party negotiations with major processors. Rhetoric by both the UFW and FLOC has emphasized farm worker self-determination as the purpose behind much of the changes sought.

Control issues appear to play a role similar to that of cooperative organizations in farmer movements in two ways. First, they provide continuity from one movement to the next so that we may be able to speak of a farm worker movement that encompasses various periods of insurgency, agricultural regions, and ethnicity and nationality of participants. Second, control issues seek to rearrange power (institutional) relationships in ways that give farm workers and their organization some influence over conditions of work and employment beyond that of income. Similarly, many cooperative organizations among farmers sought to bypass or balance the prevailing arrangements that gave the dominant positions to large economic enterprises, such as processing companies, banks, railroads, and farm implement and seed companies. Both kinds of agrarian movements have been nurtured by visions of democratic changes in institutional arrangements, whether or not they always acted consistently with this ideal.

The difficulty has been that successes of farm labor movements have been of rather short duration. In addition, as fitting their immigrant character, farm labor insurgency also has been symbolically concerned with achieving greater assimilation into the larger society as well as the ability to move on to better positions. Many of those in agricultural work a decade ago in California are no longer there. Some have left involuntarily, replaced by machines, chemicals, newer immigrants, or nonunion workers. Many have been mobile out of agriculture, however, as farm labor was seen as a transitory phase, necessary perhaps to get a niche before moving on to more desirable, and better paying, jobs. The temporary gains made through grower concessions and unionization provided some with enough economic cushion to get out of farm labor. And even for those permanent residents who make a career of agricultural labor, not many of their children appear to seek the same occupational route. These results may not have been what farm labor unions intended, but during those periods when these movements achieved substantial gains their constituency became better equipped, both economically and psychologically, for mobility to more desirable situations. The tragedy is that periods of real opportunity have tended to be brief, as grower intransigence still condemns most farm workers to lives full of hardships.

Future Prospects

Unless the U.S. should suddenly move toward the development of a coherent and comprehensive farm or rural development policy, we should expect that the specific commodity organizations (e.g., National Corn Growers Association, American Dairy Association, National Pork Producers Council, etc.) and agribusiness enterprises and their organizations such as the American Farm Bureau will continue to have extraordinary influence on the political economy of U.S. agriculture. We might even suggest that commodity organizations have an organizational and political interest in maintaining this fragmented agricultural policy that deals with each commodity on its own (political) merits. In opposition to this, we may expect continued development of grass-roots mobilizations concerned with the total fabric of rural life and food consumption. Reflecting trends of the last two decades, these movements will be better described as rural, rather than agricultural, movements. Furthermore, it seems that the label "new social movement" will best fit these contemporary tendencies.

These movements will probably continue to receive resource support from certain cooperatives and from various churches. Coordination of their wide range of interests will, however, be problematic and perhaps only overcome by strong commitment to grassroots participatory democratic organization. Bureaucratic organizational forms often only serve to compartmentalize the various issues that do, in fact, overlap and interact with one another. Democratic forms, on the other hand, allow for the representation of whole persons whose lived experience synthesizes the various interest spheres, permitting a more realistic assessment of the total environment within which problems are located. This general demand for democratization is exemplified by more specific challenges to a similar compartmentalization promoted by agricultural science. Kloppenburg argues that solutions to problems at "the local system level" depend on those "who think in terms of whole farms, those whose experiences are of whole farms" (1991, 531)—that is, through farmers, rather than agricultural scientists. Similarly, Busch has suggested the need for a "democratization of the problem formation process" itself (1984, 310).

The environment within which this struggle takes place will continue to include two of the most powerful forces that have always shaped the political and economic structure of U.S. agriculture: world markets and new technology. Both of these forces, however, appear to be on the verge of rapid transformation. GATT and NAFTA both promise/threaten to "free" agricultural markets from traditional forms of protection given by many nations. U.S. farmers will find themselves having to compete with agricultural production systems around the world, many of which use cheap labor derived from semi-feudal conditions of widespread poverty and political repression of basic human rights. The farmers of the European Union have led the protest against such trends. Ironically, the summer of 1992 saw many North American farmers join European farmers in such protests against what is defined as a U.S.-led initiative to free agricultural markets through GATT. Regardless of the outcome of these specific negotiations, U.S. farmers will face a future marked by an increased pace in the development of global capital.

Farm labor movements historically have faced a rather porous border to the south. New immigrants, particularly those without proper documentation, have been a continual threat to take away jobs, as employers have used this option to undercut unionization efforts. Currently, large numbers of recent immigrants from Mexico and Central America in California's agricultural regions have replaced much of the UFW's former organizational base. Any new organizing efforts will have to convince these workers that unionization is in their interests—something made more difficult by the overabundance of people willing to work in the fields. In addition, growers can always raise the issue of price pressures from international competition in attempts to keep farm labor demands to a minimum. Even though some agribusiness enterprises might move their operations to Mexico or another country, however, it is difficult to imagine that their domestic niches will not be filled quickly by other growers.

Another force will be the impact of new technologies in genetic engineering or biotechnology. The possibilities here sometimes seem limited only by the human imagination and often appear to reflect science fiction drama. Yet the probabilities will be shaped by very real political and economic forces. The acquisition of genetic engineering firms by petrochemical corporations will undoubtedly give priority to biotechnologies that prove profitable for these interests (Kloppenburg 1988). Here farmers and consumers have a common interest in mobilizing to influence the direction of genetic engineering research in the public interest. We have already seen a precursor to this struggle in the alliance of farmers and consumers to oppose BGH. Along these lines, renewed attention is being given to the role of the land-grant colleges of agriculture in providing research support to the genetic engineering firms. These colleges and the USDA are again being asked (as they have for the past century) to become more accountable to the public, rather than to private interests.

The challenge of biotechnology may bring together opposition to multiple forms of domination (bureaucratic, monopoly capitalist, scientific) that coalesce in the production of what is accepted as the legitimate knowledge on which agriculture is based. Kloppenburg describes the mobilization of an activist network operating at the national level but also "most importantly, in countless local groups organized around a wide variety of issues of local concern" (1991, 521). This movement seeks to "transform the scientific and technical bases of agricultural production" and find "a great deal of support in growing popular disaffection with the continuing deterioration of the environment." Reflecting the stance of this movement, Kloppenburg advocates expanding the range of voices that have the power to speak authoritatively in the debate over the reconstruction of agriculture. Indeed, he favors using "local knowledge"—the "knowledge contained in the heads of farmers and agricultural workers"—in the formation of a "successor science" that would reverse the traditional flow of power and authority between producer and the agro-scientific complex (Kloppenburg 1991, 520).

Recent developments suggest a continued bifurcation of agrarian social movements. On the one hand, some organizations will pursue the narrow economic interests of agricultural commodity producers through traditional political behavior. The assumptions embedded in this tradition will lead not only to lobbying for favorable market policy on a commodity by commodity basis but also for continued application of science toward increased productivity in a world characterized by agricultural overproduction. On the other hand, postmaterialist values oppose the limited and narrow formal rationalities of the scientific, economic, and political spheres as forms of "bounded rationality" (Kitschelt 1985, 310). Alternative values can only be realistically pursued to the extent that technological development resolves the problem of scarcity. In agriculture, scarcity in food production is no longer a problem of the forces of production, only a consequence of the relations of production (Lappé and Collins 1982). In the advanced capitalist societies the "farm problem" has in fact long been one of overproduction. Opposition to the continued commercialization of social relations in the rural United States reflects the highly developed technical base of agriculture. In short, we are arguing that the bifurcation of agrarian social movements reflects more than the willingness of an "isolated" group of farm protest leaders to "press toward increasingly radical strategies" for "comprehensive rural policy reform" in spite of the high "transaction costs" associated with this break (Browne 1991, 30–31). Rather, this bifurcation is seen here as deeply grounded in the social structure of postindustrial society: specifically in the intersection of agriculture with the new social movements.

As Kitschelt argues, unless basic reforms take place, the present structure "erodes self-organized mutual aid systems and . . . furthers the administrative control of more life spheres" (1985, 277). Alternative rationalities would limit the priority of a formal rationality bounded by the market. There are many possible objectives for agriculture: the development of a sustainable, deep ecological relationship with the earth; the production of quality, healthy food; the building of nonhierarchical, democratic communities; nonpatriarchal familial relations; and so forth. The newer social movements in rural America reflect this orientation.

These new movements suggest a break with the continuity of Taylor's farmer movement by constructing a new body of ideology and sentiments about a new set of issues, beyond the modernization of agriculture. The principal organizing element of modern agriculture has been the principle of profit-maximization. Even the three master frames or ideologies we have discussed can be seen as grounded in this broader framework of modernity. But it is only in the privileged conditions of postindustrial society and postscarcity agriculture that the new social movements' demands for total emancipation can escape entrapment in the "iron cage" of market rationality.

In various ways the new social movements represent a break from the movement with which Taylor was familiar. That Movement remained within the logic or the sphere of modernity and for this reason receives most of the attention of scholars and journalists. A fundamental break with the past represented by these new movements requires wholly new approaches to assess the logic, efficacy, and role these movements may play in postindustrial society. At the moment, alternative sources of knowledge for the reconstruction of agriculture "have no voice, or speak without authority, or simply are not heard in contemporary agroscientific discourse" (Kloppenburg 1991, 52). Their distinctiveness may best be stated by contending that the newer agrarian social movements reflect the embryonic emergence of a postmodern agriculture.

Postscript

As this book was going to press, there was evidence that the UFW was on the verge of making a dramatic shift in its strategies. In late March 1994 the union embarked on a 24-day, 330-mile march-pilgrimage through the San Joaquin Valley's vineyards and orchards, ending in Sacramento on the first anniversary of Chavez's death. Reminiscent of the union's 1966 Delano to Sacramento march, its purpose was to reestablish contact with farm workers in the valley and initiate a renewed organizing campaign. Meanwhile, the table-grape boycott would receive less of the union's attention. The new head of the union, Arturo Rodriguez, claimed that the outlook for organizing was good, since many workers were dissatisfied with falling wages and various abuses by some growers and labor contractors. At the culminating rally at the state capitol, Rodriguez called on farm workers to help the union organize their ranches and on supporters to join in this effort—appeals reminiscent of Rodriguez's father-in-law Cesar Chavez's recruitment strategies during the 1960s and early 1970s.

If the UFW does have the resources and commitment to launch another major organizing campaign, the union will confront situations that are significantly different from those of the 1960s and 1970s. Throughout the 1980s political upheavals in Central America and economic dislocations in Mexico brought hundreds of thousands of new immigrants into California, and many took farm labor jobs. A significant proportion of them are undocumented. Typically, their financial positions are considerably more desperate than were those who formed the UFW's primary constituency among Mexican-American farm workers two decades earlier.

231

Immigration reform during the 1980s also may have stimulated increased immigration from Mexico and Central America, or at least did not deter it, as was its stated purpose. One of the provisions of the 1986 Immigration Reform and Control Act (IRCA) was the Seasonal Agricultural Worker Program (SAW) that permitted undocumented residents who had worked in agriculture for a minimum of 90 days between May 1985 and May 1986 to apply for legal status. Rather than stabilize the farm labor force, the SAW program stimulated a one-time increase in immigration by those who hoped to become legalized, and instead of reducing the proportion of undocumented workers in the fields, the opposite appears to have resulted (Zabin et al. 1993, 37–38) If the U.S.-Mexico border was porous before, it became even more so during the 1980s. Also, the controversial employer-sanction provisions of the IRCA so far have been ineffective in reducing employment of undocumented workers.

Among the new immigrants coming to California during the 1980s were large numbers of Mixtec Indians from Oaxaca and surrounding states in southern Mexico, not a traditional source of farm labor. Mixtec is an Aztec word that means "cloud people," and their name refers to their mountainous homeland. Estimates are that during the early 1990s Mixtecs coonstituted 5 to 10 percent of the farm labor force in California. Some Mixtecs speak little or no Spanish, and many are undocumented. As a group they have experienced greater impoverishment than other farm workers and are subject to ethnic prejudice and discrimination, sometimes by mestizo Mexicans (those of mixed European and Indian descent), because of their distinctive culture, language, and appearance. Similar to the impact of braceros four decades earlier, there is considerable evidence that the availability of Mixtecs has precipitated a wage decline for farm labor. Furthermore, in some agricultural operations Mexican Americans and mestizo Mexican nationals have been displaced or simply not rehired by growers and labor contractors who then employed the lower paid Mixtecs (Zabin et al. 1993, vii–viii, 59–122).

Changes in the labor force have made the farm worker population in California and elsewhere in the West more heterogeneous and more stratified. The traditional division among those of Mexican origin according to citizenship status and documentation has been further complicated by differences in ethnic background, length of time in the United States, and migration patterns. Hierarchies have become more visible, with Mixtecs tending to be the most exploited. These patterns confound the task of organizing—which is difficult even under the best conditions.

Along with U.S. farmers in general, California's agricultural industry faces stiffer competition from fruits, vegetables, and other agricultural products imported from Mexico and elsewhere, owing in large part to the greater internationalization of capital. Interestingly, many of the Mixtecs now in California initially migrated to northern Mexico to work in commercial agriculture. Because several major U.S. agribusiness firms have set up operations in Mexico, any California units they own are now in effect in competition with their Mexican ones. Whatever the source of competition, California growers who were used to having a virtual monopoly on many fruits and vegetables consumed in the United States have become particularly cost-conscious. This may be another underlying reason for the decline in agricultural wages during the 1980s and early 1990s.

This competition may make growers even more resistant to unionization. Although many growers fought unionization during previous decades, once it occurred, most agricultural operations passed on their increased labor costs with little impact on consumers. The current situation makes shifting increased production costs more difficult. For much of this century one had the sense that much of agribusiness's vehement resistance to unionization reflected to a considerable degree an ideological opposition and racism; in the future this may tilt more exclusively toward economic calculations, if it has not already. One dilemma for unions is that the larger operations that have tended toward a more sophisticated outlook regarding unions and have provided the UFW with many contract breakthroughs are more capable than smaller firms of moving their operations in the face of global competition.

Notes

1. See Herbert Aptheker's volume in the Social Movements Past and Present series, *Abolitionism: A Revolutionary Movement* (Boston: Twayne Publishers, 1988).

2. Daniel Shays of Pelham, Massachusetts, had been a captain in the Revolutionary War and was subsequently prosecuted for nonpayment of debt. While Shays served as leader of his local militia, he denied any leadership role in the rebellion, claiming that he was simply a member of a committee of the people (Szatmary 1980, 99). Our account of Shays' Rebellion draws primarily from Szatmary's (1980) excellent history of that farmer movement.

3. See Gene Clanton's volume in the Social Movements Past and Present series, *Populism: The Humane Preference in America, 1890–1900* (Boston: Twayne Publishers, 1989), for an in-depth analysis of this subject.

4. For our present purposes, the "new social movements" share the following characteristics. They have more to do with life-style or "consumption" issues rather than production per se. The civil rights movement, women's movement, peace movement, and environmental movement exemplify the "new social movements" distinction from the way in which such progressive movements were once considered to be derivative of or subordinate to the labor movement. The new social movements are characterized by an interest in focusing on change in society rather than channeling energy and resources into influencing the state. Such strategies are often grounded in a prefigurative fusion of means and ends and a principled, nonnegotiable orientation toward goal achievement.

5. While such production is not always subsidized in the same way that U.S. agriculture is subsidized, it must be recognized that the cheap labor input in certain other nations is effectively subsidized by the military repression of peasant movements aimed at improving their share of the product.

6. These films included, for example, *Country, Betrayed, The River,* and *Places in the Heart* (see Mullinax and Mooney [1991] for an analysis of these films).

7. In 1993 the National Family Farm Coalition included the American Agriculture Movement, Ag Price, California Action Network, California Association of Family Farmers, Citizen Action Coalition of Indiana, Committee on Rural Affairs (New York), Community Farm Alliance of Kentucky, Dakota Resource Council (North Dakota), Dakota Rural Action (South Dakota), Empire State Farm Alliance (New York), Farm Alliance of Rural Missouri, Federation of Southern Cooperatives, Groundswell (Minnesota), Idaho Rural Council, Illinois Stewardship Alliance, Iowa Farm Unity Coalitian, Land Loss Prevention Project (North Carolina), League of Rural Voters, Minnesota COACT, Nebraska League of Rural Voters, North American Farm Alliance, North Carolina Coalition of Farm and Rural Families, Northern Indiana Farm Task Force, Northern Plains Resource Council (Montana), Oregon Common Ground, Powder River Basin Resource Council (Wyoming), Prairiefire Rural Action (Iowa), Rural Advancement Foundation International, Rural Advancement Fund (North and South Carolina), Rural Vermont, Tennessee Family Farm Alliance, Texans United, United Farmers Organization (North and South Carolina), Western Colorado Congress, Western Organization of Resource Councils, Wisconsin Farm Unity Alliance, and Wisconsin Farmland Conservancy.

8. In 1990 the North American Farm Alliance included the American Federation of Government Employees, Community Farm Alliance of Kentucky, Federation of Southern Cooperatives, Michigan Farm Unity Coalition, Minnesota Groundswell, Missouri Rural Crisis Center, National Farmers' Union of Canada, National Lawyers Guild, National Rainbow Coalition, Nebraskans for Peace, New York State Farm Alliance, Ohio Farm Alliance, Rural Vermont, and Wisconsin Farm Unity Alliance.

9. One of UCAPAWA's leaders, Dorothy Ray Healey, reiterated this explanation in an August 1990 interview with Theo Majka.

10. An interesting account of Chavez's involvement with the struggle to end the bracero system is provided by Fred Ross, the person who first recruited Chavez for the Community Service Organization in 1952 (Ross 1989).

11. The motivations for Teamster entrance into organizing farmworkers have been complex and shifting, involving (among other things) rivalries among Teamster officials. Although Teamster involvement in the DiGiorgio election may have reflected only a desire to protect the union's jurisdictional flank, later Teamster competition with the UFW from 1970 to 1977 represented attempts coordinated with agribusiness—and initially supported by officials in the Nixon administration—to undermine the effectiveness of the UFW (Majka and Majka 1982, chaps. 9–11).

12. Walsh (1978) suggests that another reason for eliminating labor contractors rather than integrating them into the contracts and union structure was that the contractors might then create a faction in the union who could oppose Chavez. This question of internal dissent and opposition would become more important in the years ahead.

13. This was the figure most often given in the media. Philip Martin, an agricultural economist at the University of California at Davis, gave a lower estimate, however, stating that in 1987 the UFW had 6,000 to 10,000 members working under 50 to 60 contracts covering 5,000 jobs. He noted that the UFW was certified in 370 elections but had contracts for only a small portion of these operations (Martin et al. 1988, 40).

14. In March 1994 the UFW indicated it may embark on its first serious organizing campaign in a decade (see Postscript).

15. These comments were made in a July 1989 interview at his office in Sacramento with Theo Majka and Linda Majka.

16. For an account of farm labor activities in a number of states as well as an overview of the difficulties involved in farm labor organizations, see Edid (1994).

17. Part of the discussion of FLOC's unionization efforts is based on a series of interviews conducted by Linda Majka and Theo Majka in 1985 and 1986 with FLOC leaders and staff members, particularly Baldemar Velasquez, president, and Ray Santiago, secretary/treasurer. It should be emphasized that the interpretation of FLOC's organizing efforts given here is *not* FLOC's own interpretation of its efforts.

FLOC leaders maintained throughout that promotion of the consumer boycott was their primary purpose.

18. In a 1982 telephone survey among Indiana residents, Ken Barger found widespread support for both basic labor rights for agricultural labor and the farm worker movement. Only 2 percent of the respondents were, however, participating in the boycott of Campbell products, including only 8 percent of those who were aware of the boycott (Barger and Reza 1994).

Works Cited

Abrahamsen, Martin A. 1976. *Copperative Business Enterprise*. New York: McGraw-Hill.

Adler, Patricia A., and Peter Adler. 1987. *Membership Roles in Field Research*. Beverly Hills, Calif.: Sage Publications.

Agricultural Labor Relations Board (ALRB). 1975–89. *Annual Reports*. Sacramento, Calif.: Agricultural Labor Relations Board.

Allison, Roger. 1990. Personal communication. Columbia, Mo. March.

Amols, George, and William Kaiser. 1984. *Agricultural Finance Statistics, 1960–1983*. Economic Research Service, Statistical Bulletin No. 706. Washington, D.C.: U.S. Department of Agriculture, National Economics Division.

Aptheker, Herbert. 1969. *Negro Slave Revolts in the United States*. New York: International Publishers.

Ash, Roberta. 1972. *Social Movements in America*. Chicago: Markham Publishing.

Baker, Gladys L. 1939. "The County Agent." In *Agriculture in the United States: A Documentary History*, vol. 2, edited by Wayne Rasmussen, 2544–49. New York: Random House.

Bakersfield Californian. 13 October 1985. "Methodists Asked to Oppose Boycott: Deukmejian Urges Traditional United Farm Workers' Ally to Support Table Grapes," by Bruce Scheidt.

Barger, W. K., and Ernesto Reza. 1994. *The Farm Labor Movement in the Midwest: Social Change and Adaptation among Migrant Farmworkers*. Austin: University of Texas Press.

Barnes, Donna. 1989. *Farmers in Rebellion: The Rise and Fall of the Southern Farmers Alliance and People's Party of Texas*. Austin: University of Texas Press.

Barrett, Charles Simon. 1909. *The Mission, History, and Times of the Farmers' Union*. Nashville: Marshall & Bruce Co.

Berger, Samuel R. 1978. *Dollar Harvest: The Story of the Farm Bureau*. The Plains, Va.: American Agriculture Movement Publication.

240 *Works Cited*

Berry, Wendell. 1994. "The Pleasures of Eating." *ACE Magazine* 6, no. 4: 10, 11, 18.

Boggs, Carl. 1986. *Social Movements and Political Power: Emerging Forms of Radicalism in the West.* Philadelphia: Temple University Press.

Bonnen, James T. 1973. "Implications for Agricultural Policy." *American Journal of Agricultural Economics* 55 (August): 391–98.

Browne, William P. 1988. *Private Interests, Public Policy, and American Agriculture.* Lawrence: University of Kansas Press.

Browne, William P., and John Dinse. 1985. "The Emergence of the American Agriculture Movement, 1977–1979." *Great Plains Quarterly* 5 (Fall): 221–35.

Browne, William P., and Mark Lundgren. 1988. "Agrarian Protest and a Grassroots Lobby." In Browne, *Private Interests, Public Policy, and American Agriculture,* 64–88. Lawrence: University of Kansas Press.

Buck, Solon Justus. 1913. *The Granger Movement: A Study of Agricultural Organization and Its Political, Economic, and Social Manifestations, 1870–1880.* Lincoln: University of Nebraska Press.

Busch, Lawrence. 1984. "Science, Technology, Agriculture, and Everyday Life." In *Research in Rural Sociology and Development,* vol. 1, edited by H. K. Schwarzweller, 289–314. Greenwich, Conn.: JAI Press.

Buttel, Frederick H., Olaf Larson, and Gilbert Gillespie. 1990. *The Sociology of Agriculture.* Westport, Conn.: Greenwood Press.

Cantor, Louis. 1969. *A Prologue to the Protest Movement: The Missouri Sharecropper Roadside Demonstration of 1939.* Durham, N.C.: Duke University Press.

Cigler, Allan J., and John Mark Hanson. 1983. "Group Formation through Protest: The AAM." In *Interest Group Politics,* edited by Allan J. Cigler and Burdett A. Loomis. Washington, D.C.: Congressional Quarterly Press.

Cochrane, Willard W. 1979. *The Development of American Agriculture: A Historical Analysis.* Minneapolis: University of Minnesota Press.

Collins, Randall. 1986. *Weberian Sociological Theory.* Cambridge: Cambridge University Press.

Crampton, John A. 1965. *The National Farmers' Union: Ideology of a Pressure Group.* Lincoln: University of Nebraska Press.

Danbom, David B. 1979. *The Resisted Revolution: Urban America and the Industrialization of Agriculture, 1900–1930.* Ames: Iowa State University Press.

Daniel, Cletus E. 1981. *Bitter Harvest: A History of California Farmworkers, 1870–1941.* Ithaca, N.Y.: Cornell University Press.

Daniels, Pete. 1985. *Breaking the Land: The Transformation of Cotton, Tobacco, and Rice Cultures since 1880.* Urbana: University of Illinois Press.

Davies, James C. 1962. "Toward a Theory of Revolution." *American Sociological Review* 27: 5–19.

Davis, John Emmeus. 1980. "Capitalist Agricultural Development and the Exploitation of the Propertied Laborer." In *The Rural Sociology of the Advanced Societies: Critical Perspectives*, edited by Frederick H. Buttel and Howard Newby, 133–54. Montclair, N.J.: Allanheld, Osmun & Co.

Dyson, Lowell. 1986. *Farmers' Organizations.* Westport, Conn.: Greenwood Press.

Edid, Maralyn. 1994. *Farm Labor Organizing: Trends and Prospects.* Ithaca, N.Y.: ILR Press.

Ellis, David Maldwyn. 1946. *Landlords and Farmers in the Hudson-Mohawk Region, 1790–1850.* Ithaca, N.Y.: Cornell University Press.

Ferree, Myra Marx, and Frederick D. Miller. 1985. "Mobilization and Meaning: Toward an Integration of Social Psychological and Resource Perspectives on Social Movements." *Sociological Inquiry* 55: 38–51.

Fine, Nathan. 1928. *Labor and Farmer Parties in the United States, 1828–1928.* New York: Rand School of Social Science.

Flacks, Richard. 1988. *Making History: The American Left and the American Mind.* New York: Columbia University Press.

Forster, G. W. 1936. "Progress and Problems . . . " *Journal of Farm Economics* 18 (February).

Friedland, William H., Amy E. Barton, and Robert J. Thomas. 1981. *Manufacturing Green Gold.* New York: Cambridge University Press.

Friedman, Harriet. 1978. "World Market, State, and Family Farm: Social Bases of Household Production in the Era of Wage Labor." *Comparative Studies in Society and History* 20, no. 4: 545–86.

Galarza, Ernesto. 1964. *Merchant of Labor: The Mexican Bracero Story.* Charlotte/Santa Barbara, Calif.: McNally & Loftin.

———. 1970. *Spiders in the House and Workers in the Fields.* Notre Dame, Ind.: University of Notre Dame Press.

———. 1977. *Farm Workers and Agri-Business in California, 1947–1960.* Notre Dame, Ind: University of Notre Dame Press.

Gamson, William. 1990. *The Strategy of Social Protest.* 2d ed. Belmont, Calif.: Wadsworth Press.

Gamson, William A., Bruce Fireman, Steven Rytina. 1982. *Encounters with Unjust Authority.* Homewood, Ill.: Dorsey Press.

Gardner, Charles M. 1949. *The Grange: Friend of the Farmer, 1867–1947.* Washington, D.C.: National Grange of the Patrons of Husbandry.

Gerlach, L. P., and V. W. Hine. 1970. *People, Power, and Change: Movements of Social Transformation.* New York: Bobbs-Merrill.

Goodwyn, Lawrence. 1978. *The Populist Movement: A Short History of the Agrarian Revolt in America.* Oxford: Oxford University Press.

Green, James R. 1978. *Grass-Roots Socialism: Radical Movements in the Southwest, 1895–1943.* Baton Rouge: Louisiana State University Press.

Gregory, James N. 1989. *American Exodus: The Dust Bowl Migration and Okie Culture in California.* New York: Oxford University Press.

Grubbs, Donald H. 1971. *Cry from the Cotton: The Southern Tenant Farmers' Union and the New Deal.* Chapel Hill: University of North Carolina Press.

Gurr, Ted Robert. 1969. *Why Men Rebel.* Princeton, N.J.: Princeton University Press.

Hackney, Sheldon, ed. 1971. *Populism: The Critical Issues.* Boston: Little, Brown.

Hansen, Merle. 1990. Personal communication. Minneapolis. March.

Harvey, David. 1982. *The Limits to Capital.* Chicago: University of Chicago Press.

Healey, Dorothy Ray. 1976. In "Activists in Radical Movements from 1930–1960." Phonotape 49A. Collected by LaRue McCormick. Regional Oral History Project, Bancroft Library, University of California, Berkeley.

Hobsbawm, E. J. 1981. *Bandits.* New York: Pantheon Books.

Hodne, Carol. 1989. Personal communication. Iowa City, Iowa. December.

Hoffman, Abraham. 1974. *Unwanted Mexican Americans in the Great Depression.* Tucson: University of Arizona Press.

Holmes, George K. 1920. "Three Centuries of Tobacco." *Yearbook of the USDA, 1919.* Washington, D.C.: U.S. Government Printing Office.

Jamieson, Stuart Marshall. 1945. *Labor Unionism in American Agriculture.* U.S. Department of Labor, Bureau of Labor Statistics, Bulletin No. 836. Washington, D.C.: U.S. Government Printing Office.

Jenkins, J. Craig. 1978. "The Demand for Immigrant Workers: Labor Scarcity or Social Control." *International Migration Review* 12.

———. "Resource Mobilization Theory and the Study of Social Movements." *Annual Review of Sociology* 9: 527–33.

———. 1985. *The Politics of Insurgency: The Farm Worker Movement in the 1960s.* New York: Columbia University Press.

Johnson, D. Gale, Kenzo Hemmi, and Pierre Lardinois, 1985. *Agricultural Policy and Trade: Adjusting Domestic Programs to an International Framework: A Task Force Report to the Trilateral Commission.* New York: New York University Press.

Kaplan, Sidney. 1952. "Veteran Officers and Politics in Massachusetts, 1783–1787." *William and Mary Quarterly* 9, no. 1.

Kile, O. M. 1948. *The Farm Bureau through Three Decades.* Baltimore: Waverly Press.

Kim, Sung Bok. 1978. *Landlord and Tenant in Colonial New York: Manorial Society, 1664–1775.* Chapel Hill: University of North Carolina Press.

Kitschelt, Herbert. 1985. "New Social Movements in West Germany and the United States." *Political Power and Social Theory* 5: 273–324.

Klandermans, Bert. 1986. "New Social Movements and Resource Mobilization: The European and the American Approaches." *International Journal of Mass Emergencies and Disasters* 4, no. 2: 13–37. Special issue: Comparative Perspectives and Research on Social Movements and Collective Behavior. Guest editor: Gary T. Marx.

Kloppenburg, Jack, Jr. 1988. *First the Seed: The Political Economy of Plant Biotechnology, 1992–2000.* New York: Cambridge University Press.

———. 1991. "Social Theory and the De/Reconstruction of Agricultural Science: Local Knowledge for an Alternative Agriculture." *Rural Sociology* 56, no. 4 (Winter): 519–48.

Kohl, Barbara A. 1979. "The AAM: Discussion and Contrast with Past Agrarian Movements." Paper presented at the North Central Sociological Society Meetings, Akron, Ohio. April.

Lappé, Frances Moore. 1989. "Saving the Family Farm Can Benefit All of Us." *Utne Reader*, July–August.

Lappé, Frances Moore, and Joseph Collins. 1982. *World Hunger: 10 Myths.* San Francisco: Institute for Food and Development Policy.

Lasker, Bruno. 1931. *Filipino Immigration to the United States.* Chicago: University of Chicago Press.

Lefler, Hugh T., and William S. Powell. 1973. *Colonial North Carolina: A History.* New York: Charles Scribner's Sons.

Levenson, Lew. 1934. "California's Casualty List." *Nation* 29 August, 243–45.

Levy, Jacques. 1975. *Cesar Chavez: Autobiography of a La Causa.* New York: W. W. Norton.

Lichter, Daniel T., Glenn V. Fuguitt, and Tim B. Heaton. 1985. "Components of Nonmetropolitan Population Change: The Controbution of Rural Areas." *Rural Sociology* 50, no. 1: 88–98.

Lipset, Seymour Martin. 1971. *Agrarian Socialism: The Cooperative Commonwealth Federation in Saskatchewan: A Study in Political Sociology.* Berkeley: University of California Press.

Lofland, John. 1985. *Protest: Studies of Collective Behavior and Social Movements.* New Brunswick, N.J.: Transaction Books.

Logsdon, Gene. 1989. "Who Says the Family Farm Is Dead? Welcome to Future Farming's Best Bet." *Utne Reader*, July–August, 82–88.

London, Joan, and Henry Anderson. 1970. *So Shall Ye Reap.* New York: Thomas Y. Crowell.

Lopez, Steven. 1990. "After the Victory: The Farm Labor Organizing Committee and the Institutionalization of Social Movement Success." Honors thesis, University of Dayton.

Los Angeles Times. 31 July 1985. "Changing ALRB Worries Chavez's Union," by Harry Bernstein.

Los Angeles Times. 18 September 1985. "Farm Union Fight," by Harry Bernstein.

Los Angeles Times. 8 December 1987. "Workers Can't Expect a Fair Shake from the Farm Board," by Harry Bernstein.

Los Angeles Times. 28 August 1988. "Deukmejian Accuses Chavez, Backers of 'Irresponsible' Charges on Grapes," by Jerry Gillam.

Los Angeles Times. 18 November 1988. "Growers' Limits on Union Access to Workers OKd," by Philip Hager.

Lynd, Staughton. 1967. *Class Conflict, Slavery, and the U.S. Constitution.* Indianapolis: Bobbs-Merrill.

McAdam, Doug. 1982. *Political Process and the Development of Black Insurgency, 1930–1970.* Chicago: University of Chicago Press.

McCarthy, John D., and Mayer N. Zald. 1973. *The Trend of Social Movements.* Morristown, N.J.: General Learning.

———. 1977. "Resource Mobilization and Social Movements." *American Journal of Sociology* 82: 1212–41.

McConnell, Grant. 1953. *The Decline of Agrarian Democracy.* Berkeley; University of California Press.

McMath, Robert C., Jr. 1977. *The Populist Vanguard: A History of the Southern Farmers' Alliance.* New York: W. W. Norton.

McNall, Scott G. 1988. *The Road to Rebellion: Class Formation and Kansas Populism, 1865–1900.* Chicago: University of Chicago Press.

McWilliams, Carey. 1939. *Factories in the Field.* Santa Barbara, Calif.: Peregrine, 1971.

———. 1942. *Ill Fares the Land: Migrants and Migratory Labor in the United States.* New York: Arno, 1976.

———. 1979. *The Education of Carey McWilliams.* New York: Simon & Schuster.

Main, Jackson Turner. 1965. *The Social Structure of Revolutionary America.* Princeton, N.J.: Princeton University Press.

Majka, Linda C. 1981. "Labor Militancy among Farm Workers and the Strategy of Protest, 1900–1979." *Social Problems* 28, no. 5: 533–47.

Majka, Linda C., and Theo J. Majka. 1982. *Farm Workers, Agribusiness, and the State.* Philadelphia: Temple University Press.

Majka, Theo J. 1978. "Regulating Farmworkers." *Contemporary Crises* 2: 141–55.

Majka, Theo J. 1980. "Poor People's Movements and Farm Labor Insurgency." *Contemporary Crises* 4: 283–308.

Majka, Theo J., and Linda C. Majka. 1984. "Power, Insurgency, and State Intervention." In *Research in Social Movements, Conflict and Change,* vol. 6, edited by Richard Ratcliff. Greenwich, Conn.: JAI Press.

Mark, Irving. 1940. *Agrarian Conflicts in Colonial New York, 1711–1775.* New York: Columbia University Press.

Martin, Philip L., Daniel Egan, and Stephanie Luce. 1988. *The Wages and Fringe Benefits of Unionized California Farmworkers*. Giannini Information Series No. 88-4, The Giannini Foundation of Agricultural Economics, University of California.

Martin, Philip L., Suzanne Vaupel, and Daniel L. Egan. 1988. *Unfulfilled Promise: Collective Bargaining in California Agriculture*. Boulder, Colo.: Westview Press, 1988.

Matthiessen, Peter. 1969. *Sal Si Puedes*. New York: Delta.

Meister, Dick, and Anne Loftis. 1977. *A Long Time Coming: The Struggle to Unionize America's Farm Workers*. New York: Macmillan.

Michie, Aruna Nayer, and Craig Jagger. 1980. *Why Farmers Protest: Kansas Farmers, the Farm Problem, and the AAM*. Kansas State University Agricultural Experiment Station Bulletin. July.

Mini, Norman. 1935. "That California Dictatorship." *Nation*, 20 February, 224–26.

Mitchell, H. L. 1987. *Roll the Union On: A Pictorial History of the Southern Tenant Farmers' Union as Told by Its Co-Founder, H. L. Mitchell*. Chicago: Charles H. Kerr Publishing.

_____. 1989. *Mean Things Happening in This Land: The Life and Times of H. L. Mitchell, Co-Founder of the Southern Tenant Farmers' Union*. Montclair, N.J.: Allanheld, Osmun & Co.

Mitchell, Theodore. 1987. *Political Education in the Southern Farmers' Alliance, 1887–1900*. Madison: University of Wisconsin Press.

Montgomery, David. 1979. *Workers Control in America*. New York: Cambridge University Press.

Mooney, Patrick H. 1983. "Toward a Class Analysis of Midwestern Agriculture." *Rural Sociology* 48, no. 4: 563–84.

_____. 1986. "The Political Economy of Credit in American Agriculture." *Rural Sociology* 51, no. 4: 449–70.

_____. 1988. *My Own Boss? Class, Rationality, and the Family Farm*. Boulder, Colo.: Westview Press.

_____. 1989. "The Farmers' Movement? An Exploration of Carl Thayer's Thesis." Paper presented at the Social Science History Meetings, Washington, D.C. November.

Mooney, Patrick H., and Scott A. Hunt. 1994 "Ideology and Agrarian Mobilization in the United States: Collective Action Frames, Abeyance Structures, and Movement Continuity." Paper presented at the Midwest Sociological Society Meetings, St. Louis, Mo., March.

Moore, Truman E. 1965. *The Slaves We Rent*. New York: Random House.

Morgan, Dan. 1979. *Merchants of Grain*. New York: Penguin Books.

Morlan, Robert. 1955. *Political Prairie Fire: The Non-Partisan League, 1915–1922*. Minneapolis: University of Minnesota Press.

Morris, Aldon D. 1984. *The Origins of the Civil Rights Movement: Black Communities Organizing for Change.* New York: Free Press.

National Organization for Raw Materials (NORM). n.d. Pamphlet.

O'Connor, John. 1990. "Environment and Agriculture." Address given at North American Farm Alliance Leadership Training Institute, Minneapolis. March.

Ostendorf, David. 1989. Personal communication. Des Moines. July.

Petrulis, Mindy, et al. 1987. *How Is Farm Financial Stress Affecting Rural America?* Agricultural Economics Report No. 586. Washington, D.C.: U.S. Department of Agriculture, Economic Research Service. June.

Pfeffer, Max J. 1983. "Social Origins of Three Systems of Farm Production in the United States." *Rural Sociology* 48, no. 4: 540–62.

Powell, William S. 1949. *The War of the Regulation and the Battle of Alamance, May 16, 1771.* Raleigh, N.C.: State Department of Archives and History.

Press Enterprise (Riverside, Calif.). 25 June 1989. "Farm Workers' Union Leaving the Field," by Bob LaBarre.

Quinn, Thomas. 1989. Personal communication. Downing, Wis. December.

Reisler, Mark. 1976. *By the Sweat of Their Brow: Mexican Immigrant Labor in the United States, 1900–1940.* Westport Conn.: Greenwood Press.

Ringer, Darrell T. 1990. "The Missing Link to Rural Economic Development." Unpublished manuscript.

Ritchie, Mark. 1985. "Parity Not Charity." In *Farm Gate Defense*, ed. Allen Wilford, 243–56. Toronto: New Canada Publications.

Ross, Fred. 1989. *Conquering Goliath: Cesar Chavez at the Beginning.* Keene, Calif.: El Taller Grafico Press.

Rowell, Willis. 1984. *Mad as Hell: A Behind the Scenes Story of the NFO.* Corning, Ia.: Gauthier Publishing.

Rude, George. 1980. *Ideology and Popular Protest.* New York: Pantheon Books.

Rural America. 1977. *Platform for Rural America.* Washington, D.C.: Rural America.

Saloutos, Theodore. 1960. *Farmer Movements in the South, 1865–1933.* Lincoln: University of Nebraska Press.

Saloutos, Theodore, and John D. Hicks. 1951. *Twentieth-Century Populism: Agricultural Discontent in the Middle West, 1900–1939.* Lincoln: University of Nebraska Press.

Schwartz, Michael. 1976. *Radical Protest and Social Structure: The Southern Farmers' Alliance and the Cotton Tenancy, 1880–1890.* New York: Academic Press.

Scott, James. 1990. *Domination and the Art of Resistance: Hidden Transcripts.* New Haven: Yale University Press.

Shover, John L. 1965. *Cornbelt Rebellion: The Farmers' Holiday Association.* Urbana: University of Illinois Press.

Sigelman, Lee. 1983. "Politics, Economics, and the American Farmer: The Case of 1980." *Rural Sociology* 48, no. 3: 367–85.

Slaughter, Thomas P. 1986. *The Whiskey Rebellion: Frontier Epilogue to the American Revolution.* New York: Oxford University Press.

Snow, David A., and Robert D. Benford. 1988. "Master Frames and Cycles of Protest." Paper presented at the Workshop on Frontiers in Social Movement Theory, Ann Arbor. June.

Snow, David A., et al. 1986. "Frame Alignment and Mobilization." *American Sociological Review* 51, no. 4: 464–81.

Starkey, Marion. 1955. *A Little Rebellion.* New York: Knopf.

Stein, Walter J. 1971. *California and the Dust Bowl Migration.* Contributions in American History, No. 21. Westport, Conn.: Greenwood Press.

Steinbeck, John. 1936. "Dubious Battle in California." *Nation*, 12 September, 302–304.

_____. 1938. *Their Blood Is Strong.* San Francisco: Simon J. Lubin Society.

Stover, Fred W. 1968. *The Truth about the Farm Betrayals.* Des Moines: U.S. Farmers Association.

Strange, Marty. 1988. *Family Farming: A New Economic Vision.* Lincoln: University of Nebraska Press and Institute of Food and Development Policy.

Szatmary, David P. 1980. *Shays' Rebellion: The Making of an Agrarian Insurrection.* Amherst: University of Massachusetts Press.

Taylor, Carl C. 1953. *The Farmers' Movement, 1620–1920.* Westport, Conn.: Greenwood Press.

Taylor, Paul W. 1975. Personal communication. Berkeley, Calif. August.

Taylor, Ronald B. 1975. *Chavez and the Farm Workers.* Boston: Beacon Press, 1975.

Taylor, Verta. 1989. "Social Movement Continuity: The Women's Movement in Abeyance." *American Sociological Review* 54 (October): 761–75.

Theorin, Lee. 1990. Personal communication. Connorsville, Wis. March.

Thomas, Robert J. 1985. *Citizenship, Gender, and Work.* Berkeley: University of California Press.

Thompson, John B. 1990. *Ideology and Modern Culture: Critical Social Theory in the Era of Mass Communication.* Stanford, Calif.: Stanford University Press.

Tilly, Charles. 1978. *From Mobilization to Revolution.* Reading, Mass.: Addison-Wesley.

Touraine, Alain. 1988. *Return of the Actor: Social Theory in Postindustrial Society.* Minneapolis: University of Minnesota Press.

U.S. Congress. 1940. [La Follette Committee Hearings.] Senate Committee

248 *Works Cited*

on Education and Labor, Subcommittee to Investigate Violations of the Rights of Free Speech and Assembly and Interference with the Right of Labor to Organize and Bargain Collectively, Pursuant to S. Res. 226, 74th Congress. Hearings, pts. 47, 49, 54, 55.

U.S. Congress. 1941. [Tolan Committee.] House Select Committee to Investigate the Interstate Migration of Destitute Citizens, Pursuant to H. Res. 63, 491, 629, 76th Congress, and H. Res. 16, 77th Congress. Report on Interstate Migration, pt. 4.

U.S. Congress. 1942. [La Follette Committee, Reports.] Senate Subcommittee of the Committee on Education and Labor, Report no. 1150, Violations of Free Speech and Rights of Labor, 77th Congress, 2nd session, pt. 4.

U.S. Department of Agriculture. 1940. *Farmers in a Changing World: The Yearbook of Agriculture, 1940*. House Document #696. Washington, D.C.: U.S. Government Printing Office.

U.S. Department of Agriculture. 1967. *Agricultural Statistics*. Washington, D.C.: U.S. Government Printing Office.

U.S. Department of Agriculture. 1980. *Agricultural Handbook*. House Document #574. Washington, D.C.: U.S. Government Printing Office.

U.S. Department of Agriculture. 1982. *Agricultural Handbook*. House Document #609. Washington, D.C.: U.S. Government Printing Office.

U.S. Department of Agriculture. 1984. *Agricultural Handbook*. House Document #637. Washington, D.C.: U.S. Government Printing Office.

Valdez, Dennis Nodin. 1984. "From Following the Crops to Chasing the Corporations: The Farm Labor Organizing Committee, 1967–1983." In *The Chicano Struggle: Analyses of Past and Present Efforts*. Binghamton, N.Y.: National Association for Chicano Studies/Bilingual Press.

_____. 1991. *El Norte: Agricultural Workers in the Great Lakes Region, 1919–1970*. Austin: University of Texas Press.

Vogt, Stanley W. 1948. *The Last Frontier*. Denver: Farmers' Education and Cooperative Union of America.

Waldie, Jerome. 1989. Personal communication. Placerville, Calif. August.

Wall Street Journal. 9 September 1986. "Its Ranks Eroding, Farm Workers' Union Struggles to Survive," by Constanza Montana and John Emshwiller.

Walsh, Edward J. 1978. "Mobilization Theory vis-à-vis a Mobilization Process: The Case of the United Farm Workers' Movement." In *Research in Social Movements, Conflict and Change*, vol 1., edited by Louis Kreisberg, 155–77. Greenwich, Conn.: JAI Press.

Walters, Charles, Jr. 1968. *Holding Action*. New York: Halcyon Books.

Weber, Max. 1946. *From Max Weber: Essays in Sociology*, edited by H. H. Gerth and C. Wright Mills. New York: Oxford University Press.

_____. 1978. *Economy and Society*, edited by Guenther Roth and Claus Wittich. Berkeley: University of California Press.

Wood, David Truman. 1961. "The National Farmers' Organization in Transition." Ph.D. dissertation, University of Iowa.

Wright, Erik Olin. 1978. *Class, Crisis, and the State.* London: New Left Books.

Yronwode, Peter. 1984. "First Penny Auction since 1930s Held in Missouri." *North American Farmer,* 3 October, 1, 7.

Zabin, Carol; Michael Kearney; Anna Garcia; David Runsten; and Carole Nagengast. 1993. *Mixtec Migrants in California Agriculture: A New Cycle of Poverty.* Davis: California Institute for Rural Studies.

Zald, Mayer N., and John D. McCarthy, eds. 1979. *The Dynamics of Social Movements.* Cambridge, Mass.: Winthrop Publishers.

Zald, Mayer N., and John D. McCarthy. 1987. *Social Movements in an Organizational Society.* New Brunswick, N.J.: Transaction Books.

Zwerdling, Daniel. 1980. "The Food Monsters: How They Gobble up Each other—and Us." *Progressive* 44, no. 3: 16–27.

Index

AAA. *See* Agricultural Adjustment Act
AAM. *See* American Agriculture
  Movement
activists: characteristics of xxvi–xxviii;
  the Regulators, 16; religious groups,
  108
adult basic education programs, 46–47.
  See also education
AFL. *See* American Federation of Labor
AFL-CIO. *See* American Federation of
  Labor–Congress of Industrial
  Organizations
agrarian fundamentalism, xxx, 220
agrarian social movements: and economic strategies, xxx; bifurcation of, 229;
  characteristics of activists,
  xxvi–xxvii; in colonial period, xix;
  pre-Revolutionary, 4–11; resource
  mobilization and political process
  models, xxvi–xxix
agribusiness: ability to resist unionization, 147–48; impact of strategies,
  196–98; in California, xxii, 123–25,
  178, 199; and international competition, 232–33; legal and political
  means, 178; profit-gaining methods,
  xxii–xxiii; strategies of, xxii, 197
Agricultural Adjustment Act: acreage
  reduction, 74; purpose of, 135
Agricultural Adjustment Administration,
  80
agricultural crisis of 1980s: conferences,
  112, 115; declining farm values, 107;

escalation of debt/asset ratio, 107;
  increase in farm foreclosures, 106;
  NAFA actions, 112; NAFA's analysis
  of,113; political action, 115–16; solutions to NFFC actions, 112
Agricultural Labor Relations Act: access
  rule, 176–78, 196; bad faith bargaining, 194–95; changes in administration, 191–96; comparison with NLRA,
  196, 198; founding of, xxv, 174; legislature begins resolving capital-labor
  conflicts, 190; limits on agribusiness,
  176–77; reasons of its passage, 190;
  terms of, 174; transformed from pro-
  union law into union obstacle-
  creator, 191–92
Agricultural Labor Relations Board: and
  bad-faith bargaining, 194–95; budget
  cutbacks, 195; founding of, 174;
  results of temporary operations suspension, 177–78; UFW calls for eliminating of budget of, 196
Agricultural Wheel, 41
Agricultural Workers Freedom to Work
  Association, 162
Agricultural Workers Industrial League,
  127
Agricultural Workers Organizing
  Committee, 154; affiliated with AFL-
  CIO, 154; merger with NFWA, 158
agriculture, future objectives of, 229–30
Alatorre, Richard, 173
Alinsky, Saul, xxix, 153

251

successful strikes in early 1930s, 127; primary shortcoming of, 130; and strike issues, 128
capitalist production, 221
Capper-Volstead Act, 73
Carter, Jimmy, 100, 103, 106, 178, 180
CAWIU. *See* Cannery and Agricultural Workers Industrial Union
Chambers, Pat, 130–32
Chandler, Alfred J., 133
Chavez, Cesar: ambivalence regarding institutionalization of UFW, 189; charismatic leadership of, 164, 188–91; death of, xxv, 184, 197; desire to incorporate agricultural labor into NLRA, 162; fasting for nonviolence, 161; favors boycotts, 181; originally a leader of Community Service Organization, xxix,153, 223; seeks money for strikers, 156; as UFW leader, xxiv, 150
Christian Labor Association, 179
Church, Bruce, 182, 197
CIO. *See* Congress of Industrial Organizations
Citizens for Farm Labor, 153
civil disobedience, 8, 17, 22
CLA. *See* Christian Labor Association
Cleburne Demands, 39
Clements, George, 136
cognitive liberation, xxviii–xxix, 218
Cohen, Jerry, 166, 173, 186
collective bargaining: and the NFO, xxi, 93; and tobacco, 5; as economic strategy, xxx; three ideologies guiding collective action, 220–22. *See also* free rider
colonial farm movements, xix
Colorado Farmers' Union, 58
Colored Farmers' National Alliance, 41
Colson, Charles, 170
commodity associations, specialized: National Cattlemen's Association, 97; National Corn Growers, 97
Community Service Organization, xxix, 153
competitive capitalism, xxx, 220

Confederacion de Uniones Obreras Mexicanas, 127, 225
Confederation of Mexican Labor Unions. *See* Confederacion de Uniones Obreras Mexicanas
Congress of Industrial Organizations, 87, 138
Contreras, Rufino, 180
cooperative economics, xx, 91
cooperative elevators, 54, 60
cooperative movement in the South, xxviii
cooperatives: anti-capitalist ideology, 57; farmers lose control of, 94; founded by the Grange, 35; lead to lobbying, xx; marketing, xx, 33, 38; purchasing, xx, 33, 34, 38; to combat crop lien system, 38
corporate agriculture, 123
Country Life Commission, 68
county agent: as defense attorneys for landlords, 81; salaried through fundraising, 69–70
cow war: causes of, 76–77; resulting confrontations of, 77–80
criminal syndicalism law, 132, 134
crop lien system: and the Farmers' Alliance, 38; defined, 31; in cotton production, 45
Cross, Ira B., 129
Cummings, Homer, 85

Daifullah, Nagi, 171
Dakota Alliance, 43
Daws, S. O., 38
de la Cruz, Juan, 171
Decker, Caroline. *See* Gladstein, Caroline Decker
depression: and protests, xx; causes of farmers' increased debts, 75; conditions for farmers, 75; farm labor movement during, 127
Deukmejian, George, 191, 197
DiGiorgio Corporation, 153, 156–59 233n. 11
Dunlop Commission, xxv, 206–208, 214
Dust Bowl: devaluation and surplus of agricultural goods, 134–35; draught,

The Authors

Patrick H. Mooney received his Ph.D. from the University of Wisconsin-Madison in 1985 and is an associate professor of sociology at the University of Kentucky. He is the author of *My Own Boss? Class, Rationality, and the Family Farm* (1988) and has written several articles and book chapters on agricultural class structure and farmers' movements. He is currently involved in research on agrarian transformation in post-Communist Poland, the sustainable agriculture movement in the United States, oral histories of African-American farmers in Kentucky, and the representation of family farming in popular film.

Theo J. Majka received his Ph.D. from the University of California at Santa Barbara in 1978 and is an associate professor of sociology at the University of Dayton. He is co-author, with Linda Majka, of *Farm Workers, Agribusiness, and the State* (1982) and has written several articles on farm labor movements. He is currently involved in research on the maintenance of residential stability and community ties in racially integrated neighborhoods, the effectiveness of neighborhood-based collective actions, and the cyclical patterns of social movements.